IN THE NAME OF NATIONAL SECURITY

By the Same Author

Political Dynamics of Constitutional Law (with Neal Devins, 4th ed. 2006)

Military Tribunals and Presidential Power: American Revolution to the War on Terrorism (2005)

Nazi Saboteurs on Trial: A Military Tribunal & American Law (2d ed. revised 2005)

American Constitutional Law (6th ed. 2005)

Presidential War Power (2d ed. 2004)

The Politics of Executive Privilege (2004)

The Democratic Constitution (with Neal Devins, 2004)

Religious Liberty in America: Political Safeguards (2002)

Congressional Abdication on War and Spending (2000)

The Politics of Shared Power: Congress and the Executive (4th ed. 1998)

Constitutional Conflicts Between Congress & the President (4th ed. 1997)

Encyclopedia of the American Presidency (with Leonard W. Levy, 1994)

Constitutional Dialogues: Interpretation as Political Process (1988)

The Constitution Between Friends: Congress, the President, and the Law (1978)

Presidential Spending Power (1975)

President and Congress (1972)

IN THE NAME OF
NATIONAL SECURITY

Unchecked Presidential Power and the
Reynolds Case

Louis Fisher

UNIVERSITY PRESS OF KANSAS

© 2006 by the University Press of Kansas
All rights reserved

Published by the University Press of Kansas (Lawrence, Kansas 66045), which was organized by the Kansas Board of Regents and is operated and funded by Emporia State University, Fort Hays State University, Kansas State University, Pittsburg State University, the University of Kansas, and Wichita State University

Library of Congress Cataloging-in-Publication Data

Fisher, Louis.
   In the name of national security : unchecked presidential power and the Reynolds case / Louis Fisher.
      p.   cm.
   Includes bibliographical references and index.
   ISBN 0-7006-1464-8 (cloth : alk. paper)
   1. Reynolds, Patricia J.—Trials, litigation, etc.   2. United States—Trials, litigation, etc.   3. National security—Law and legislation—United States.   4. Executive privilege (Government information)—United States.   5. Official secrets—United States.   6. Government liability—United States.   7. Liability for aircraft accidents—United States.   I. Title.
   KF228.R485F57 2006
   342.73'06—dc22   2006013490

British Library Cataloguing-in-Publication Data is available.

Printed in the United States of America

10 9 8 7 6 5 4 3 2 1

The paper used in this publication meets the minimum requirements of the American National Standard for Permanence of Paper for Printed Library Materials Z39.48–1992.

To Cathy, Judy, Pat, Susan, and Wilson
for speaking Truth to Power

CONTENTS

PREFACE

The midair explosion of an Air Force B-29 over Waycross, Ga., in October 1948 triggered a series of judicial rulings over "state secrets." The widows of three civilians killed in the crash sued the government for negligence and won in district court and the Third Circuit. At each level, they asked for the accident report and statements of three crew survivors, but the government refused to release the documents to the plaintiffs or even to the district judge. Only at the Supreme Court, in *United States v. Reynolds* (1953), did the judiciary support the government's right to withhold evidence from private parties when disclosure, according to the government, would prejudice national security. This series of rulings formalized the state secrets privilege.

What makes the case intriguing is the uneven track record of the government. Initially it relied on unpersuasive—and losing—arguments in district court and the Third Circuit. Rebuffed twice in a row, the government turned increasingly to a jerry-built state secrets privilege that prevailed at the Supreme Court. Although the lower courts had insisted that sensitive and confidential documents should be submitted to the district judge, to be read in his chambers, the Supreme Court declined to look at the documents. It simply took at face value the government's assertion that disclosure of the material would do harm to the national security. The Court's decision presents many inconsistent and incoherent themes.

Doubts about the government's justifications were rekindled in the year 2000, when the daughter of one of the men killed in the crash browsed the Internet and discovered the accident report, which was by now declassified. It revealed not only serious negligence by the government, but also contained nothing that could be called state secrets. There was no discernible reason why the government could not have shared the accident report and the survivor statements with the plaintiffs during pretrial proceedings, except that they would have shown negligence on the part of the military. In legal terms, the government's conduct had the makings of a *coram nobis* ("before us") suit. This is a writ of error directing a court to review its earlier judgment because it was based on errors of fact. The plaintiffs in *Reynolds* could now charge that the government, by withholding the documents, had contributed to a court ruling that was wrong and unjust. It was a case of fraud against the court. By 2002 the second round of *Reynolds* litigation was underway. Papers filed with the Supreme Court early in 2003 asked it to recognize that the Justices in 1953 had been misled by the government. Because of the false impression left with the Court, it should have affirmed the lower court rulings.

Fundamental questions of constitutional law and public policy are at stake with the state secrets privilege. If the government can designate agency documents "secret" and withhold them from trial, private litigants are prevented from making their case in court. Why should the executive branch decide questions of evidence? Isn't that the province of the judge? Should the court examine the disputed documents to determine whether the government accurately described them? An independent judiciary could tell the government to either surrender the documents (perhaps in modified form, to delete sources and methods) or lose the case. What if the government, in these struggles over documents, provides false or misleading explanations to a court? What kind of remedies exist to correct the injustice and hold government accountable? These questions have special significance in the period after the terrorist attacks of September 11, 2001, with the government increasingly relying on the state secrets privilege.

Mike Briggs of University Press of Kansas saw the value of a book on this issue and asked if I'd like to do it. With my previous work in constitutional law, war powers, military law, and executive privilege, the project fit like a glove. Many people helped me pull the story together. Judith Loether, daughter of one of the crash victims (Albert Palya), discovered the accident report on the Internet and decided that the case should be reopened. She responded to my many questions and shared documents from her collection. Other family members urged that the case be reopened: Patricia J. Herring (wife of Robert E. Reynolds) and Cathy and Susan Brauner (daughters of William H. Brauner). They also gave me documents and helped clarify a number of issues. There is a chance of holding government accountable when individuals with this persistence and energy press for justice.

The law firm of Drinker Biddle & Reath represented the original plaintiffs in *Reynolds* and took up the fight again a half century later. It shared documents from their files with me. Special thanks to the firm's Wilson M. Brown III and Lori Rapuano. Wilson Brown, the lead attorney for the families who decided to relitigate the *Reynolds* case, meticulously read the manuscript and gave me important guidance and insights drawn from his years of appellate practice. I am much indebted to his close reading and his valuable suggestions.

Judy Loether discovered the accident report by tapping into a collection kept by Michael Stowe, whose interest in military accidents dates back to his years as a teenager in New Jersey. A careful reading of the accident report paved the way for the charge that the government had misled the Supreme

Court into believing that the report contained sensitive national security information. Stowe's unique collection opened the gates to a second round in the courts.

My brother Lee flew combat missions with the P-38 in World War II. He found the circumstances of the B-29 crash and the government's handling of the case highly intriguing. Twenty-two years with the Air Force gave him a practical education on the capacity of government to dissemble. He spent time analyzing the accident report, reading the interviews with survivors, and searching for other documents to determine the cause of the crash and the degree of negligence by the government.

Lee sent out many letters to obtain additional material and turned to friends and colleagues who possessed expertise with military aircraft. One was Robert A. Mann, author of *The B-29 Superfortress* (2004). Bob served in the Air Force from 1948 to 1952 and worked as both an engine and aircraft mechanic for the B-29 ground crew. He spent much time poring through the accident report and a vast array of related documents, trying to understand what went wrong on October 6, 1948. I was treated to a rich education by reading the many e-mails that sailed between Lee and Bob to debate the likely causes of the accident.

A number of friends and colleagues have, over the years, helped me further my understanding of government secrecy and national security law. I can't name them all, but at least I want to express my appreciation to John Barrett, Tom Blanton, David Danelski, Jennifer Elsea, Clare Feikert, Meredith Fuchs, Robert Pallitto, Harold Relyea, and Morton Rosenberg. Mort closely read Chapter 7 and helped clarify the kinds of legal issues and options available to judges when confronted with claims of state secrets. At the end of the book, I express my appreciation to the many people who provided valuable access to archival materials.

I was fortunate to have my manuscript read by four seasoned, savvy experts on national security law: Steven Aftergood, William Banks, Scott Silliman, and William Weaver. It would be difficult to find a quartet so knowledgeable and experienced. My thanks to all for offering incisive comments. Larisa Martin of the University Press of Kansas exercised her skills and talents as production editor in reviewing the final manuscript.

The book is dedicated to five people who pressed for justice: Cathy Brauner, Susan Brauner, Pat Herring, and Judith Palya Loether, who combined their energy and sense of justice with the legal talents of Wilson Brown. All five decided that the government's conduct had to be challenged. To each I extend my respect and admiration.

1

A B-29 EXPLODES IN MIDAIR

On October 6, 1948, a B-29 lifted off from Warner Robins Air Force Base in Georgia, scheduled to fly five hours on a research and development mission before landing at a base in Florida. The plane carried a crew of eight: pilot, copilot, flight engineer, radio operator, navigator, left and right scanner, and auto pilot mechanic. Joining the crew were five civilian electronic experts who had worked on the research project. Three of the civilians were employed by the Radio Corporation of America and two by the Franklin Institute of Technology.

The four-engine plane exploded high over Waycross, Ga., shortly before 2 o'clock in the afternoon.[1] Newspapers the next day reported that witnesses saw the plane fall to pieces and heard a roar "like a terrific thunder clap."[2] According to the newspaper stories, two of the engines failed, and a third caught fire at an altitude of about 20,000 feet.[3] The copilot, who survived, said that a fire started in the No. 1 engine, the No. 2 engine failed, and the aircraft fell into a spin.[4] When the bomb bay doors were opened to allow men to jump from the plane, the open bay intensified the spin.[5] Nine men died, including four of the five civilians. The plane tore apart during its plunge to earth. Four bodies were found in the tail section, which snapped from the main fuselage. Five other bodies were found scattered in low marshland at the edge of town, which is just north of the Okefenokee Swamp. Four men managed to parachute to safety, landing in a farm field.[6]

Harold R. Daniels, a public relations officer at the plane's air base, told reporters that the bomber was on a special research mission to test secret

---

1. Waycross Journal-Herald, October 7, 1948, at 1 (aerial photo).
2. "Survivors Tell Story of Two Engine Fires Before B-29 Blast," [Washington] Evening Star, October 7, 1948, at A6.
3. "9 Killed in B-29 Blast, Phila. Scientist Escapes," Philadelphia Inquirer, October 7, 1948, at 1.
4. "Survivors Describe Plane Wreck over Waycross Costing 9 Lives," Atlanta Journal, October 7, 1948, at 4.
5. "9 Killed in B-29 Blast, Phila. Scientist Escapes," Philadelphia Inquirer, October 7, 1948, at 1.
6. "Exploding Plane Kills 8, but Four Parachute Safely," Boston Daily Globe, October 7, 1948, at 13.

electronic equipment.[7] Newspaper stories spoke openly about the plane's secret equipment and the civilians on board who provided technical expertise. The *San Francisco Chronicle* speculated that the plane's experimental flight might have involved cosmic ray research.[8] The Air Force volunteered that the bomber was engaged in "electronic research on different types of radar."[9] The *Chicago Daily Sun Times* featured a front-page headline: "BLAST IN SECRET PLANE KILLS 9."[10]

This description of the crash is drawn from a variety of newspapers across the country. One would expect a more detailed and expert coverage in the *Air Force Times,* but a search of eight issues published on October 9, 16, 23, and 30 and November 6, 13, 20, and 27 found not a single mention of the accident. Over this same time period, the *Air Force Times* managed to run stories about other plane crashes. An article on October 2 reported on a crash rate of about 14 F-47s per month in Turkey, leading to a grounding of the aircraft.[11] A story on October 11 described successful efforts to prevent aircraft disasters at an Air Force base in California.[12] An article on October 23 explored the causes of aircraft accidents and the steps taken by the Air Force to minimize them.[13] The *Air Force Times* even had space for an article that explained the recovery of the bodies of two women who drowned after a collision between a motorpower skiff and a motorboat in Alabama.[14] Not a word, however, was written about the B-29 crash over Waycross. Why the news blackout? Why keep from readers of the *Air Force Times* what was common knowledge to the general public in every state of the country?

Additional information on the B-29 accident would surface with the *Reynolds* litigation, especially from interrogatories submitted to the government by the wives of three civilians who died in the crash. But the government withheld from them and the courts several key documents, including the accident report and the depositions of three crew survivors. Those documents, consid-

7. "Blast Wrecks B-29; 9 Killed," Chicago Daily Tribune, October 7, 1948, at 1.

8. "Air Force Hunts Clues to B-29 Blast," San Francisco Chronicle, October 8, 1948, at 6.

9. Id. For other newspaper coverage, see "B-29 Explodes While Testing Secret Devices, Killing Eight," Los Angeles Times, October 7, 1948, at 1; "B-29 Explodes, Killing 9," New York Times, October 7, 1948, at 25; "B-29 Testing Electronic Device Explodes in Midair, Killing 9," Washington Post, October 7, 1948, at 4.

10. "Blast in Secret Plane Kills 9," Chicago Daily Sun Times, October 7, 1948, at 1, 2.

11. "F-47 Trouble in Turkey," Air Force Times, October 2, 1948, at 6.

12. "Men Who Avert Crashes Praised," Air Force Times, October 16, 1948, at 11.

13. "AF Fights Pilot Error, Mechanical Failure," Air Force Times, October 23, 1948, at 13.

14. "Ft. Benning Rescue Squad Helps Recover Two Bodies," Air Force Times, October 16, 1948, at 13.

ered by the government too confidential or secret to be released to litigants and judges, would later be declassified and discovered through an Internet search by Judith Palya Loether, daughter of one of the civilians killed on the plane. Her discovery made it clear that the government had misled the courts into believing that it was necessary to withhold the documents in the interests of national security. Those details, and the litigation that followed beginning in 2003, are explored in Chapter 6.

Deciding to Sue Government

The widows of three civilians who died in the crash initiated a lawsuit, claiming that the accident was the result of negligence by the government. The complaint, filed on June 21, 1949, charged that the accident and deaths of their husbands "were caused solely and exclusively by the negligent and wrongful acts and omissions of the officers and employees of the defendant while acting within the scope of their office and employment."[15] The widows sued under the Federal Tort Claims Act, a statute passed in 1946 that waived the doctrine of sovereign immunity to allow citizens to sue government for wrongful acts. Under this law, Congress directed federal courts to treat the government in the same manner as a private individual, deciding the dispute on the basis of facts and with no partiality in favor of the government.

Joining in the litigation were Phyllis Brauner, wife of William H. Brauner of the Franklin Institute of Technology, Philadelphia, Pa.; Patricia J. Reynolds, wife of Robert Reynolds of RCA, Camden, N.J.; and Elizabeth Palya, wife of Albert H. Palya, also of RCA at Camden. Representing the women were Charles J. Biddle and Francis Hopkinson of Drinker Biddle & Reath, a prominent law firm in Philadelphia.

Their decision to sue the government was a natural response to a value deeply held in any society: the desire to see a wrong made right. If government errs, we believe it should acknowledge the mistake and correct it. In Federalist No. 51, James Madison said that justice "is the end of government. It is the end of civil society. It ever has been and ever will be pursued until it be obtained, or until liberty be lost in the pursuit."[16] However, it is very difficult to sue government, and even more difficult to sue successfully. Citizens typically lack the time, money, persistence, contacts, and professional assistance to fight government effectively. Agency attorneys are ready to do battle against

15. Transcript of Record, Supreme Court of the United States, October Term, 1952, No. 21, United States of America v. Reynolds, at 5.
16. Federalist 358 (Benjamin Fletcher Wright ed. 1961).

private parties and are especially skilled in erecting a series of hurdles designed
to prevent access to evidence and documents needed by plaintiffs, even when
Congress has specifically authorized these lawsuits.

The odds improve a bit when citizens join forces through associations and
private organizations. Even with concerted efforts and a willingness to continue the fight over many years, government has a decided advantage. A tight
grip over internal documents is one privilege, and that position of strength
is buttressed by a general unwillingness on the part of government to share
documents with anyone, including the coordinate branches of Congress and
the judiciary. Executive agencies have at their disposal a lengthy list of reasons why documents cannot, must not, and will not be shared. Many of the
justifications turn out to be bunkum, but it takes time and energy to knock
down one barrier only to confront another. Although the courts are supposed
to serve as neutral arbiters, judges frequently defer to executive claims about
national security. In doing so, they lose independent judgment and become
an arm of the executive branch.

Discouraging and daunting as this task is, there is no substitute for the
solitary individual willing to go head to head against the government. Only
the individual feels the grievance, the sting, the indignation, the anger. Only
the individual decides that something must be done. Challenges to government need a trigger, and often it is one person who, through personal experience, knows that government has committed a wrong and must be called
to account. For all the failed private lawsuits that litter the landscape, an im-
pressive list of triumphs have fundamentally changed the law and reshaped
national values.[17] What makes a difference is not merely having a good case
but being able to persevere, attract supporters, detect vulnerable spots in the
government's argument, pursue every possible lead, and hope that luck runs
in your direction.[18]

Sovereign Immunity

A principal hurdle in suing government is the doctrine of sovereign immunity. From monarchical times comes the principle that a sovereign cannot be
sued without its consent. The doctrine has roots in English practice, but even
in British times, sovereign immunity was never a total bar to relief: "If the

17. See Peter Irons, The Courage of Their Convictions: Sixteen Americans Who Fought
Their Way to the Supreme Court (1988).
18. For strategies on how to sue government effectively, see Peter H. Schuck, Suing Government: Citizen Remedies for Official Wrongs (1983).

subject was the victim of illegal official action, in many cases he could sue the King's officers for damages."[19] As explained in one study, the expression "the King can do no wrong" has been misunderstood. Originally it had an entirely different meaning: "'It meant that the king must not, was not allowed, not entitled, to do wrong. . . .' It was on this basis that the King, though not suable in his court (since it seemed an anomaly to issue a writ against oneself), nevertheless endorsed on petitions 'let justice be done,' thus empowering his courts to proceed."[20]

Lawsuits against the United States are allowed if Congress enacts legislation to permit them. From 1789 on, Congress could authorize executive departments to settle certain claims and Congress could do the same through private bills. Suing the government, however, was a different matter. In *Cohens v. Virginia* (1821), Chief Justice John Marshall stated: "The universally received opinion is, that no suit can be commenced or prosecuted against the United States; that the judiciary act does not authorize such suits."[21] Two decades later, in *United States v. McLemore* (1846), the Supreme Court noted that "the government is not liable to be sued, except with its own consent, given by law."[22] In 1926, the Court said that "in the absence of a statute directly authorizing it, courts will not give judgment against the United States for costs and expenses."[23] In recognizing the sovereign prerogative not to pay costs, federal courts pointed out that Congress "alone has power to waive or qualify that immunity."[24]

With the federal government moving into economic activities formerly handled by the private sector, sovereign immunity came under increasing attack. In a 1939 case, Justice Frankfurter spoke about "the enlarged scope of government in economic affairs," the greater reliance on independent corporate facilities to satisfy government objectives, and the growing practice of Congress allowing these corporations to be sued.[25] This trend, he said, "is partly an indication of the present climate which has brought governmental immunity from suit into disfavor."[26] Yet seven years later, just before Congress passed the Federal Tort Claims Act, he said that the federal and state governments are immune from suit "unless they agree to be sued." Finding the

19. Louis L. Jaffe, "Suits Against Governments and Officers: Sovereign Immunity," 77 Harv. L. Rev. 1, 1 (1963).

20. Id. at 4.

21. 6 Wheat. 265, 411–12 (1821).

22. 4 How. (45 U.S.) 286, 288 (1846).

23. United States v. Chemical Foundation, Inc., 272 U.S. 1, 20 (1926).

24. Id. See also Federal Housing Administration v. Burr, 309 U.S. 242, 244 (1940).

25. Keifer & Keifer v. R.F.C. 381, 390 (1939).

26. Id. at 390–91.

immunity "embodied in the Constitution," he still regarded it as "an anach-
ronistic survival of monarchical privilege, and runs counter to democratic
notions of the moral responsibility of the State."[27]

Claims Against the Government

Although it took Congress many decades to develop statutory procedures
to handle disputes against the government, various systems were in place as
early as the Revolutionary War. To support military operations against the
British, the Continental Congress entered into contracts with private parties
to provide ammunition, food, clothing, and other necessities. Legal disputes
over these contracts were inevitable and some mechanism was needed to settle
them. In 1782, Superintendent of Finance Robert Morris appointed an inspector to examine and resolve these claims.[28] It was customary to include
arbitration clauses in contracts. In some cases the government was forced to
compensate individuals and companies when it canceled a contract.[29] Unless government developed a system to handle contractual disputes fairly and
credibly, private parties would have no reason to do business with government. A rigid application of the doctrine of sovereign immunity would have
isolated the government from the public support it desperately needed.

Private Bills

Citizens were always at liberty to seek a private bill from Congress to satisfy
a financial claim. The right is implicit in the freedom of citizens to petition
their government for grievances. The American colonies spoke these words
to King George III in the Declaration of Independence: "In every stage of
these Oppressions We have Petitioned for Redress in the most humble terms:
Our repeated Petitions have been answered only by repeated injury. A Prince,
whose character is thus marked by every act which may define a Tyrant, is
unfit to be the ruler of a free People." The concept of petition was incorpo-
rated into the First Amendment: "Congress shall make no law . . . abridging
. . . the right of the people . . . to petition the Government for a redress of
grievances."

From an early date Congress passed legislation to benefit private parties.
The first private bill, enacted on June 4, 1790, compensated Frederick Wil-

---

27. Kennecott Copper Corp. v. Tax Comm'n, 327 U.S. 573, 580 (1946) (Frankfurter, J.,
dissenting).
28. James F. Nagle, A History of Government Contracting 52 (2d ed. 1999).
29. Id. at 52, 53.

liam de Steuben for "the sacrifices and eminent services made and rendered to the United States" during the Revolutionary War.[30] The first private bill to pay a tort claim (to rectify damages caused by the government) came in 1792, when Congress enacted a law to compensate the corporation of trustees of a public grammar school and academy of Wilmington, Del., after those buildings had been occupied and damaged by U.S. troops during the Revolutionary War. The bill authorized accounting officers in the government to determine a reasonable compensation and draw funds from the Treasury.[31]

Petitions for various claims were filed in such numbers that lawmakers were soon overwhelmed. To improve their chance of success, claimants hired agents and attorneys who knew how to navigate the halls of Congress. Private bills were referred to a Committee on Claims in each chamber, where the bills were analyzed on their merits. The legislative process had serious deficiencies, particularly because committee hearings were entirely ex parte (heard from one side). Committees took evidence from the claimant but did not hear from a representative of the executive branch.[32]

The next section explains, in some detail, how Congress searched for a remedy that would be fair to the private claimant. Eventually Congress would settle on a Court of Claims to act as a neutral referee, which meant that the government in these cases would be treated as any private party and not be given any special preference. Congress adopted that model when it passed the Federal Tort Claims Act in 1946. In the *Reynolds* case, the district judge and the Third Circuit followed the values of neutrality established by Congress, but the Supreme Court did not.

Court of Claims

The legislative process for handling claims cases became so burdensome and frustrating to Congress that lawmakers drafted bills in 1854 to create some sort of outside board or commission to review claims and pass judgment on them.[33] Legislative language gradually evolved into statutory authority to create a Court of Claims to investigate—but not decide—claims against the government. Once the court was established, Congress continued to delegate

30. 6 Stat. 2 (1790). See also Louis Fisher, The Politics of Executive Privilege 7–10 (2004).

31. 6 Stat. 8 (1792). For legislative debates in the House and Senate, see Annals of Cong., 2d Cong., 1st–2d Sess. 527, 538, 117, 118, 119, 120, 121 (1792).

32. Cong. Globe, 33d Cong., 2d Sess. 108 (1854) (Senator Brodhead).

33. Id. at 15 (Senator Brodhead introducing a bill to establish a "commission for the examination and adjustment of private claims"), 24 (Brodhead reporting a bill for "a board of commissioners"), 68 (Brodhead's "Board of Claims"), 69 (Brodhead's "board of claims") (1854).

additional duties to it, eventually authorizing the court to make binding judg-ments. A key issue was whether the court should function as an agency of government, and therefore partial to it, or as a body capable of operating with full independence of mind and judgment.

During floor debate on December 18, 1854, Senator Richard Brodhead offered a proposal "to remedy an evil which has been a crying one for the last twenty or twenty-five years."[34] He described the unyielding, stark congressio-nal workload: "Two days of every week—one third of the time, to say nothing of the time spent by committees—is set apart for the consideration of private bills and reports, and yet not much more than half are acted upon."[35] He objected that "we are run down by private claimants, and their agents or at-torneys."[36] Senator John Clayton wanted the board to operate independently of the claimant and the government:

> My friend from Pennsylvania [Senator Brodhead] thinks that the com-missioners themselves will be agents of the Government. Sir, I do not wish them to stand in that relation to the Government. I wish them to be impartial arbiters and judges between the United States and the individual claimant, feeling themselves as much bound to look to the interest of the claimant as to the interest of the Government. . . . These commissioners ought to be independent. If they are not judges nomi-nally, they are so in fact, and ought to have that best of all qualities pertaining to a judge—perfect independence. . . . This is a court; call it what you please.[37]

Senator Clayton did not like language in the bill stating that the commission-ers "shall hold their office until the time appointed for the expiration of this act, unless sooner removed by the President." He wanted the words "unless sooner removed by the President" struck from the bill: "I do not wish these commissioners to sit in this high tribunal, liable, at any moment, to be dis-missed by the President or anybody else."[38] Congress stripped that language from the bill.

Senator John Pettit dismissed the doctrine of sovereign immunity as strained and overrated. Even in England, where the maxim "the sovereign cannot be sued" first arose, practice had long supplanted doctrine. The king himself was not sued, but "the law provides that the suit shall be against the Crown, . . .

34. Id. at 70.
35. Id.
36. Id.
37. Id. at 72.
38. Id.

and, if judgment be rendered against the Crown, that the sum shall be paid from the treasury."[39] In the United States, executive departments routinely settled claims against the government: "When Congress refers a question to the head of one of the Departments, or to an inferior officer, as an auditor or comptroller, and say he shall settle the accounts upon principles of equity and justice, what do they do but allow themselves to be sued, and constitute the officer to whom the subject is so referred a tribunal, a judge, from whose decision their [*sic*] is no appeal whatever, but whose determination is final?"[40]

A number of senators thought it would be best to establish an actual court, with appeals taken to the Supreme Court, rather than rely on a board or commissioners to simply make recommendations to Congress. The commission would relieve Congress of some disputes when they resolved the matter in favor of the claimant, but Senator James Jones pointed out that the disappointed claimant, "the most annoying of all, those litigated claims of doubtful propriety, will fall back upon the Congress of the United States, and we shall not have relieved ourselves at all, in my judgment."[41] Brodhead replied that even a purely judicial remedy would not protect Congress from that type of litigant. If a claimant lost in court nothing would prevent the person from turning to Congress and petitioning for relief.[42] As Congress gathered experience and searched for effective remedies, it would convert the advisory commission to a court authorized to make binding judgments.

After the bill cleared the Senate, the House entered into desultory debate and passed the measure 150 to 46.[43] The House Committee on Claims approved the Senate-passed bill, with an amendment prepared to be debated, but the committee recommended that its amendment be withdrawn so that "the bill will now be put before the House just as it came from the Senate."[44] Unlike the Senate, not a single provision of the bill was subject to analysis or debate.[45]

As enacted into law in 1855, the Court of Claims performed an advisory role, acting as an investigatory agency to analyze claims. Congress directed the court to "hear and determine all claims founded upon any law of Congress, or upon any regulation of an executive department, or upon any contract, express or implied, with the government of the United States, which may be suggested to it by a petition filed therein; and also all claims which may be

39. Id. at 73.
40. Id.
41. Id. at 74.
42. Id.
43. Id. at 909.
44. Id.
45. Id. at 127, 388, 400–401, 636–37, 732, 773, 891, 909.

referred to said court by either house of Congress."[46] After hearing witnesses, the court would report to Congress on the cases acted upon, along with its opinion on the claim. The three-judge ruling could include dissents. Favorable rulings would be limited to "less than one thousand dollars."[47] Claims reported adversely by the court would be placed on the calendar of Congress, which could choose to override the court if it wished. Claims reported favorably by the court would have to be enacted into law by Congress.

Congress empowered the court "to call upon any of the departments for any information or papers it may deem necessary," and have the use of all recorded and printed reports made by House and Senate committees. However, the statute contained this discretion on the part of executive officials: "the head of no department shall answer any call for information or papers if, in his opinion, it would be injurious to the public interest."[48]

Subsequent statutes made some of the judgments of the court binding, gradually transforming it into an adjudicatory body. In his first annual message to Congress on December 3, 1861, President Abraham Lincoln turned his attention to providing "some more convenient means" for adjusting claims against the government, "especially in view of their increased number by reason of the war." He highlighted the need for equity: "It is as much the duty of Government to render prompt justice against itself in favor of citizens as it is to administer the same between private individuals." To Lincoln, the investigation and adjudication of claims "in their nature belong to the judicial department." He recommended that the Court of Claims be granted the power of making final judgments, with a right of appeal on questions of law to the Supreme Court.[49] Congress passed legislation in 1863 to implement those objectives.[50]

Legislation in 1883 underscored the determination of Congress to keep itself in the game, ready to interpose its legislative will against judgments by the claims court. When certain claims were pending before congressional committees, the court could not enter final judgment. Instead, it would report its recommendations to Congress.[51] The same procedure applied to pending claims in an executive department that "may involve controverted questions of fact or law." Departmental papers would go to the court, which "shall not

46. 10 Stat. 612, § 1 (1855).

47. Id. at 613, § 7.

48. Id. at 614, § 11.

49. 7 A Compilation of the Messages and Papers of the Presidents 3252 (Richardson ed. 1897).

50. 12 Stat. 765 (1863); see also 14 Stat. 9 (1866).

51. 22 Stat. 485, § 1 (1883).

enter judgment thereon" but report its findings to the department.[52] Amendments in 1885 gave the court jurisdiction over claims arising from the Quasi-War with France (1798 to 1800). In delegating some responsibilities to the court, Congress specified that any finding by the court "shall be taken to be merely advisory as to the law and facts found."[53] Whether the claim would actually be granted depended on legislation enacted by Congress.

Authorizing Tort Actions

In 1886, Congress considered legislative language to allow citizens to sue government for wrongful and negligent acts (tort claims). This was part of an ongoing effort by Congress to reduce the number of private claims requiring legislative consideration.[54] Representative John Tucker drafted a bill to extend the jurisdiction of the Court of Claims "beyond the mere contract obligations of the Government to obligations of all kinds, as well those that could be asserted in a court of law as those which could be asserted in a court of equity or in admiralty."[55] The judgment of the court, he explained, would be final.[56] The House passed the bill 166 to 3.[57]

The Senate, objecting to the sweep of this delegation, reported legislation with important restrictions. The Court of Claims would have jurisdiction to hear and determine all claims "founded upon the Constitution of the United States, or any law of Congress, except for pensions, or any regulation of an Executive Department, or upon any contract, expressed or implied, with the Government of the United States, or for damages, liquidated or unliquidated, *in cases not sounding in tort.*"[58] The bill that emerged from conference kept the Senate prohibition on tort actions.[59]

In separate legislation, covering specific areas, Congress allowed suits against the government for negligence or wrongful acts. In 1910, Congress authorized the Secretary of the Navy to "consider, ascertain, adjust and determine the amounts due on all claims for damages, where the amount of the

---

52. Id. at 485, § 2.

53. 23 Stat. 284, § 6 (1885).

54. 17 Cong. Rec. 663 (1886). See also H. Rept. No. 562, 49th Cong., 1st Sess. (1886) and H. Rept. No. 3497, 49th Cong., 2d Sess. (1886).

55. 18 Cong. Rec. 622 (1887).

56. Id.

57. Id. at 624.

58. Id. at 2175 (emphasis added).

59. Id. at 2676. See also statement of House conferees, paragraph 1, at 2677, Rep. Tucker's explanation at 2678 (middle of left column), and 24 Stat. 505 (1887).

claim does not exceed the sum of five hundred dollars, hereafter occasioned by collision, for which collisions vessels of the navy shall be found to be responsible."[60] Legislation in 1922 increased the amount to $1,000 and authorized agency heads to adjust any claim for property loss or damage caused by the negligence of an officer or employee of the government acting within the scope of official duties. Executive employees included enlisted men in the Army, Navy, and Marine corps.[61]

Legislation in 1920 authorized suits against the United States in admiralty. The suits would proceed "and shall be heard and determined according to the principles of law and to the rules of practice obtaining in like cases between private parties."[62] As it did with cases before the Court of Claims, Congress placed government in the same category as a private party. If sued, it was not to have any special advantages. Also in 1920 Congress passed legislation to give federal courts jurisdiction over the death of a person "caused by a wrongful act, neglect, or default occurring on the high seas."[63] The statute did not specifically mention legal actions against the government, but in 1925 Congress authorized suits against the United States in admiralty for damages caused by vessels belonging to the United States.[64]

Coolidge's Pocket Veto

After proceeding in piecemeal fashion, Congress decided in the late 1920s to pass a general tort claims bill. On January 16, 1928, the House Committee on Claims reported the Federal Tort Claims Bill to relieve Congress "from an intolerable situation" in trying to adjudicate private claims. Legislative machinery no longer served as "a medium of justice or equity toward our citizens."[65] The bill created a liability in the United States for "damages to or loss of privately owned property caused by the negligence or wrongful act or omission of an officer or employee of the United States acting within the scope of his office or employment, and permission is given for the recovery of such liability."[66] The total compensation allowable for personal injury and

60. 36 Stat. 607 (1910).
61. 42 Stat. 1066 (1922).
62. 41 Stat. 526, § 3 (1920).
63. Id. at 537, § 1.
64. 43 Stat. 1112 (1925). These types of admiralty suits are currently covered in 46 U.S.C. §§ 741–90 (2000).
65. H. Rept. No. 286, 70th Cong., 1st Sess. 1 (1928).
66. Id. at 3.

death claims could not exceed $7,500.[67] The committee offered these comments about the doctrine of sovereign immunity:

> The idea that government is immune from the jurisdiction of the courts seems to have arisen from the application of the principles of the Roman law and the adoption of the monarchical principle that the sovereign can do no wrong. This theory of immunity on the part of the sovereign has been found to be impracticable and has been departed from materially by legislative or judicial action in all countries. In some it has been abandoned altogether. In the United States a large measure of indirect action in the form of proceedings against governmental officers and governmental property has been sanctioned by the courts.[68]

During floor action in the House, Representative Charles Lee Underhill (R-Mass.) explained some of the factors that merited a tort claims act. For one, the federal government was "daily directing itself more and more into the affairs of the individual. Therefore the chances of injury because of carelessness of Government employees or because of unavoidable accident becomes greater all the time."[69] Second, the Fifth Amendment guaranteed that "no person shall be deprived of life, liberty, or property without the due process of law, nor shall private property be taken for public use without just compensation." However, in the "greatest and wealthiest country in the world," the U.S. government and its agents "destroys private property and human lives without recompense, compensation, or due process of law."[70] Citizens with claims of personal injury or death had to submit private bills to Congress and hope for the best. After extensive debate, the bill passed the House 280 to 65.[71]

The Senate Committee on Claims reported a very different bill on February 7, 1929. It granted authority to adjudicate disputes not exceeding $50,000 if the damage or loss "proximately resulted from the negligence or wrongful act or omission of any officer or employee of the Government within the scope of his office or employment and not out of contract."[72] The heads of executive departments would investigate these claims "under such regulations as the Comptroller General shall prescribe" and transmit for settlement any claim for damages to the General Accounting Office (GAO) "together with

67. Id. at 5 (Section 204).
68. Id. at 7.
69. 69 Cong. Rec. 2186 (1928).
70. Id.
71. Id. at 2180–81, 2184–204, 3112–31, 3179.
72. S. Rept. No. 1699, 70th Cong., 2d Sess. 1 (1929).

the record and their report and recommendations as to the amount to be allowed, if any."[73] The matter would be left to GAO to settle and adjust the claim, subject to review by the Court of Claims.[74]

In reporting the legislation, the Senate Committee on Claims explained why it decided to depend on the GAO. First, there was no general law providing for the adjustment of tort claims against the United States by the GAO, administrative officers, or the courts.[75] Second, the claims committees were burdened with private bills to pay tort damages caused by acts of omission or commission by officers of the United States.[76] The purpose of the bill was to have claims settled and reported to Congress "by a disinterested agency of the Government [GAO] and thereby uniformity of settlements also secured."[77] If settlement were left to executive departments, the committee anticipated that the Treasury Department would have one idea of liability and the Agriculture Department another: "there is no justification for as many different rules of settlement as there are different departments and establishments of the Government."[78]

The bill passed the Senate, cleared conference committee, and was agreed to by both chambers.[79] However, President Calvin Coolidge pocket vetoed the bill.[80] Senator Robert LaFollette later recalled that Coolidge refused to sign the bill because it made the Comptroller General the counsel for the government instead of the Attorney General.[81] Even though the legislation failed because of this separation of power dispute, both branches recognized the need to develop a system capable of handling tort claims against the government.

Federal Tort Claims Act

On January 14, 1942, President Franklin D. Roosevelt sent a message to Congress, urging it to act on legislation to handle private tort claims and bridge construction. Because of the need to concentrate on the national defense effort, he wanted both branches relieved of the annual burden of passing bills

73. Id.
74. Id. at 2, 7.
75. Id. at 3.
76. Id.
77. Id. at 6.
78. Id.
79. 70 Cong. Rec. 4836–39, 4885, 4940, 4956, 5015, 5181 (1929); H. Rept. No. 2812, 70th Cong., 2d Sess. (1929).
80. Presidential Vetoes, 1789–1988, S. Pub. 102–12, at 236 (1992) [H.R. 9285].
81. 92 Cong. Rec. 6373 (1946).

for private claims and individual bridges. He said that "more than 2,000 private claim bills are introduced in each Congress, and that a substantial percentage of these bills present claims for property damage or personal injury." The executive departments were authorized to settle claims up to $1,000 for property loss or damage and, in a few instances, claims for personal injury up to $500. Many of the private claim bills introduced each year did not fall into those categories. Of the bills Roosevelt vetoed during the previous three Congresses, one-third consisted of private claim bills.[82] He urged Congress to pass legislation that would make available "a means of dispensing justice simply and effectively to tort claimants against the Government and give them the same right to a day in court which claimants now enjoy in fields such as breach of contract, patent infringement, or admiralty claims."[83]

As part of the Legislative Reorganization Act of 1946, Congress enacted legislation to address the growing problem of tort claims. The Joint Committee on the Organization of Congress reported that too much congressional time was devoted to private claims and matters that could be better delegated to executive agencies and the courts. Because of this workload, Congress was "drifting away from its traditional function as a truly representative assembly," draining it of capacity to legislate on matters of national and international importance.[84] The committee regarded Congress as

poorly equipped to serve as a judicial tribunal for the settlement of private claims against the Government of the United States. This method of handling individual claims does not work well either for the Government or for the individual claimant, while the cost of legislating the settlement in many cases far exceeds the total amounts involved.

Long delays in consideration of claims against the Government, time consumed by the Claims Committees of the House and the Senate, and crowded private calendars combine to make this an inefficient method of procedure.

The United States courts are well able and equipped to hear these claims and to decide them with justice and equity both to the Government and to the claimants. We, therefore, recommend that all claims for damages against the Government be transferred by law to the United States Court of Claims and to the United States district courts for proper adjudication.[85]

82. 88 Cong. Rec. 313 (1942).
83. Id. at 314.
84. S. Rept. No. 1011, 79th Cong., 2d Sess. 24 (1946).
85. Id. at 25.

The Federal Tort Claims Act of 1946 authorized federal agencies to settle any claim against the United States "caused by the negligent or wrongful act or omission of any employee of the Government while acting within the scope of his office or employment."[86] Employees of the government included "members of the military or naval forces of the United States, and persons acting on behalf of a Federal agency in an official capacity, temporarily or permanently in the service of the United States, whether with or without compensation."[87] The phrase "acting within the scope of his office or employment," as applied to a member of the U.S. military or naval forces, meant "acting in line of duty."[88] Claims settled by executive agencies could be for money only and could not exceed $1,000.[89]

Other tort suits involving greater sums of money would be handled by federal district courts—again, for money only. The claims would be those that the United States, if a private person, "would be liable to the claimant for such damage, loss, injury, or death in accordance with the law of the place where the act or omission occurred."[90] Several provisions of the bill underscored the point (later raised in the *Reynolds* litigation) that in tort actions the federal government would be treated on a par with the private claimant. The United States would be liable in respect of such claims "in the same manner, and to the same extent as a private individual under like circumstances, except that the United States shall not be liable for interest prior to judgment, or for punitive damages."[91] The district courts would allow costs to the successful claimant "to the same extent as if the United States were a private litigant, except that such costs shall not include attorneys' fees."[92] Congress also authorized the Attorney General to "arbitrate, compromise, or settle any claim cognizable" under the Federal Tort Claims Act, after a suit has been filed and with the approval of the court in which the suit was pending.[93]

To limit the number of tort suits against the government, Congress excluded claims arising out of the loss or negligent transmission of letters or postal matter, the assessment or collection of any tax or customs duty, the imposition or establishment of a quarantine by the United States, injuries to vessels passing through the locks of the Panama Canal or while in Canal Zone

---

86. 60 Stat. 843, § 403(a) (1946).
87. Id., § 402(b).
88. Id., § 402(c).
89. Id., § 403(a).
90. Id., § 410(a).
91. Id.
92. Id.
93. Id., § 413.

waters, combatant activities of the military or naval forces during time of war, and activities of the Tennessee Valley Authority.[94]

Another huge exception consists of what are called "discretionary functions." The tort claims statute does not apply to any claim based upon an act or omission of a federal employee, "exercising due care, in the exercise of a statute or regulation, whether or not such statute or regulation be valid, or based upon the exercise or performance or the failure to exercise or perform a discretionary function or duty on the part of a Federal agency or an employee of the Government, whether or not the discretion involved be abused."[95] In the same year that the Supreme Court decided *Reynolds*, it handled another tort claims case, *Dalehite v. United States* (1953), which focused on the discretionary function exception.[96] This case also involved a military matter, and the Justices split along similar lines. Both cases featured dissents by the same Justices: Jackson, Black, and Frankfurter. *Dalehite* will be looked at more closely in Chapter 4.

Other than the exceptions listed in the statute, Congress authorized courts to adjudicate claims against the government and to decide them fairly. Congress empowered the courts to exercise independent judgment. As with the Court of Claims, a dispute between a private party and the government was to be decided on the facts and the law, with no preferential treatment granted to government. There was no reason for judges to accept at face value the government's claim that an agency document requested by plaintiffs was somehow privileged, without the court itself examining the document to verify the government's judgment.

To uncritically accept the government's word would be to abdicate the court's duty to exercise independent judgment, leaving control entirely in the hands of unchecked and self-interested executive claims. Nothing in the Federal Tort Claims Act implied that courts could deny claims on the basis of any government privilege, much less the state secrets privilege. If the executive branch claimed that a document was too sensitive to be shared with a private party, a judge could always insist that the document be placed in the hands of the court to be read in chamber. That was the position of the district court and the Third Circuit in *Reynolds*, but the Supreme Court unwisely tilted toward the government and embraced, without any independent analysis, the state secrets privilege.

94. Id., § 421.
95. Id., § 421(a). See William G. Weaver and Thomas Longoria, "Bureaucracy that Kills: Federal Sovereign Immunity and the Discretionary Function Exception," 96 Am. Pol. Sci. Rev. 335 (2002).
96. 346 U.S. 15 (1953).

Having shifted tort actions to the courts, Congress banned the type of private bill that had been used for tort actions in the past. The same statute that provided for federal tort claims also stated:

No private bill or resolution (including so-called omnibus claims or pension bills), and no amendment to any bill or resolution, authorizing or directing (1) the payment of money for property damages, for personal injuries or death for which suit may be instituted under the Federal Tort Claims Act, or for a pension (other than to carry out a provision of law or treaty stipulation); (2) the construction of a bridge across a navigable stream; or (3) the correction of a military or naval record, shall be received or considered in either the Senate or the House of Representatives.[97]

The Curtain of Secrecy

Even when plaintiffs are assured that a court has statutory authority to hear a tort case, and a statute directs that government be treated on a par with private litigants, access to the agency documents needed to win a case is always an uphill climb. A preoccupation with secrecy and confidentiality is a natural characteristic of administrative institutions.[98] Max Weber noted that every bureaucracy seeks to increase its superiority "through the means of *keeping secret* its knowledge and intentions. Bureaucratic administration always tends to exclude the public, to hide its knowledge and action from criticism as well as it can."[99] This strategy, he explained, is followed by every bureaucracy, public or private.[100] The concept of the "office secret"

is the specific invention of bureaucracy, and few things it defends so fanatically as this attitude which, outside of the specific areas mentioned, cannot be justified with purely functional arguments. In facing a parliament, the bureaucracy fights, out of a sure power instinct, every one of the institution's attempts to gain through its own means (as, e.g., through the so-called "right of parliamentary investigation") expert knowledge from the interested parties. Bureaucracy naturally prefers a

97. Id. at 831, § 131.
98. Francis E. Rourke, "Secrecy in American Bureaucracy," 72 Pol. Sci. Q. 540 (1957).
99. 3 Max Weber, Economy and Society: An Outline of Interpretive Sociology 992 (Guenther Roth and Claus Wittich eds. 1968) (emphasis in original).
100. Id.

poorly informed, and hence powerless, parliament—at least insofar as this ignorance is compatible with the bureaucracy's own interests.[101]

It has long been the practice of federal agencies to vastly overclassify documents. Approximately two million federal employees, civil and military, are authorized to classify information at some level.[102] Those doing this work are unlikely to get in trouble by overclassifying a document. Underclassifying a document, however, or not classifying it at all, might result in punitive actions against the employee. These individual calculations within an agency make it much more difficult for plaintiffs, lawmakers, and judges to obtain the information needed to adjudicate a case fairly.

It would be a misconception to believe that executive officials are uniquely and steadfastly dedicated to keeping secrets for the purpose of safeguarding national security. Their motivations and conduct are much more mixed. The same agency that is adept at withholding documents can swing in the opposite direction and declassify or leak sensitive records for the purpose of discrediting a private litigant or prevailing in an interagency contest. These abrupt reversals can come at the cost of national security. Officials who unload sensitive documents and information into the public domain are rarely investigated, sanctioned, or punished.

Although executive officials often announce that members of Congress cannot be trusted with sensitive information because they will leak it to the press or the public, the executive branch is by far the greatest source of leaks. President John F. Kennedy spoke accurately in saying that "the Ship of State is the only ship that leaks at the top."[103] When President Richard Nixon was furious about leaks, leading to the creation of a "plumbers" unit and the Watergate break-in, the leaks he worried about came not from Congress but from his own administration.

Official Secrets Acts

The United States has never followed the lead of Great Britain by having an Official Secrets Act. Part of the reason is the comparatively stronger role of Congress in a system of separated powers and America's traditional reliance on checks and balances to prevent a dangerous concentration of power in a single branch. The legislature in a parliamentary system is dominated by the

101. Id. at 992–93.
102. Secrecy, Report of the Commission on Protecting and Reducing Government Secrecy, S. Doc. 105-2 (1997), at xxii.
103. Elie Abel, Leaking: Who Does It? Who Benefits? At What Cost? 17 (1987).

prime minister and executive departments, and has comparatively weak powers of legislative oversight. Moreover, U.S. courts have greater authority to scrutinize and override presidential judgments about classified information than is the case with British courts.

Great Britain adopted the first Official Secrets Act in 1889 to deal with the leak of government secrets. The statute applied to situations where a person "for the purpose of wrongfully obtaining information" enters into a military facility (arsenal, factory, dockyard, camp, etc.), without authority to be there, and "lawfully or unlawfully . . . either obtains any document, sketch, plan, model, or knowledge of any thing which he is not entitled to obtain, or takes without lawful authority any sketch or plan." Anyone who then attempts to communicate that information to "any person to whom the same ought not, in the interest of the State, to be communicated at that time," was subject to imprisonment for a term not exceeding one year, to a fine, or to both.[104] Efforts to give that information "to any agent of a foreign State" were subject to longer terms in prison.[105]

England revised the statute in 1911 in response to concerns about spying by German nationals and German sympathizers in Britain. Previous language "for the purpose" or "wilfully" was dropped and replaced by unqualified punishment for leaking official secrets. The law now applied to individuals "for any purpose prejudicial to the safety or interests of the State." For prosecution, it was not necessary to show that the accused "was guilty of any particular act tending to show a purpose prejudicial to the safety or interests of the State."[106] Section 2 applied the law to government employees at every level (such as ministers and civil servants) and covered those who received government contracts. It applied as well to any person, including the press, who received the documents, "unless he proves that the communication to him of the sketch, plan, model, article, note, document, or information was contrary to his desire."[107] Individuals convicted of violations of Section 2 were subject to imprisonment for up to two years and/or unlimited fines.[108] Other revisions to the Official Secrets Acts were made in 1920, 1939, and 1989.[109]

104. Public General Acts 52 & 53 Vict., 1889, at 269.
105. Id. at 270.
106. Public General Acts 1 & 2 George V, 1911, at 102.
107. Id. at 103.
108. See James B. Christoph, "A Comparative View: Administrative Secrecy in Britain," 35 Pub. Adm. Rev. 23, 26 (1975).
109. Public General Acts 10 & 11 George V, 1920, at 492; Public General Acts 2 & 3 and Part of 3 & 4 George VI, 1938–39, at 1408; Public General Acts Elizabeth II, 1989, Part I, Chapters 1–25, at 101.

The United States has never adopted this kind of statute. An effort in the early 1970s to define and incorporate the state secrets privilege in the Federal Rules of Evidence was unsuccessful (Chapter 5). By statute, Congress has singled out a number of activities that can be punished by fines and prison sentences for individuals who mishandle classified information (Chapter 7). The only provision in the U.S. Constitution relating to secrecy is for *legislative* procedures: "Each House shall keep a Journal of its Proceedings, and from time to time publish the same, excepting such Parts as may in their Judgment require Secrecy."[110]

In 2000, Congress passed a bill that would have established criminal penalties for leaking classified information. Fines and imprisonment for up to three years were included to punish any current or former government employee who "knowingly and willfully discloses, or attempts to disclose," any classified information to a person not authorized to receive the information, "knowing that the person is not authorized access to such classified information."[111] Criminal liability did not apply to the disclosure of classified information to federal judges established under Article III or to any member or committee of Congress. Both the chairman and the ranking member of the House Judiciary Committee opposed this provision, citing "profound First Amendment implications."[112] Nancy Pelosi, Democrat from California, and Bob Barr, Republican from Georgia, warned that the bill would be the first time in American history that Congress had passed an "official secrets act."[113] Although President Clinton recognized the need to deter and punish unauthorized disclosures, he vetoed the bill because it was too restrictive on public discussion. He also noted that there had been no public hearings on the language, and that deliberations within his own administration "lacked the thoroughness this provision warranted."[114]

Agency Resistance

Executive officials stand prepared with a long list of ready-made reasons and doctrines why a member of Congress, a judge, or a citizen may not see a requested document. Agencies can argue that the release of a document will damage the "deliberative process" within the executive branch, or that the

---

110. U.S. Const. art. I, § 5, cl. 3.
111. Section 304 of H.R. 4392, as reported from conference committee; H. Rept. No. 106–969, 106th Cong., 2d Sess. 6–7 (2000).
112. 146 Cong. Rec. 22387, 22389 (2000).
113. Id. at 22390, 22394.
114. Public Papers of the Presidents, 2000–2001, III, at 2467.

document falls within the supposedly protected category of "decisional memoranda." The government can label (properly or artificially) the document as "enforcement sensitive" or "litigation sensitive."[115] In the face of a determined and skilled adversary, the government may eventually have to back down. Congress has a number of tools, including the subpoena power and the threat of holding an executive official in contempt, to force the release of documents and compel testimony.[116] Private litigants have far less leverage.

When the subject matter turns to "national security," agency officials feel especially emboldened to block access to documents. Those who serve in the executive branch, especially experts in national security, often have little difficulty lying or engaging in deception, whether the adversary is Congress, the judiciary, the public, or the international community. They believe they possess superior information, even if the information is later shown to be patently false. Experts who believe they have a unique hold on the truth will resist sharing information with people not in the know. That attitude leads officials to deny information not only to parties outside the executive branch, but even within.

Sissela Bok, in her book *Lying*, explains that individuals who are convinced they know the truth can easily justify lies and deception: "They may perpetuate so-called pious frauds to convert the unbelieving or strengthen the conviction of the faithful. They see nothing wrong in telling untruths for what they regard as a much 'higher' truth."[117] Those who have worked in the executive branch caution that it "is in the nature of things that government officials engage in deception. The healthiest thing, though, is not to wring your hands about it and talk moralistically about how that shouldn't happen, but just be aware that that's part of the game."[118]

Just as "unity" within the White House and the executive branch is considered a virtue for assuring coherent planning and execution, so does it provide an opportunity for deliberate, calculated, and coordinated lying. That pattern was detailed in Bruce Ladd's *Crisis in Credibility* (1968) and John Orman's *Presidential Secrecy and Deception* (1980). The centralized structure of the White House, operating in a culture that values personal loyalty and one-party discipline, enables executive officials to present false and misleading information to Congress, the courts, and the public with almost virtual impunity. A recent article concludes that "it is costless for the president to

115. Louis Fisher, The Politics of Executive Privilege (2004).

116. Id.

117. Sissela Bok, Lying: Moral Choice in Public and Private Life 7 (1978).

118. John Prados and Margaret Pratt Porter, eds., Inside the Pentagon Papers 29 (2004). Statement by Howard Margolis.

assert a secrecy privilege: the overwhelming odds are that the assertion will be successful, and even if unsuccessful, the process of overturning claims of privilege is lengthy and the only potential cost of excessive claims of national security is in bad publicity."[119]

In 1969, the Nixon administration wanted Congress to authorize and fund the supersonic transport plane (the SST). The administration received a report from a panel of scientists commissioned to study the plane. Although the report had been prepared and written with appropriated funds, the White House refused to release it to Congress or the public. Denied full and accurate information, Congress initially provided funds. Close votes in 1971, however, eventually doomed the project. After those votes, litigation forced the administration to release the report and it became public. The report cited numerous reasons why Congress should not fund the aircraft.[120]

A more recent example of White House deceit is the prescription drug program, enacted in 2004. Members of Congress were told by the administration that the bill would cost $395 billion over a ten-year period. Republicans warned that if the estimate topped $400 billion they would withdraw their support. What was withheld, instead, were calculations by administration experts that the cost would likely be $500 billion or higher. The chief actuary of the Department of Health and Human Services, responsible for assuring the integrity of cost projections, was ordered by his superiors not to share the higher figure with Congress, including the committees of jurisdiction.[121]

It had been the understanding of Congress for decades that the chief actuary had a duty to share cost estimates with lawmakers to assist them with their legislative duties. The statute authorizing this office appeared to anticipate a nonpartisan expert who would have "superior expertise in the actuarial sciences" and who would exercise official duties "in accordance with professional standards of actuarial independence."[122] The administration, however, insisted that it could order the chief actuary to withhold information as part of the President's constitutional duty to supervise and control the executive branch. According to this legal analysis, the administration is empowered to

119. William G. Weaver and Robert M. Pallitto, "State Secrets and Executive Power," 120 Pol. Sci. Q. 85, 86 (2005).

120. Paul N. McCloskey Jr., Truth and Untruth: Political Deceit in America 75–84 (1972).

121. Amy Goldstein, "Official Says He Was Told to Withhold Medicare Data," Washington Post, March 13, 2004, at A1; Robert Pear, "Democrats Demand Inquiry into Charge by Medicare Officer," New York Times, March 14, 2004, at 1; Christopher Lee, "Ex-Medicare Chief's Pay Illegal, GAO Says," Washington Post, September 8, 2004, at A21; Robert Pear, "Inquiry Proposes Penalties for Hiding Medicare Data," New York Times, September 8, 2004, at A16.

122. 42 U.S.C. § 1317 (2000).

prevent the chief actuary from communicating accurate information, compiled at taxpayer expense, to Congress.[123] As a result, lawmakers voted on the prescription drug program with inaccurate and misleading cost estimates. The administration knew the facts, but not Congress (or the public). After Congress passed the law, the White House announced that the cost of the drug benefit would be at least $720 billion over the next decade.[124]

Executive deception in the field of national security has a unique history, full of various self-serving justifications. Overclassification and a penchant for secrecy narrows the circle of policy makers. Those who happen to be privileged to read classified documents, even if the documents are false and unreliable, regard others as uninformed and thus unqualified and ineligible to participate in the formulation of policy. It does not matter whether the excluded party is Congress, a court, a private litigant, or another agency.

Justified Lying

Lying about national security is necessary and appropriate at times. If a President, acting as Commander in Chief, indicates to an enemy that U.S. forces are likely to mount an attack from the north, when the planned attack all along is from the south, no one would question both the morality and propriety of the deception. That type of feint is common practice by both sides in time of war. During the 1960 presidential campaign, Senator John Kennedy raised the issue whether the Eisenhower administration was planning to use military force against Cuba. Vice President Richard Nixon, knowing that a covert operation had indeed been prepared, decided to dismiss Kennedy's suggestion in order not to put Fidel Castro on notice.[125] A number of deceptive statements can be justified. A country may decide to allow the enemy to bomb an unprotected city, even if it knew of the attack in advance, rather than reveal to the enemy that it has broken its secret code. Cruel choices of that nature are part of war.

Presidents have broad discretion in deciding how to classify agency documents. In an executive order issued in 1940, President Franklin D. Roosevelt provided guidelines on the categories of Secret, Confidential, and Re-

123. Letter of May 21, 2004 from Jack L. Goldsmith III, Assistant Attorney General, Office of Legal Counsel, U.S. Department of Justice, to Alex M. Azar II, General Counsel, Department of Health and Human Services.

124. Robert Pear, "New White House Estimate Lifts Drug Benefit Cost to $720 Billion," New York Times, February 9, 2005, at A1.

125. James P. Pfiffner, The Character Factor: How We Judge America's Presidents 22–23 (2004).

stricted.[126] President Harry Truman kept those classifications but added Top Secret.[127] He provided further details a year later.[128] As explained in another executive order issued in 1982 by President Ronald Reagan, classification and declassification are performed not merely to safeguard national security information, but also to recognize that "it is essential that the public be informed concerning the activities of its Government."[129] Moreover, "[i]n no case shall information be classified in order to conceal violations of law, inefficiency, or administrative error; to prevent embarrassment to a person, organization, or agency; to restrain competition; or to prevent or delay the release of information that does not require protection in the interest of national security."[130] Those are excellent standards, but their enforcement depends entirely on the executive branch.

The Limits of Lying

Lying to an enemy is understandable. What justifies lies to Congress, the judiciary, and the public? Executive officials who lie to Congress may face contempt citations and prosecutions for perjury, but such cases are rare. In extreme circumstances, presidential lies (and obstruction of justice) can result in impeachment and removal from office. For the most part, individuals in the executive branch who engage in lies go unpunished. With little accountability, the learning curve for honesty and integrity is modest. Executive officials do learn, but it is the knowledge that deception to Congress, the courts, and the public comes at little personal cost.

False statements and deception by executive officials are especially damaging in court, where litigants are given reason to expect a fair chance of presenting their case before a neutral judge. If, however, the administration invokes the state secrets privilege to block access to agency documents, the judge has to decide how to maintain independence and impartiality. To accept the government's assertion without actually looking at the disputed documents puts the court in league with the executive branch and eliminates the possibility of a fair trial for the private litigant. Alternatively, a court may look at the document in chambers to subject the government's decision to independent scrutiny. A court can also inform the government that if it wants to insist on the state secrets privilege, the private party will prevail because it was unable to obtain documents needed for its lawsuit. That result is especially justified

---

126. Executive Order 8381, 5 Fed. Reg. 1147 (1940).
127. Executive Order 10104, 15 Fed. Reg. 597, 598 (1950).
128. Executive Order 10290, 16 Fed. Reg. 9795 (1951).
129. Executive Order 12356, Public Papers of the Presidents, 1982, I, at 412.
130. Id. at 414, § 1.6 (a).

when the government tries to prosecute someone for criminal activities on the basis of documents it will not share with the defendant or with the court. Those choices are explored in detail in Chapter 7.

The Price of Secrecy

Secrecy does not assure either security or success. Executive lies and deception inflict severe and long-lasting damage to the nation. David Wise, in *The Politics of Lying* (1973), wrote: "The excuse for secrecy and deception most frequently given by those in power is that the American people must sometimes be misled in order to mislead the enemy. This justification is unacceptable on moral and philosophic grounds, and often it simply isn't true. Frequently the 'enemy' knows that is going on, but the American public does not."[131] When the U.S. government waged a "secret war" in Laos, American citizens were kept in the dark—but the Laotians certainly were not. During the Vietnam War, the Johnson administration entered into secret commitments to provide funds to the Philippines, Thailand, and South Korea for their support.[132] The allocation of those funds had been kept from Congress and the public, but of course not from the allies.

Secrecy can damage national security. The Bay of Pigs operation in 1961 failed because it was "too secretive, too compartmentalized, no accountability or review, no notes."[133] Extreme CIA secrecy and compartmentalization prevented the Joint Chiefs of Staff "from fully auditing the soundness of plans as many changes were made."[134] In analyzing why the Reagan presidency ran afoul of the Iran-Contra scandal, the Tower Commission Report attributed the failures to "the obsession with secrecy." The "concern for preserving the secrecy of the initiative provided an excuse for abandoning sound process. . . . The effect of this informality was that the initiative lacked a formal institutional record."[135]

On August 6, 2001, President Bush received a Presidential Daily Briefing (PDB) entitled "Bin Ladin Determined to Strike in US." PDBs are so secret that only a select group of executive officials are allowed to see them, and they are not shared with members of Congress. This particular PDB was declassified and approved for release on April 10, 2004. The text begins: "Clandes-

131. David Wise, The Politics of Lying: Government Deception, Secrecy, and Power 344 (1973).
132. Louis Fisher, Presidential War Power 135–37 (2d ed. 2004).
133. David M. Abshire, Saving the Reagan Presidency: Trust Is the Coin of the Realm 66 (2005).
134. Id. at 45. See Richard M. Bissell Jr., Reflections of a Cold Warrior 152–204 (1996).
135. The Tower Commission Report 68, 69–70 (1987).

tine, foreign government, and media reports indicate Bin Ladin since 1997 has wanted to conduct terrorist attacks in the US. Bin Ladin implied in US television interviews in 1997 and 1998 that his followers would follow the example of World Trade Center bomber Ramzi Yousef and 'bring the fighting to America.'" The text reported that Bin Ladin "wanted to hijack a US aircraft to gain the release of 'Blind Shaykh' Umar Abd al-Rahman and other US-held extremists." FBI information "indicates patterns of suspicious activity in this country consistent with preparations for hijackings or other types of attacks, including recent surveillance of federal buildings in New York."[136]

After public release of this document, the White House prepared a "Fact Sheet" stating that the PDB "did not warn of the 9–11 attacks. Although the PDB referred to the possibility of hijackings, it did not discuss the possible use of planes as weapons."[137] Even if the PDB did not predict that planes would be flown into the World Trade Center and the Pentagon, the knowledge that Al Qaeda was planning attacks in the United States by using aircraft was of public importance. Had the document been published in August 2001, it would have put U.S. airports on alert and might have done some good. It appeared to have little use kept secret.

As a second example of dysfunctional secrecy, on February 7, 2002, President Bush signed a secret memorandum entitled "Humane Treatment of al Qaeda and Taliban Detainees." He accepted the legal conclusion of the Justice Department that none of the provisions of the Geneva Conventions apply to Al Qaeda because it was not a High Contracting party to the treaties. He also determined that Taliban detainees did not qualify as prisoners of war under Geneva. However, he also stated that "our values as a Nation, values that we share with many nations in the world, call for us to treat detainees humanely, including those who are not legally entitled to such treatment. Our Nation has been and will continue to be a strong supporter of Geneva and its principles. As a matter of policy, the United States Armed Forces shall continue to treat detainees humanely and, to the extent appropriate and consistent with military necessity, in a manner consistent with the principles of Geneva." He said that the United States "will hold states, organizations, and individuals who gain control of United States personnel responsible for treating such personnel humanely and consistent with applicable law."[138]

This memo was not declassified until June 17, 2004, after the international community was stunned to see photographs of prisoner abuses by American

136. Available from a Web site, but the document has no Internet markings.

137. Office of the Press Secretary, the White House, "Fact Sheet: The August 6, 2001 PDB," April 10, 2004, at 1; http://www.fas.org/irp/news/2004/04/wh041004.html.

138. Available from a Web site, but the document has no Internet markings. The bottom of the first page states: "Declassified in Full on 6/17/2004."

personnel at the Abu Ghraib facility in Iraq. Prisoners were also abused in U.S. camps located in Afghanistan, Guantánamo, and CIA "black sites" in various countries. Had the Bush policy of humane treatment of detainees been posted at U.S. prisons and made public as administration policy, there would have been both a policy and a mechanism in place to enforce a presidential order. Secrecy permitted the excesses to go unchecked and unmonitored, at great cost to U.S. prestige.

In a book published in 2004, Eric Alterman analyzed the price of executive branch dishonesty. Presidents end up "not only in fooling the nation but also in fooling themselves." Heavy costs can pile up against the President, his party, and the nation. Although public officials and some academics continue to explicitly or implicitly condone stealth and deception by Presidents, Alterman views presidential dishonesty as "ultimately and invariably self-destructive."[139] Sissela Bok reminds us: "Truth and integrity are precious resources, easily squandered, hard to regain. They can thrive only on a foundation of respect for veracity."[140]

In the B-29 case, the government's decision to withhold documents from the three widows prompted the district court and the Third Circuit to decide the tort claims case in their favor. At those stages, the courts played their assigned task by protecting the ability of each party to present its case fairly in court. If the women were unable to argue their case effectively because the government refused to release key documents—even to the district judge—the judiciary decided that government must pay a price by losing the case. At the level of the Supreme Court, however, the Justices accepted what the government alleged about the accident report and the survivor statements, without ever making an independent inspection of the materials. Not only did that undermine the case brought by the widows, it also signaled that the Court functioned as part of the executive branch rather than as an independent institution. The picture looked worse, a half century later, when it was discovered that the documents had been falsely described by the government and the courts had been misled.

139. Eric Alterman, When Presidents Lie: A History of Official Deception and Its Consequences 22 (2004).
140. Bok, Lying, at 249.

2

IN DISTRICT COURT

After the crash of the B-29 on October 6, 1948, Phyllis Brauner began to prepare to sue the government for the wrongful death of her husband. Her family lawyer, Theodore Mattern, learned in early 1949 that Elizabeth Palya would be interested in joining the suit. Their attorneys agreed it would be best to try the case in the Philadelphia area rather than in Georgia.[1] On June 21, 1949, Brauner and Palya filed their lawsuit in district court in the Eastern District of Pennsylvania to recover damages for the deaths of their husbands. They sued under the Federal Tort Claims Act. At that stage, the case was styled *Brauner and Palya v. United States*. Patricia Reynolds filed her case later that year, on September 27, and on December 8, the two cases were consolidated for trial. Charles Biddle of Philadelphia provided legal representation for the three women and handled oral argument in court.

The case was assigned to Chief Judge William H. Kirkpatrick. After graduating from the University of Pennsylvania law school, he practiced for several years and joined the Army Judge Advocate's Corps during World War I. Discharged as a lieutenant colonel, he spent a term in the U.S. House of Representatives from 1921 to 1923 and was nominated by President Calvin Coolidge to a district judgeship in 1927. He served as chief judge from 1948 to 1958.[2]

The three wives charged that the accident and the deaths of their husbands "were caused solely and exclusively by the negligent and wrongful acts and omissions of the officers and employees of the defendant [the U.S. government] while acting within the scope of their office and employment, and were due in no manner whatsoever to any act or failure to act on the part" of the civilians who died.[3] The complaint pointed out that William Brauner left a wife, a daughter Susan (age four), and a daughter Catherine born on February 12, 1949. An amount of $300,000 was requested for Phyllis Brauner "or such

---

1. Letter from Mrs. Palya's attorney, W. J. Perryman, to Theodore Mattern, January 7, 1949; letter given to author by Cathy Brauner.
2. Directory of American Judges (Charles Liebman ed. 1955); Biographical Directory of the Federal Judiciary, 1789–2000, at 602 (2001).
3. Transcript of Record, Supreme Court of the United States, October Term, 1952, No. 21, United States v. Reynolds, at 5 (hereafter "Transcript of Record").

larger amount to which this Honorable Court may determine she is legally entitled."[4] Albert Palya left a wife, a son Robert (age nine), a son William (age six), and a daughter Judith (seven weeks old). The complaint also asked for $300,000 for Elizabeth Palya, or a larger amount if the court so decided.[5]

In a response dated November 22, 1949, the Justice Department replied that "there were no negligent and wrongful acts and omissions on the part of any officers or employees" of the government, and claimed that the government "was in no manner responsible for the accident."[6] The court denied a motion to dismiss the case. The three wives moved for an order requiring the government to produce (1) written statements of the three crewmen who survived the crash and (2) the government's report and findings of the official investigation. The government opposed the motion on the grounds that the plaintiffs had not shown "good cause" for the production of the documents, and that the report and findings of investigation were "privileged."[7]

Preparing for Trial

In an effort to understand the cause of the B-29 accident and the government's level of culpability, the wives were entitled to obtain facts and information from the government to assist them at the pretrial stage. Federal Rules of Civil Procedure provide for various tools of discovery: depositions, interrogatories (written questions), and production of documents. Rule 27 provides for depositions before trial and pending appeal. Parties to a lawsuit may identify the names and addresses of the persons to be examined and the substance of the testimony that the party expects to obtain. Under Rule 33, any party may serve upon any other party written interrogatories to be answered by the party served.[8] Each interrogatory shall be answered separately and fully in writing under oath. At the time of the *Reynolds* litigation, answers were due 15 days after service of the interrogatories, "unless the court, on motion and notice and for good cause shown, enlarges or shortens the time." Within ten days of service, the party receiving the interrogatories may respond with written objections.

Access to documents is governed by Rule 34. Upon motion of any party "showing good cause" and upon notice to all other parties, the court may

4. Id.
5. Id. at 6.
6. Id. at 7.
7. Brauner v. United States, 10 F.R.D. 468, 469–70 (D. Pa. 1950).
8. 28 U.S.C. 3300 (1946 ed.).

order any party "to produce and permit the inspection and copying or photographing" of any designated documents, papers, books, accounts, letters, photographs, objects, "or tangible things not privileged," within the scope of examination permitted by discovery.[9] The order specifies the time, place, and manner of making the inspection and taking the copies "and may prescribe such terms and conditions as are just."[10]

Failure to cooperate in discovery is covered by Rule 37. If a party refuses to answer any question during a deposition, the remainder of the deposition shall be completed. Afterward, on reasonable notice to all affected persons, the party that asked the question may request from the court an order compelling an answer. Refusals to comply with depositions and interrogatories may result in court orders that require the parties to pay reasonable expenses, including attorney's fees. Rule 37 contains other sanctions. If a party refuses to be sworn or refuses to answer any question after being directed to do so by the court, the refusal may be considered a contempt of court.[11]

Interrogatories

On November 28, 1949, Charles Biddle submitted 31 questions to the government, requesting that it provide answers and submit copies of identified records and documents. The first question asked whether the government had directed an investigation into the crash. If so, the government was to attach to its answer a copy of the reports and findings of the investigation (or investigations, if more than one).[12] On January 5, 1950, the government responded to the interrogatories. It acknowledged that there had been an investigation, but the report would not be produced "as it is not within the scope of an interrogatory filed pursuant to Rule 33, Federal Rules of Civil Procedure, as amended."[13] No claim of state secrets was advanced at that point.

Biddle's second question asked whether the government required that current aircraft maintenance records be maintained. He requested copies of the records, "covering the entire history of the aircraft." The government affirmed that such records were required but said they were destroyed in the crash. In response to Questions 3 and 4, the government acknowledged that it was required to maintain flight engineering records and also records or logs show-

9. Id. at 3301.
10. Id.
11. Id. at 3303.
12. Transcript of Record, at 8.
13. Id. at 12.

ing mechanical condition, maintenance of equipment, and flight records. It attached copies of those materials.

Question 5 asked whether the government had obtained statements, either oral or written, concerning the events that led up to the crash, the mechanical condition of the plane immediately prior to the crash, the cause or probable cause of the crash and loss of lives, and other matters concerning the crash. The government confirmed that such statements and records existed. However, it refused to release the materials on the ground that they were beyond the scope of an interrogatory filed pursuant to Rule 33. It did provide, as requested in Question 6, the names and addresses of the four survivors who gave statements: Captain Herbert W. Moore (copilot), S/Sgt. Walter J. Peny (left scanner), T/Sgt. Earl W. Murrhee (flight engineer), and "Eugene Mechlir." The latter refers to Eugene A. Mechler, the only civilian who survived.

Question 7: "Was any engine trouble experienced with the said B-29 type aircraft on October 6, 1948, prior to the crash?"[14] The government's unhelpful reply: "Yes, almost immediately before the crash." Question 8 asked for the altitude that trouble was first experienced and the details of the trouble. The government answered that the trouble occurred at 18,500 feet at approximately 2 P.M. Eastern standard time. At between 18,500 or 19,000 feet, the manifold pressure on engine No. 1 dropped to 23 inches. The pilot "feathered" that engine (shut it down and changed the angle of the blade to make it parallel to the line of flight). A fire broke out in engine No. 1 but was extinguished. (Plaintiffs later learned that the fire was not put out.) In response to Question 9, as to whether any of the engines caught fire prior to the crash, the department said that engine No. 1 caught fire at approximately 20,000 feet and at approximately 2:05 P.M. Eastern time, and that one fire occurred.

Questions 10 and 11 asked what orders had been issued to the civilians on the plane to adjust their parachutes and prepare to bail out. At what altitude and time? Was the order ever given to the civilians to bail out? At what altitude and time, and "how was it given"? Also, was the plane in normal flight at the time? The government answered that the pilot instructed all personnel—military and civilian—to put their chutes on immediately after leveling out at 20,000 and prior to the outbreak of the fire. At the moment the gear was extended and the bomb bay doors opened to facilitate parachuting from the plane, the aircraft fell into a "violent spin," and the "centrifugal force probably made it difficult to bail out."[15] The government said that testimony did not indicate whether or not an order to bail out had been given. It did not say whether the civilians had been given instructions on how to use a parachute.

14. Id. at 9.
15. Id. at 12.

Question 12 asked whether the plane was equipped with an automatic pilot. If so, was it functioning properly on the day of the crash, when was the equipment first turned on, and was it operating at the time the order to bail out was given? "If not, why not?" The government answered that the plane did have an automatic pilot, that it was functioning on the climb, and that the autopilot was not being used at the time of the accident. The pilot turned it off. "The erratic action of the aircraft after the gear was extended and the bomb bay doors opened would have precluded using the auto pilot to hold the aircraft while bailing out."[16] Question 13: What was the time of the crash, and at what altitude above sea level? Answer: the plane crashed at approximately 2:08 P.M. Eastern time and at about 500 feet above sea level.

The interrogatory explored the plane's fire-fighting equipment. Did it have that equipment? Was the equipment standard for the plane? If not, describe the difference. Did the equipment include a capacity for smothering engine fires? If the equipment existed, how recently before the crash had the equipment been tested? Was the equipment functioning properly immediately before the crash? Was the crash due in any way to a failure on the part of the equipment to function properly? The plaintiffs requested any reports regarding the failure of the fire-fighting equipment, either at the time of the accident or previously. Responding to these Questions 14 and 15, the government said that fire-fighting equipment existed, it was standard equipment, it had a carbon dioxide fire extinguisher system for smothering engine fires, the fire-fighting equipment had been tested in June 1948, it was functioning properly immediately before the crash, and the crash was not due in any way to a failure on the part of the fire-fighting equipment. In view of the government's answer that the equipment was functioning properly, it said that no reports existed on the failure of the equipment.

Question 16 asked for the date the plane was first placed in an operational status. Answer: October 19, 1945. Next question: How many hours in flight had been logged by the plane prior to the crash? Answer: 304 hours and ten minutes. Question 18: Had the plane been involved in any accident or accidents prior to October 6, 1948? If so, provide details and attach copies of official reports of investigation. Response: The plane had never been involved in a prior accident. Question 19: Did the government have in force on the day of the accident any written standard regulations with reference to the operation of Army aircraft and the carrying of civilian personnel? The government replied in the affirmative and attached copies of the regulations.

Questions 20 and 21 asked for the names of the pilot and copilot and whether the government required that a log or record of their flying experi-

16. Id. at 12–13.

ence be maintained. The government provided the names of Captains Ralph W. Erwin and Herbert W. Moore Jr., and attached the records of their flying experience. Question 22: Was the plane fitted with emergency escape hatches? If so, provide the size and location of each escape hatch and the number of doors that must be opened to escape from each hatch. Answer: The plane was equipped with emergency escape hatches. An attached exhibit indicated their size and location. The government explained that two doors must be opened to exit from the rear pressurized compartments, and one door must be opened to exit from the front compartment.

Question 23 requested the weight of the B-29 when empty and its gross weight loaded on the day of the accident. Also, what was the maximum gross weight allowable for the plane under normal conditions, and was there anything unusual about the distribution of weight or personnel on October 6, 1948? Answer: 69,121 pounds empty and a gross weight of 109,000 pounds on the day of the accident. Under normal conditions, the "gross weight allowable is 102,000 pounds."[17] The government said there was nothing unusual about the distribution of weight or personnel on October 6, 1948.

Question 24: Did the engines of the B-29 tend to overheat when run at full power? If so, for what periods, and at what times were the engines run at full power on October 6, 1948? Did the engines give any evidence of overheating on that date? If so, provide details, including time and temperature. The government responded that the engines of all aircraft, including the B-29, tend to overheat when run at full power. It said that the engines of the B-29 on October 6, 1948, were never run at full power. Only the prescribed takeoff, climb, and cruise power settings were used, and they never approached full power. The engine head temperatures of engine Nos. 1, 2, and 4 were high after takeoff, and the manifold pressure was reduced to 40 inches of mercury. The airspeed was kept at 195 miles per hour, and no further high head temperature was experienced. The engine reaction, the government said, was not unusual for the B-29 on climbs after takeoff.

Two questions related to keeping a radio log. Question 25 asked whether a radio log was kept on the B-29 showing communications with other aircraft and with ground stations. If so, a copy of the radio log for October 6, 1948, was requested. Question 26: Was a radio log kept at Robins Air Force Base of messages sent to and received from the B-29 on the day of the accident? If so, provide a copy of the radio log. The government answered that if the B-29 kept a radio log, "it was destroyed in the aircraft crash." A radio log was kept by the control tower at Robins of messages sent to and received by the B-29 for takeoff instruction, but the military airways logs "are destroyed after one

17. Id. at 13.

year and if there were any en route messages to any airways station from said aircraft they are no longer available."[18] The government attached a copy of the radio log from the air base tower.

Question 27: Did the pilot bail out with his parachute? If so, at what altitude? Question 28 requested the same information about the copilot. The government said that the pilot "did not appear to have bailed out. Body was found near wreckage, with no parachute attached."[19] The copilot bailed out at approximately 15,000 feet. Question 29 asked for copies of any pictures taken by the government of the wreckage after the crash. The government provided them.

The last two questions sought information about possible mechanical or engineering defects on the B-29 for three months immediately preceding the crash. Was it necessary at any time to postpone a scheduled flight of the plane because of those defects? The government's answer to Question 30 is confusing: "No. Scheduled flight was postponed for mechanical and engineering defects for three months prior to October 6, 1948."[20] Perhaps it was supposed to read: "No scheduled flight was postponed for mechanical and engineering flight for three months prior to October 6, 1948." The last question asked whether the government had prescribed modifications for the B-29 engines to prevent overheating and to reduce fire hazards. If so, when were the modifications prescribed? If any modifications had been carried out, the interrogatory asked for details. The government's answer to this crucial question was a blunt and abrupt "No."[21] When the declassified accident report was discovered on the Internet in 2000, the falsity of that answer became apparent.

Pressing for Documents

After the government's response on January 5, 1950, Charles Biddle filed a motion for the production of documents. Acting under Rule 34, he moved to compel the government to permit plaintiffs to inspect and copy the following documents: the report and findings of the official investigation of the B-29 crash and the three statements taken by the government of the surviving crew members, Moore, Peny, and Murrhee. Biddle stated that the government "has the possession, custody and control of each of the foregoing documents, and has refused to provide copies of same although requested to do so pursuant to

18. Id. at 14.
19. Id.
20. Id.
21. Id.

interrogatories propounded by plaintiffs for answer under Rule 33." Each of the documents, he said, "constitutes or contains evidence or information relevant and material to the action and necessary to the plaintiffs in preparation for trial of this action, as more fully shown in Exhibit A hereto attached."[22] Exhibit A, signed by Elizabeth Palya, stated that "all of said documents are material and necessary . . . to enable her counsel to prepare for trial and that she cannot safely proceed to trial without them." She asked the court to allow her attorney, "during the ordinary business hours for such a period as the court shall direct," to take photostatic copies of the documents.[23]

On January 25, the government offered five reasons to withhold the documents. The first: "Report and findings of official investigation of air crash near Waycross, Georgia, are privileged documents, part of the executive files and declared confidential, pursuant to regulation promulgated under authority of Revised Statute 161 (5 U.S. Code 22)."[24] The citation is to the Housekeeping Statute, which dates back to 1789 and merely directed agency heads to keep custody of official documents. It did not in any way authorize withholding documents from plaintiffs or the courts. The classification "confidential" was standard practice for an airplane investigation and did not, by itself, raise a question of national security or state secrets. That claim would come later.

The second reason: "Report and findings of the official investigation of air crash near Waycross, Georgia, are hearsay."[25] The government did not elaborate on why the documents should be called hearsay, which is usually considered to be evidence based not on a witness's personal knowledge but on another's statement not made under oath. Reasons 3 to 5 were also based on the hearsay argument. According to the government, the statements made by Moore, Peny, and Murrhee were all hearsay, "and if the same is desired plaintiffs could take his deposition."[26]

Lower Court Guidance

Judge Kirkpatrick did not decide the case until June 30, 1950. By that time, several district and appellate courts had issued important rulings on access to government documents in cases involving military accidents. Federal judges had heard the government argue in previous cases that certain documents were too sensitive, privileged, or secret to be shared with a private plaintiff. In

22. Id. at 15.
23. Id. at 16.
24. Id. at 17.
25. Id.
26. Id.

such cases, the judges reasoned, the documents should be given to the court to independently determine and verify whether the government had accurately characterized the contents.

A district court decision in 1944, *United States v. Haugen,* seemed to endorse total judicial deference to military claims—at least in time of war—that a requested document was confidential and could not be shared with private parties or the courts. As one follows the litigation through its various stages, however, the case does not support so sweeping a proposition. Richard Roland Haugen was charged with possessing, publishing, and circulating counterfeit meal tickets with intent to defraud the United States. He said he did not know that the meal tickets, issued by the Olympic Commissary Company, were in any way associated with an agency of the United States. The "national security" quality of the case arose because Olympic Commissary was a government contractor in the secret defense project at Hanford, Washington, a project designed to create fission of uranium derivatives and the construction of an atomic bomb.

The government needed to show that the company was indeed a federal agency. To do that, it needed to produce the contract between the United States and the company, but the originals were in the office of the Comptroller General of the General Accounting Office in Washington, D.C. Instead of obtaining the contract and showing it to Haugen or the court, the government relied on oral testimony from a major. The district judge initially seemed to find this argument acceptable: "The right of the Army to refuse to disclose confidential information, the secrecy of which it deems necessary to national defense, is indisputable."[27] In support of this assertion (which other courts had rejected), the judge cited only two lower court cases.[28] It also quoted this language from an Army regulation: "Secret Material—a. Documents, information or material, the unauthorized disclosure of which would endanger national security, cause serious injury to the interests or prestige of the Nation, or any Governmental activity thereof, or would be of great advantage to a foreign nation, shall be classified secret."[29]

It would be quite remarkable for a court to allow the government to prosecute an individual on the basis of a document it refused to release, yet the court seemed willing to read itself out of the picture: "The determination of what steps are necessary in time of war for the protection of national security lies exclusively with the military and is not subject to court review."[30] Not-

27. United States v. Haugen, 58 F.Supp. 436, 438 (E.D. Wash. 1944).
28. Id.; Firth Sterling Steel Co. v. Bethlehem Steel Co., 199 F. 353, and In re Grove, 180 F. 62.
29. 58 F.Supp. at 438 (Note 1).
30. Id.

withstanding that rhetoric, the court did not proceed in such a passive and subservient manner. It asked whether "secondary evidence" (not the contract but the oral testimony from the major) was admissible in a courtroom.[31] While stating that the "exigencies of war require the withholding of the original document,"[32] it also found it unsatisfactory to rely on "a copy of the copy."[33] Because the major "could not introduce a copy of the copy, it is clear that he cannot testify as to his recollection of the copy."[34] Further: "No showing was made that the plaintiff [the government] could not produce a witness who had seen the original."[35]

Because the government had "failed to present the best evidence available to it," the judge concluded that he should have sustained the initial objection to the major's testimony. Without such evidence, the government "has failed to sustain its burden of proving that the Olympic Commissary was an agency of the United States and that the counterfeiting of its meal tickets was calculated to defraud the United States."[36] The court therefore dismissed the government's effort to prosecute Haugen. In short, the government could withhold a requested document, but exercising that privilege would come at a price: Keep the document and lose the case. That is precisely what happened in district court and the Third Circuit with the *Reynolds* case.

In *Haugen,* the government decided in its appeal to the Ninth Circuit to share the disputed document with the trial court. After the district judge dismissed the indictment against Haugen, five days later the government moved to reopen the case "and proposed to submit the evidence which the court stated in its opinion 'it seems not unreasonable to . . . require.'"[37] The trial then proceeded. The Ninth Circuit said there was no question that Haugen "was a counterfeiter and forger of the meal tickets and that he had possessed them and sold some as charged in the second and third counts."[38] The question was solely one of adequate evidence. To meet the test established by the district judge and at the suggestion of Haugen's attorney, the government handed the contract to the court "for its consideration."[39] Having examined the contract and concluding that the Olympic Commissary was an agency of the United States, the Ninth Circuit affirmed the conviction and sentencing

31. Id. at 439.
32. Id.
33. Id. at 440.
34. Id.
35. Id.
36. Id.
37. Haugen v. United States, 153 F.2d 850, 851 (9th Cir. 1946).
38. Id. at 852.
39. Id.

of Haugen.[40] Although the district court initially argued that the military had exclusive control in determining what steps are necessary in time of war to protect national security, and that courts had no power or authority to conduct an independent review, the Ninth Circuit looked at the disputed document and formed its own judgment.

Struggles over access to government documents appear in several other cases decided just before district court action in *Reynolds*. In *Bank Line Limited* (1946), the plaintiffs requested a copy of a record prepared by the U.S. Naval Board of Investigation regarding collisions between inbound and outbound vessels of a convoy. The plaintiff relied on Rule 32 of the Admiralty Code, but the government withheld the record by making a claim of privilege and arguing that disclosure would seriously hamper the administration of the Navy Department. A district court ruled that the plaintiff was entitled to the record. No reasons of national security had been presented to justify the claim of privilege.[41] In the government's appeal to the Second Circuit, letters were received from the Judge Advocate of the Navy and the Acting Secretary of the Navy, both urging the appellate court to refuse access to the Navy Board's record because it would interfere with the Navy's investigatory and fact-finding procedure and would be prejudicial to the department's best interests.[42] (Similar letters were forwarded to the courts in the *Reynolds* case.) After the Second Circuit turned aside the government's petition to deny production of the record, the district court in 1948 allowed access to the documents.[43] In referring to the sovereign's command *Soit droit fait al partie* (Let right be done to the party), it added this observation: "But right cannot be done if the government is allowed to suppress the facts in its possession."[44]

Wunderly v. United States (1948) involved a collision between the plaintiff's automobile and an Army jeep. The government furnished plaintiff with copies of statements made by the driver and his immediate superior but refused to furnish a copy of the statement of a major.[45] A district court pointed out that the Federal Tort Claims Act places the United States, with respect to claims dealt with by the act, on a par with private litigants.[46] The court ruled that the plaintiffs were entitled to compel the United States to answer interrogatories concerning statements by a major in official Army correspondence with his commanding officer about the accident.

40. Id. at 853.
41. Bank Line Limited v. United States, 68 F.Supp. 587, 588 (D. N.Y. 1946).
42. Bank Line v. United States, 163 F.2d 133, 135–36 (2d Cir. 1947).
43. Bank Line v. United States, 76 F.Supp. 801 (D. N.Y. 1948).
44. Id. at 804.
45. Wunderly v. United States, 8 F.R.D. 356, 357 (D. Pa. 1948).
46. Id. at 357.

The court overruled the government's objection that the major's statement was privileged. No contention had been made "that any military secrets, possibly protected by the scope of common law privilege, are involved."[47] It relied in part on *O'Neill v. United States*, a district court decision handed down a few months earlier, on August 23, 1948. The author of that decision was Judge Kirkpatrick. The case involved a tort action under the Admiralty Act brought by a seaman for personal injuries after damage to a tanker. Like the Federal Tort Claims Act, the Suits in Admiralty Act put the government in all respects on a par with private individuals in litigation. Judge Kirkpatrick held that the seaman was entitled to receive written statements, taken by the Federal Bureau of Investigation, made by witnesses who had personal knowledge of the damage done to the tanker.[48]

At the appellate level, with the case now called *Alltmont*, the Third Circuit vacated Kirkpatrick's order on June 3, 1949, because of confusion about which documents the government would be compelled to hand over.[49] Kirkpatrick entered a new decree on June 28 to clarify what he meant by witnesses to the accident.[50] The Third Circuit was now in a position, on November 23, to rule whether there had been a prior showing of good cause (required by Admiralty Rule 32) to obtain the FBI statements. The Third Circuit reversed Kirkpatrick, requiring him to determine whether the plaintiffs had shown good cause. Access to the statements might be unnecessary because the plaintiffs had the names and addresses of the persons who made statements to the FBI and could therefore interview them directly.[51] Many of those themes would later appear at all three levels of the *Reynolds* case: district court, Third Circuit, and Supreme Court.

In *Cresmer v. United States* (1949), the plaintiff directed the government to produce for inspection and copying the record or report of the investigation conducted by the Navy Board of Investigation of an air crash in Bayside, Long Island, resulting in the death of a private citizen.[52] The plaintiff claimed that government neglience contributed to the accident. The government argued that the person operating the plane, although an employee of the government, was acting unlawfully and not within the scope of his office and employment. The government also opposed the motion for production of documents on the ground that the report was privileged.[53]

47. Id.
48. O'Neill v. United States, 79 F.Supp. 827 (D. Pa. 1948).
49. Alltmont v. United States, 174 F.2d 931 (3d Cir. 1949).
50. Alltmont v. United States, 87 F.Supp. 214 (D. Pa. 1949).
51. Alltmont v. United States, 177 F.2d 971, 978–79 (3d Cir. 1949).
52. Cresmer v. United States, 9 F.R.D. 203 (D. N.Y. 1949).
53. Id. at 204.

The district judge reminded the government that the Federal Tort Claims Act places the United States in respect to claims on a par with private litigants. To make sure that the report did not contain military secrets that would be detrimental to the interest of U.S. armed forces or national security, the judge directed the government to produce the report for his examination. The judge received the report, read it, and saw "nothing in it which would in any way reveal a military secret or subject the United States and its armed forces to any peril by reason of complete revelation."[54] In the absence of a showing of a war secret or a threat to national security, the judge ruled that "it would appear to be unseemly for the Government to thwart the efforts of a plaintiff in a case such as this to learn as much as possible concerning the cause of the disaster."[55] The court granted the plaintiff's motion for production of the report.

Two other important decisions were handed down by federal courts before Judge Kirkpatrick issued his ruling in the B-29 case. In *Cotton Valley* (1949), a district court warned the United States of what would happen if it failed to comply with a court order to produce documents requested by a private party. The government could first submit the documents to the court for independent scrutiny to test the government's claim of privilege. Failure to follow that procedure would mean that the court would dismiss the government's effort to file an antitrust action against the company.[56] The Supreme Court affirmed that judgment on April 24, 1950.[57]

The other case was *Evans v. United States,* decided by a district court on May 23, 1950. A private party brought an action against the government under the Federal Tort Claims Act for an alleged negligent death caused by the crash of an Air Force plane. The government refused to permit the private parties to see public documents, including the official investigative report of the accident.[58] The government also withheld the names of any witnesses and their statements. The case was on all fours with the B-29 litigation. The court underscored its duty under the Federal Tort Claims Act to adjudicate disputes in an independent manner and to assure that plaintiffs have adequate access to documents to prepare their case:

It is not the exclusive right of any such agency of the Government to decide for itself the privileged nature of any such documents, but the Court is the one to judge of this when contention is made. This can be done by presenting to the Judge, without disclosure in the first instance

54. Id.
55. Id.
56. United States v. Cotton Valley Operators Committee, 9 F.R.D. 719 (D. La. 1949).
57. United States v. Cotton Valley Operators Committee, 339 U.S. 940 (1950).
58. Evans v. United States, 10 F.R.D. 255, 257 (D. La. 1950).

to the other side, whatever is claimed to have that status. The Court then decides whether it is privileged or not. This would seem to be the inevitable consequence of the Government submitting itself either as plaintiff or defendant to litigation with private persons.[59]

In this manner the court announced that it—and not the executive branch—was in charge of the conduct of the trial. It would decide what evidence could be introduced. In view of the allegations of the *Evans* complaint and the motion to produce information, documents, and witnesses with respect to what caused the accident, the court ruled that the plaintiffs had shown good cause to have the requested materials submitted to them by the government.[60]

Kirkpatrick's Decision in *Reynolds*

Judge Kirkpatrick decided the B-29 case on June 30, 1950. An initial question was whether the three wives had demonstrated "good cause" to seek the requested documents. After ruling in their favor, he analyzed the government's arguments for withholding the documents, ranging from the so-called Housekeeping Statute to possible reliance on the state secrets privilege or some combination of the two.

Did the Plaintiffs Have Good Cause?

Building on *Alltmont* and earlier cases, Judge Kirkpatrick first turned to the question whether the wives had shown good cause to obtain the accident report and survivor statements. He noted that the women lived within a few miles of Philadelphia and that the three witnesses "are Army Air Force personnel stationed in three different Army air bases in Florida."[61] One factor was the burden, expense, and inconvenience of having the plaintiffs take depositions in those locations, "though of themselves they do not necessarily establish good cause."[62] Kirkpatrick said that the Justice Department had suggested at argument that the government might bring the witnesses to Philadelphia or even pay the expenses of the plaintiffs' attorney to travel to Florida, "but I do not understand that any binding commitment to that effect has been made nor have I the power to order it under this motion to produce."[63] He had re-

59. Id. at 257–58.
60. Id. at 258.
61. Brauner v. United States, 10 F.R.D. at 470.
62. Id.
63. Id.

ceived no intimation that the government's suggestion would be approved or carried into effect by Army Command.

Assuming that it would be possible to take the depositions of the witnesses without undue burden on the plaintiffs, Kirkpatrick turned to a second issue. In view of the nature of the case, "disclosure of the contents of their written statements is necessary to enable the plaintiffs to properly prepare their cases for trial, and furnishes good cause for production."[64] The plaintiffs, he said, "have no knowledge of why the accident happened."[65] To the extent that such knowledge existed, the government had it. When the plane crashed, "it was wrecked and much of the evidence of what occurred was destroyed."[66] Only persons with long experience in investigating plane accidents "could hope to get at the real cause of the accident under such circumstances."[67] The Air Force was able to question the surviving witnesses "while their recollections were fresh."[68] By using those statements as a starting point, the board of investigators could explore the reasons for the accident. The statements by witnesses and the board's report "undoubtedly contain facts, information and clues which it might be extremely difficult, if not impossible, for the plaintiffs with their lack of technical resources to obtain merely by taking the depositions of the survivors."[69]

Kirkpatrick said he was not suggesting that the witnesses, if deposed, would not attempt to answer the questions put to them truthfully. Yet in this particular case, "in which seemingly trivial things may, to the expert, furnish important clues as to the cause of the accident, the plaintiffs must have accurate and precise firsthand information as to every relevant fact, if they are to conduct their examination of witnesses properly and to get at the truth in preparing for trial."[70] Denied access to essential documents, it would be difficult to effectively question witnesses: "they are employees of the defendant, in military service and subject to military authority and it is not an unfair assumption that they will not be encouraged to disclose, voluntarily, any information which might fix responsibility upon the Air Force."[71]

The interrogatories had flushed out some basic facts, but the government's answers "are far short of the full and complete disclosure of facts which the spirit of the rules requires."[72] Although the government produced a number

64. Id.
65. Id.
66. Id. at 470–71.
67. Id. at 471.
68. Id.
69. Id.
70. Id.
71. Id.
72. Id.

of documents, "these refer to the past performance of the plane and service records of the pilots and are essentially negative."[73] Kirkpatrick noted that in response to the question, "Describe in detail the trouble experienced," the government answered: "At between 18,500 or 19,000 feet manifold pressure dropped to 23 inches on No. one engine."[74] To Kirkpatrick, it was "obvious" that the government, in possession of the report and findings of its official investigation, "knows more about the accident than this."[75]

Depositions had limited value for another reason. The accident happened "more than 18 months ago and what the crew would remember now might well differ in important matters from what they told their officers when the event was fresh in their minds."[76] Kirkpatrick explained that even in simple accident cases "requiring no technical knowledge to prepare for trial, the fact that a long period of time has elapsed between the accident and the taking of the deposition of a witness gives a certain unique value to a statement given by him immediately after the accident when the whole thing was fresh—particularly when given to an employer before any damage suit involving negligence has begun."[77] For those reasons, Kirkpatrick concluded that "good cause appears for the production of all documents which are subject to the motion."[78]

The Housekeeping Statute

Judge Kirkpatrick then focused on the government's assertion that the findings of an official investigation could be withheld from plaintiffs on the basis of the Housekeeping Statute, originally enacted in 1789. Nothing in the history of that statute implies authority for executive departments to exclude from private parties—or judges—documents and papers in the possession of U.S. agencies, especially in matters of litigation. The Housekeeping Statute was simply designed to make executive officials responsible for safeguarding the public documents in their possession.

The need for this type of legislation was recognized by the Continental Congress when it created single executives in 1781 to handle the business of foreign affairs, war, and finance. On February 22, 1782, the Continental Congress adopted language to guide the duties of the new secretary for the department of foreign affairs:

73. Id.
74. Id.
75. Id.
76. Id.
77. Id.
78. Id.

That the books, records and other papers of the United States, that relate to this department, be committed to his custody ~~subject always to the inspection of Congress or of such persons as they may appoint~~ [to which (and all other papers of his office,) any member of Congress shall have access: provided that no copy shall be taken of matters of a secret nature without the special leave of Congress:][79]

The deleted words were replaced by the bracketed material, giving any member of Congress access to the documents. At this time in the nation's history, the authority of Congress to obtain departmental records was assured because only one branch of government existed: the Continental Congress. All other agencies, including executive departments and adjudicatory bodies, functioned as agents of the legislative branch and were responsible to it. Records or papers "of a secret nature" were protected from disclosure unless Congress so provided.

When Congress created the executive departments of Foreign Affairs, War, and Treasury in 1789, each statute placed upon the heads of those departments the responsibility for having "the custody and charge of all records, books and papers" in the secretary's office. Those statutes were enacted on July 27, August 7, and September 2.[80] Congress then enacted, on September 15, a freestanding statute entitled "An Act to provide for the safe-keeping of the Acts, Records and Seal of the United States, and for other purposes." It changed the name of the Department of Foreign Affairs to the Department of State, called the head of that department the Secretary of State, made the Secretary of State responsible for handling bills, orders, and resolutions passed by both Houses, and agreed to this language:

> Sec. 7. *And be it further enacted,* That the same Secretary shall forthwith after his appointment be entitled to have the custody and charge of the said seal of the United States, and also of all books, records and papers, remaining in the office of the late Secretary of the United States in Congress assembled; and such of the said books, records and papers, as may appertain to the Treasury department, or War department, shall be delivered over to the principal officers of the said departments respectively, as the President of the United States shall direct.[81]

This language evolved over the years and changed its designation in the U.S. Code. Under the Revised Statutes of 1878 it was referred to as R.S. §

79. 22 Journals of the Continental Congress 88 (1914).
80. 1 Stat. 29 (§ 4), 50 (§ 4), 67 (§ 7).
81. Id. at 69.

161: "The head of each Department is authorized to prescribe regulations, not inconsistent with law, for the government of his Department, the conduct of its officers and clerks, the distribution and performance of its business, and the custody, use, and preservation of the records, papers, and property appertaining to it." At the time of the *Reynolds* litigation, the language was found at 5 U.S.C. § 22. Currently the citation is 5 U.S.C. § 301. It provides:

> The head of an Executive department or military department may prescribe regulations for the government of his department, the conduct of its employees, the distribution and performance of its business, and the custody, use, and preservation of its records, papers, and property. This section does not authorize withholding information from the public or limiting the availability of records to the public.[82]

The last sentence was added in 1958, after Congress concluded that the executive branch had abused this statutory language and inappropriately withheld information from the public. The legislative history of this change in 1958 is detailed in Chapter 5. What was meant by the Housekeeping Statute at the time of the *Reynolds* litigation is covered here.

Several lower court decisions issued before the B-29 litigation discussed the Housekeeping Statute. In the *Bank Line* case in 1947, the Second Circuit cited the statute but did not regard it as a general source of authority to withhold documents from a private litigant.[83] The Second Circuit referred to *Boske v. Comingore,* a Supreme Court decision from 1900 that is limited to a unique dispute between the United States and Kentucky. A state court held a U.S. collector of internal revenue in contempt because he refused, while giving his deposition in a case pending in the state court, to provide copies of certain reports made by distillers. A Treasury Department regulation, issued pursuant to the Housekeeping Statute, provided:

> All records in the offices of collectors of internal revenue or of any of their deputies are in their custody and control for purposes relating to the collection of the revenues of the United States only. They have no control of them and no discretion with regard to permitting the use of them for any other purpose. Collectors are hereby prohibited from giving out any special tax records or any copies thereof to private persons or to local officers, or to produce such records or copies thereof in a state

82. 5 U.S.C. § 301 (2000).
83. Bank Line v. United States, 163 F.2d at 138.

court, whether in answer to *subpœnas duces tecum* [subpoenas for a document] or otherwise.[84]

Here the documents were created solely for the purpose of collecting U.S. revenue, and for no other purpose. The restriction on making the records available to the judiciary applies only to a state court. The Treasury regulation provides no legal authority for the government to withhold documents needed by plaintiffs in federal courts who seek tort claims, such as in the B-29 case. When *Bank Line* returned to the district court, it interpreted *Boske v. Comingore* in this manner: "Disclosure of papers in the possession of the government may be sought in cases in which the government is merely a witness and in cases in which it is a party."[85]

Wunderly, in 1948, discussed the reliance of the Justice Department on the Housekeeping Statute to prevent a plaintiff from interrogating a major. The case refers to Order 3229 issued by Attorney General Frank Murphy on May 2, 1939, entitled "Disclosure or Use of Confidential Records and Information." He issued the order pursuant to R.S. § 161, the Housekeeping Statute. As with the Treasury regulation discussed above, Murphy provided the following guidance for Justice Department records:

All official files, documents, records and information in the offices of the Department of Justice, including the several offices of United States Attorneys, Federal Bureau of Investigation, United States Marshals, and Federal penal and correctional institutions, or in the custody or control of any officer or employee of the Department of Justice, are to be regarded as confidential. No officer or employee may permit the disclosure or use of the same for any purpose other than for the performance of his official duties, except in the discretion of the Attorney General, The Assistant to the Attorney General, or an Assistant Attorney General acting for him.

Whenever a subpoena *duces tecum* is served to produce any of such files, documents, records or information, the officer or employee on whom such subpoena is served, unless otherwise expressly directed by the Attorney General, will appear in court in answer thereto and respectfully decline to produce the records specified there in [*sic*], on the ground that the disclosure of such records is prohibited by this regulation.[86]

84. 177 U.S. 459, 460 (1900).
85. Bank Line v. United States, 76 F.Supp. at 803.
86. 11 Fed. Reg. 4920 (1939).

Nothing in this order necessarily bars the production of documents needed by a plaintiff in litigation, and certainly nothing in the order would automatically override a court ruling requiring that a document be turned over to a private party, or be read in a judge's chamber. In the *Wunderly* case, the court allowed the interrogatory of the major, adding: "No contention is made—in fact, the contrary is conceded—that any military secrets, possibly protected by the scope of common law privilege, are involved."[87]

The *O'Neill* litigation made several references to the Housekeeping Statute. The district court cited the order issued by Attorney General Murphy and the fact that it was based on R.S. § 161, 5 U.S.C. § 22.[88] Still, the court did not support the Justice Department's effort to prevent the plaintiff from receiving statements taken by the FBI.

In the *Reynolds* case, Judge Kirkpatrick took guidance from those cases in analyzing the government's claimed immunity to withhold the accident report and other findings of the investigation "based upon the express provision of the Statute, R.S. § 161, 5 U.S.C.A. § 22, and the rules and regulations of the Department of Justice."[89] Those arguments had been fully considered by the lower courts and had not been sustained. Kirkpatrick thus rejected the Housekeeping Statute as a ground for preventing plaintiffs from gaining access to needed documents.

Access to State Secrets Documents

As a general concept, the doctrine of state secrets was referred to in legal literature on some occasions. The standard treatise on evidence by John Henry Wigmore flatly stated: "There must be a privilege for *secrets of State, i.e.* matters whose disclosure would endager [*sic*] the Nation's governmental requirements or its relations of friendship and profit with other nations." Yet he cautioned that this privilege "has been so often improperly invoked and so loosely misapplied that a strict definition of its legitimate limits must be made."[90]

To avoid the murkiness and inutility associated with general categories, Wigmore separated state secrets into eight categories: (1) where the "chief Executive and subordinate executive officers are in some respects *exempt from liability for torts* of violence and defamation," (2) whether the chief Executive "is *procedurally exempt from the legal process of the Judiciary* for any purpose whatever," (3) the question whether the Executive is exempted from the "or-

---

87. Wunderly v. United States, 8 F.R.D. at 357.
88. O'Neill v. United States, 79 F.Supp. at 828–29.
89. Brauner v. United States, 10 F.R.D. at 471.
90. 8 John Henry Wigmore, Evidence in Trials at Common Law § 2212a (3d ed. 1940) (emphasis in original).

dinary *duty to give testimony*," (4) a question whether executive officers are exempt from the general duty to attend court, though still liable to give evidence by deposition while remaining at their offices, (5) the doctrine that "*official records are irremovable* and cannot be required to be taken, in the original, from their place of official custody to the court-room," (6) the privilege permitting "secrecy for communications by *informers to official prosecutors*, by parties or witnesses to a *judge*, and by citizens making *compulsory reports* to the State," (7) "a genuine *topical privilege* for facts constituting *secrets of State*, and this, by improper extension," has often been made to include (8) an "anomalous *communications-privilege* for *communications by or to or between officials of the government*."[91]

Several of these categories do not apply to *Reynolds*, particularly (4) and (6), whereas (5) is easily overcome by making copies of the official records. On the duty to give evidence, Wigmore said: "Let it be understood, then, that there is no exemption, for officials as such, or for the Executive as such, from the universal testimonial duty to give evidence in judicial investigations."[92] An exemption from attendance in court "does not involve any concession either of an exemption from the Executive's general testimonial duty to furnish evidence or of a judicial inability to enforce the performance of that duty."[93]

Regarding access to official records, Wigmore remarked: "the *illegality* of removing such records . . . is no ground for refusing to receive them."[94] Moreover, copies of official records are admissible "whenever the original is not removable," and there is "the right of a citizen or taxpayer to *inspect official records* in their place of custody."[95] Wigmore came to the key question. Who should determine the necessity for secrecy? The executive or the judiciary? As with other privileges, he concluded it should be the court: "Shall every subordinate in the department have access to the secret, and not the presiding officer of justice? Cannot the constitutionally coördinate body of government share the confidence? . . . The truth cannot be escaped that a Court which abdicates its inherent function of determining the facts upon which the admissibility of evidence depends will furnish to bureaucratic officials too ample opportunities for abusing the privilege. . . . Both principle and policy demand that the determination of the privilege shall be for the Court."[96]

The lower court cases that preceded the B-29 case made passing reference to the state secrets doctrine but never squarely confronted it. The Second

91. Id. at § 2367 (emphasis in original).
92. Id. at § 2370.
93. Id. at § 2371.
94. Id. at § 2373 (emphasis in original).
95. Id. (emphasis in original).
96. Id. at § 2379.

Circuit in *Bank Line* said that the "existence of governmental privileges must be established by the party invoking them and the right of government officers to prevent disclosure of state secrets must be asserted in the same way procedurally as that of a private individual."[97] When the case returned to the district court the judge observed, without deciding: "Perhaps there is an area of military and diplomatic secrets where the national interest must prevail even at the expense of private justice."[98]

The judge in *Wunderly* noted that the government had not claimed "any military secrets."[99] The district court in *O'Neill* underscored that "the general policy of the common law, prohibiting disclosure of state secrets . . . is not involved in this case."[100] The district judge in *Cresmer* read the investigative report by the Navy Board and found "nothing in it which would in any way reveal a military secret."[101]

Guided by those precedents, Judge Kirkpatrick stated that the government "does not here contend that this is a case involving the well-recognized common-law privilege protecting state secrets or facts which might seriously harm the Government in its diplomatic relations, military operations or measures for national security."[102] Yet he saw that the government was relying on something more than the Housekeeping Statute: "In effect, the Government claims a new kind of privilege."[103] The government maintained that the proceedings of military investigatory bodies "should be privileged in order to allow the free and unhampered self-criticism within the service necessary to obtain maximum efficiency, fix responsibility and maintain proper discipline." Kirkpatrick found "no recognition in the law of the existence of such a privilege."[104] He recognized that substantially the same claim had been "considered and rejected" at the district court level in *Bank Line* and *Cresmer*. In agreeing with the results of those decisions, Kirkpatrick concluded in his decision of June 30, 1950, that the accident report and the findings of the Air Force's investigation "are not privileged."[105] He accordingly denied the government's motion and granted the plaintiff's motion to have the documents produced.

97. Bank Line v. United States, 163 F.2d at 138.
98. Bank Line v. United States, 76 F.Supp. at 804.
99. Wunderly v. United States, 8 F.R.D. at 357.
100. O'Neill v. United States, 79 F.Supp. at 829.
101. Cresmer v. United States, 9 F.R.D. at 204.
102. Brauner v. United States, 10 F.R.D. 468, 471–72 (D. Pa. 1950).
103. Id. at 472.
104. Id.
105. Id.

Edging Toward the State Secrets Privilege

On July 20, Judge Kirkpatrick issued an order permitting plaintiffs to inspect the requested documents. This notice was mailed to the parties the next day.[106] He set a deadline of August 7 for the government to produce the documents.[107] The government began to claim that the requested documents possessed a sensitivity beyond the purpose or scope of the Housekeeping Statute and beyond merely classifying a report as "confidential." It did not flatly assert the state secrets privilege, but it was headed in that direction after its earlier arguments had failed.

On July 24, the Justice Department presented Kirkpatrick with a letter from Eugene M. Zuckert, Assistant Secretary of the Air Force. Acting under the Housekeeping Statute, he said it had been determined "that it would not be in the public interest to furnish this report of investigation as requested by counsel in this case." The report was prepared under regulations "designed to insure the collection of all pertinent information regarding aircraft accidents in order that all possible measures will be developed for the prevention of accidents and the optimum promotion of flying safety." Under Air Force regulations, "this type of report is not available in courts-martial proceedings or other forms of disciplinary action or in the determination of pecuniary liability."[108] However, blocking the availability of these reports in courts-martial does not necessarily block their availability in Article III courts, where federal judges exercise constitutional independence.

Zuckert confined his analysis to the Housekeeping Statute and the argument previously tried in court (and often rejected there) that internal investigations of aircraft accidents have a special privilege meriting nondisclosure in judicial proceedings. He closed with this plea: "It is hoped that the extreme importance that the Department of the Air Force places upon the confidential nature of its official aircraft accident reports will be fully appreciated and understood by your Honorable Court."[109] Zuckert appeared to concede that executive departments did not have exclusive and final authority over the release of documents, or that courts must necessarily defer to the superior authority and judgment of the Air Force. The government might have decided to draft

106. Docket Sheet, Phyllis Brauner and Elizabeth Palya v. United States, Docket 9793, entry for July 20, 1950.

107. Transcript of Proceedings, August 9, 1950, Brauner and Palya v. United States, Civil Action No. 9793, and Reynolds v. United States, Civil Action No. 10142 (E.D. Pa. 1950), at 4 (hereafter "Proceedings for August 9, 1950").

108. Letter of July 21, 1950, signed by Eugene M. Zuckert, Assistance of the Air Force, directed to "The Honorable, the Judges, United States District Court for the Eastern District of Pennsylvania, Philadelphia, Pennsylvania."

109. Id.

the statement in a tactful and respectful manner, rather than bluntly telling a judge what he could and could not see.

On August 9, Judge Kirkpatrick met in court to hear from Francis Hopkinson for the plaintiffs, two attorneys from the Justice Department, and two colonels from the Judge Advocate General's Office of the Air Force. Thomas J. Curtin, Assistant U.S. Attorney, discussed with Kirkpatrick new claims of privilege to support a petition for rehearing the case. One claim stated that there had been no showing of good cause, while a second offered what seemed to be a new form of privilege. Curtin brought with him an affidavit signed by Maj. Gen. Reginald C. Harmon, Judge Advocate General of the U.S. Air Force, who pledged to make the three surviving crew members "available at the expense of the United States for interrogation by the plaintiffs at a place and time to be designated by the plaintiffs," and that the three witnesses would be authorized "to testify regarding all matters pertaining to the cause of the accident except as to facts and matters of a classified nature."[110] The witnesses would be authorized to "refresh their memories by reference to any statements made by them before Aircraft Accident Investigating Boards or Investigating Officers, as well as other pertinent and material records that are in the possession of the United States Air Force."[111]

Harmon's affidavit further stated that information and findings of the accident report and survivor statements, which had been demanded by the plaintiffs, "cannot be furnished without seriously hampering national security, flying safety and the development of highly technical and secret military equipment," and that the disclosure of statements made by witnesses before Accident Investigative Boards "would have a deterrent effect upon the much desired objective of encouraging uninhibited admissions in future inquiry proceedings instituted primarily in the interest of flying safety."[112] Those statements talked about the sensitivity of the documents but did not seem to rise to the level of state secrets, where the government may claim exclusive authority over agency documents. To Curtin, the Harmon affidavit went "to the common law claim we have in this case separately and apart from our constitutional claim as embodied in the Constitution and Revised Statute 161."[113]

---

110. Affidavit of the Judge Advocate General, United States Air Force, Reynolds v. United States, Civil Action No. 10142, U.S. District Court for the Eastern District of Pennsylvania, August 7, 1950, signed by Major General Reginald C. Harmon (hereafter "Harmon affidavit"). This affidavit was not filed with the court until October 10, 1950. However, Thomas J. Curtin of the Justice Department brought this affidavit with him to the August 9 hearing; Proceedings for August 9, 1950, at 6–8.

111. Harmon affidavit, at 2.

112. Id.

113. Proceedings for August 9, 1950, at 8.

At the August 9 hearing, Curtin also brought along an undated claim of privilege by the Secretary of the Air Force, Thomas K. Finletter. The document repeated the argument that the disclosure of statements taken during an official investigation on an aircraft accident would have a deterrent effect on the objective of encouraging uninhibited statements in future inquiry proceedings instituted primarily in the interest of flying safety, and described the "confidential mission" of the B-29 that crashed over Waycross, Ga. The plane carried "confidential equipment on board and any disclosure of its mission or information concerning its operation or performance would be prejudicial to this Department and would not be in the public interest."[114]

This document seems like a diversion. The plaintiffs had not asked for anything about the confidential mission or confidential equipment. Was Finletter implying that he could not surrender the accident report and the survivor statements without at the same time revealing the confidential mission and the confidential equipment? When the report and statements were later declassified and made available on the Internet, to be discovered there in 2000, it was clear that Finletter could have released the documents without disclosing anything about the confidential mission or the confidential equipment. He further stated:

It has been the historic position of the executive branch of the Government, as the Attorney General of the United States has informed this Honorable Court by statement filed by him in *Nathan Alltmont et al. v. United States,* Civil Action No. 10019, 177 F.(2d) 971, that executive files and investigative reports are confidential and privileged and that their disclosure would not be in the public interest.[115]

Finletter may have been breaking new ground. Not only could the government claim a privilege over state secrets, confined to the areas of national security and foreign affairs, but it could more broadly assert a policy of nondisclosure for anything it regarded as "not in the public interest." It is true, as Finletter said, that the executive branch has often argued that executive files and investigative reports are confidential and privileged and that their disclosure would not be in the public interest. It is equally true that Congress and

---

114. Claim of Privilege by the Secretary of the Air Force, Reynolds v. United States, Civil Action No. 10142 (E.D. Pa. 1950), at 2, filed with the court on October 10, 1950 (hereafter "Finletter statement"). The five-page statement, signed by Secretary of the Air Force Thomas K. Finletter, is not paginated. It was not filed with the court until October 10, 1950, but Thomas J. Curtin of the Justice Department brought it with him to the August 9 hearing. Proceedings of August 9, 1950, at 5, 13.

115. Finletter statement, at 3.

the federal courts have often successfully insisted on their right to see these documents and have never automatically deferred to broad executive claims of privilege.[116]

The statement by Finletter cites 21 examples, from 1796 to 1948, where Presidents supposedly refused to furnish documents to Congress and the courts. The list is of uneven quality in terms of accuracy and relevance to the B-29 controversy. The first example is President Washington refusing in 1796 "to furnish the instructions to the U.S. Minister concerning the Jay Treaty."[117] The actual outcome of this dispute is far more complex and does not support exclusive executive control over agency documents.[118] A second example: "President Jefferson in 1807 refused to furnish confidential letters relative to the Burr conspiracy." This description is extremely misleading. The Jefferson administration understood that Burr, charged with treason and facing a death penalty, was constitutionally entitled to whatever documents he needed to defend himself. The administration offered to show the letters to the court (see Chapter 7 for details). A third example: "President Polk in 1846 refused to furnish evidence of payments made by the State Department on President's certificates." Polk, however, was not advancing a constitutional claim. He was exercising discretionary authority that Congress had given him by *statute*.[119] Few of the examples cited by Finletter have anything to do with investigative reports, and none of them, given the time period, involved the statutory authority given by Congress to litigants under the Federal Tort Claims Act.

The Finletter statement claimed that the position of the executive branch over files and investigative reports "is historically approved and authorized by authority of R.S. § 161, 5 U.S.C. 22, and Air Force Regulations issued pursuant thereto."[120] Nothing in the history of the Housekeeping Statute justifies exclusive and unreviewable executive control over files and investigative reports, especially when needed in court. In fact, abuse of the statute by the executive branch in keeping documents from the public prompted Congress in 1958 to add this sentence: "This section does not authorize withholding information from the public or limiting the availability of records to the public." The reason for making that change is explained in Chapter 5.

Finletter concluded by regarding the compulsory production of the investigative report as "prejudicial to the efficient operation of the Department of the Air Force, is not in the public interest, and is inconsistent with national

116. Louis Fisher, The Politics of Executive Privilege (2004).
117. Finletter statement, at 3.
118. Fisher, The Politics of Executive Privilege, at 33–39.
119. Louis Fisher, "Confidential Spending and Governmental Accountability," 47 G.W. L. Rev. 347, 355–56 (1979).
120. Finletter statement, at 4.

security. Accordingly, pursuant to the authority vested in me as the head of the Department of the Air Force, I assert the privileged status of reports here involved and must respectfully decline to permit their production."[121] Three points need to be made. First, Finletter was not relying primarily on common law or the state secrets privilege. He was relying on the statutory authority given by the Housekeeping Statute regarding the safekeeping of agency records. Two: lower courts had on a number of occasions rejected his interpretation of the Housekeeping Statute. Three: Finletter's last line about declining to permit their production can be seen as an assertion of the state secrets privilege in the sense that no matter what a federal judge ordered, the executive branch could refuse. As the government learned at the district court and Third Circuit levels, refusal could be accompanied by something the government did not want: losing the case.

At the August 9 hearing, Judge Kirkpatrick said it was his impression that the government was not contending "that this is a case involving the well recognized common law privilege in regard to secrets or facts which might seriously harm the Government in its diplomatic relations, military operations or the national security." Curtin replied: "I might say with regard to that point I wish you would pass that for a minute, because that does come into this case in the second document."[122]

As to the Housekeeping Statute and the insistence of lower court judges to submit disputed documents to the court for examination, Curtin told Kirkpatrick: "We do not believe that is good law. We contend that the findings of the head of the Department are binding, and the judiciary cannot waive it."[123] Kirkpatrick pursued the point:

It is an important question. I suppose, just to state a wholly imaginary and rather fantastic case, suppose you had a collision between a mail truck and a taxicab, and the Attorney General came in and said that in his opinion discovery in the case would imperil the whole military position of the United States, and so forth. Would the Court have to accept that? Is that where your argument leads?[124]

Curtin stuck to his guns: "Under the statute we contend [the department's judgment] is final."[125] Putting the statutory question to the side, Kirkpatrick wanted to know that if the government claimed a common law privilege over

121. Id. at 5.
122. Proceedings for August 9, 1950, at 6.
123. Id. at 9.
124. Id.
125. Id. at 10.

military secrets, would the government's decision be final and unreviewable by a court? Curtin: "There is no other interpretation. In other words, I say that the Executive is the person who must make that determination, not the Judiciary."[126] It had to be wrung out of Curtin and was never expressly claimed in Justice Department briefs, but the state secrets privilege had made its appearance. The government was on the record.

After the August 9 hearing, Judge Kirkpatrick issued an amended order on September 21, directing the government to produce for examination by the court several documents "so that this court may determine whether or not all or any parts of such documents contain matters of a confidential nature, discovery of which would violate the Government's privilege against disclosure of matters involving the national or public interest." The documents included the report and findings of the official investigation of the B-29 crash on October 6, 1948, and the statements taken from Moore, Peny, and Murrhee. Examination of the documents would take place at the U.S. courthouse in Philadelphia on October 4, after which the government would be required to permit the plaintiffs and their attorneys "to inspect the said documents and make copies of the same, with the exception of any part or parts of the said documents which may have been determined by this court to be privileged from discovery."[127]

In Camera Review Fails

The issue was now the status of Judge Kirkpatrick's order directing the government to produce the disputed documents for his review in his chambers. On October 10, the government petitioned for a rehearing on the motion to produce the documents, citing three reasons. One, Judge Kirkpatrick's order "is contrary to law." Two, the order "is in violation of revised statute 161 (5 U.S. Code 22)" (the Housekeeping Statute). And three, the plaintiffs "have failed to show good cause sufficient to compel production of the documents sought under Rule 34 of the Federal Rules of Civil Procedure."[128] Curiously, having developed the state secrets privilege at the hearing on August 9, Curtin excluded it from this petition for a rehearing. Why wave the Big Weapon and then pull it back? Following the government's arguments and affidavits, Judge Kirkpatrick on October 12 issued an "Order that Facts Be Taken as

126. Id.

127. Amended Order, September 21, 1950, Brauner and Palya v. United States, Civil Action No. 9793, and Reynolds v. United States, Civil Action No. 10142 (E.D. Pa. 1950), at 2.

128. Petition for Rehearing on Motion to Quash Order and Motion for Production of Documents Under Rule 34, Brauner and Palya v. United States, Civil Action No. 9793 (E.D. Pa. October 10, 1950).

Established." He said that the government, "having failed to comply with the order of this court dated September 21, 1950, requiring defendant to produce certain documents at Room 2096, United States Courthouse, Philadelphia, Pennsylvania, on October 4, 1950, for discovery purposes; and it appearing that the said documents are in the possession and control of defendant, that there was no sufficient excuse for defendant's failure to produce the same." He ordered that the following facts be taken as established "for the purposes of this action, that plaintiffs need produce no further proof with respect to said facts, and that defendant will not be permitted to introduce evidence controverting said facts." The two facts in the order were these:

1. The deaths of William H. Brauner, Albert Palya and Robert E. Reynolds occurred as the result of the crash near Waycross, Georgia, on October 6, 1948, of a B-29 airplane owned and operated by defendant, United States of America.
2. The said crash and the resulting deaths of the aforesaid persons were caused solely and exclusively by the negligence and wrongful acts and omissions of the officers and employees of defendant while acting within the scope of their office and employment.[129]

As earlier cases had signaled, the government's refusal to produce requested documents—either to plaintiffs or to a trial court—always ran a risk. The court could simply decide in favor of the plaintiff. That is the course Judge Kirkpatrick chose. The task was now to determine the amount of money to be granted to each of the widows. On November 27, Kirkpatrick heard evidence presented by Biddle and Hopkinson for the plaintiffs and Curtin for the government. At the time of the hearing, Patricia J. Reynolds had remarried and was now Patricia J. Herring, living in Indianapolis, Ind.[130]

Biddle offered into evidence certain facts, agreed to by the government, about the accident and the employment records of Brauner, Palya, and Reynolds. Each had boarded the B-29 "as a civilian observer, for the purpose of observing and testing the operation of certain confidential electronic equipment which was installed in the said airplane."[131] The names of the wives and

129. Order that Facts Be Taken as Established, October 12, 1950, Brauner and Palya v. United States of America, Civil Action No. 9793, and Reynolds v. United States of America, Civil Action No. 10142 (E.D. Pa. 1950).

130. Statement in the chambers of Judge Kirkpatrick, November 21, 1950, in the case of Brauner and Palya v. United States, Civil Action No. 9793, and Reynolds v. United States, Civil Action No. 10142 (E.D. Pa. 1950), at 2.

131. Transcript of the Trial Record, November 27, 1950, Brauner and Palya v. United States of America, Civil Action No. 9793, and Reynolds v. United States, Civil Action No. 10142 (E.D. Pa. 1950), at 3.

the names and ages of the children were entered into the record, as well as "the ages, life expectancy, education, previous employment, et cetera, of the respective decedents."[132] The employment records and salaries of the three men were introduced into evidence.[133] The court heard testimony from Douglas Hancock Ewing, who had worked with Palya at RCA in Camden, N.J. Ewing offered views on Palya's professional competence and prospects for future earnings.[134] Ewing gave similar evaluations about Reynolds and Brauner, who worked under Ewing's supervision at RCA.[135] Testimony was taken from other RCA officials to estimate the earnings potential of the three men.[136] Brauner's supervisor at the Franklin Institute testified about his work performance and future earnings.[137]

With the government determined to withhold the documents, even for in camera review, Judge Kirkpatrick issued a ruling that awarded damages to the three widows. On February 20, 1951, he granted a total of $225,000 in damages: $80,000 each to Phyllis Brauner and Elizabeth Palya, and $65,000 to Patricia Herring.[138]

At the district court level, the government never formally or consistently asserted the state secrets privilege. It relied partly on the Housekeeping Statute and partly on the claim that access by the plaintiffs to the accident report and survivor statements would interfere with the capacity of executive agencies to conduct effective investigations into problems that exist within their organizations. At the August 9 hearing, Curtin for the Justice Department seemed to be heading in the direction of the state secrets privilege, but then declined to cite it in his October 10 petition for a rehearing. After losing the case at district court, the government would search for other authorities to justify withholding documents from the plaintiffs.

132. Id. at 11.
133. Id. at 12–15.
134. Id. at 16–23.
135. Id. at 23–30.
136. Id. at 30–45.
137. Id. at 47–55.
138. Sur Pleadings and Proof, Brauner and Palya v. United States, Civil Action No. 9793, and Reynolds v. United States, Civil Action No. 10142 (E.D. Pa. February 20, 1951). See also "3 Widows Get $225,000 in B-29 Crash During Tests," Philadelphia Inquirer, February 23, 1951, at 15; "3 Crash Widows Win Suit," New York Times, February 23, 1951, at 29.

3

AT THE APPELLATE LEVEL

The government lost in district court after refusing to give agency documents to Judge Kirkpatrick to examine in his chambers. It decided to withhold what it regarded as privileged materials, trusting that its underlying argument would find favor on appeal. The first test came at the Third Circuit. If the government failed there, it could take its case to the next and final level: the U.S. Supreme Court. At each of these appellate forums, the government would have an opportunity to revisit and refashion legal justifications for withholding documents, placing greater weight on the state secret privilege if necessary.

The Third Circuit

The *Reynolds* litigation took shape at a time of heightened conflicts: the outbreak of the Korean War in June 1950, confrontations with the Soviet Union, and a concerted campaign against communism at home. In this climate, it must have been strategically tempting for the government to play the national security card. During periods of national emergency, federal judges have a track record of acquiescing to executive judgments, especially claims made by the President in his capacity as Commander in Chief. But the government did not urge the lower courts to abandon judicial independence and entrust constitutional interpretation to the executive branch. The general principles and issues identified in trial court moved with little change to the Third Circuit. The case was heard by a panel of three judges—Albert Branson Maris, Herbert F. Goodrich, and Harry E. Kalodner—at the federal courthouse in Philadelphia.

Maris served as a federal district judge from 1936 to 1938 before joining the Third Circuit on June 24, 1938. A graduate of Temple Law School, he served in the U.S. Army in 1918 and was discharged as a second lieutenant. Goodrich received his law degree from Harvard, taught at the University of Michigan and University of Pennsylvania law schools, and took his seat on the Third Circuit on May 10, 1940. Kalodner graduated from the University of Pennsylvania Law School, worked in private practice from 1919 to 1936, became a state judge and federal district judge (1938 to 1946 for the latter), and began his service with the Third Circuit on September 4, 1946. Kalodner was the only one of the three with a background in military law, having served in the Judge Advocate General's office of the U.S. Army from 1917 to 1918.[1]

The government gave notice on April 20, 1951, that it would appeal Judge Kirkpatrick's decision.[2] The plaintiffs, the district court, and the Third Circuit were unaware of changes that the Air Force made to the classification levels of the accident report and the survivor statements. The accident report, submitted October 18, 1948, was originally classified as Restricted. Of the four levels—Top Secret, Secret, Confidential, and Restricted—Restricted was the lowest.[3] Some of the documents were upgraded to Secret on January 3, 1949, but returned to Restricted on September 14 or 15, 1950. In later years, in response to Freedom of Information Act requests, the government began to release heavily redacted reports. In the 1990s, the government declassified the B-29 documents and made them available to the public at a price.

The Government's Brief

The government identified four issues for the Third Circuit. The first: whether Judge Kirkpatrick could find the facts against the United States "without requiring the production of evidence by the plaintiffs." Next, whether he could evaluate plaintiffs' showing of good cause "without considering the assertion by the Secretary of the Air Force that disclosure of the departmental records involved was contrary to the public interest; and, if so, did the district court properly find a showing of good cause." Third, where the head of an executive department, "acting independently in an area of constitutional and statutory power entirely separate from litigation, declines to disclose departmental records, can a district judge penalize such action without bringing the validity of the refusal under adjudication." Fourth, the government asked whether the agency records involved in the case were "privileged" and thus free from discovery.[4] The questions raised statutory and constitutional issues, but the state secret privilege was not singled out.

---

1. Directory of American Judges (Charles Liebman ed. 1955); Biographical Directory of the Federal Judiciary, 1789–2000 (2001).

2. Notice of Appeal to the United States Court of Appeals for the Third Circuit, Brauner and Palya v. United States, Civil Action No. 9793, and Reynolds v. United States, Civil Action No. 10142 (E.D. Pa. 1951).

3. 15 Fed. Reg. 597–98 (1950).

4. Brief of the United States, Reynolds v. United States, No. 10,483 (3d Cir. 1951), at 1 (hereafter "Government's Brief").

The government challenged "the coercion" exercised by the district court with regard to the production of official documents, "the custody and control of which is, by Constitution and statute, entrusted to the head of an executive department, here the Secretary for Air [*sic*], and made his sole responsibility."[5] The question of custody had been addressed by statute (the Housekeeping Statute), not the Constitution. To the government, the ultimate issue was whether the statute "and the Constitutional doctrine of separation of powers creates in the head of an executive department a discretion, to be exercised by him, to determine whether the public interest permits disclosure of official records."[6] The government thus argued that access to evidence in a trial would be decided not by the judiciary but by one of the parties to the case: the executive branch.

No doubt the Housekeeping Statute conferred a discretion and duty on department heads over the safekeeping of records, but it made no mention of an exclusive and overriding power to withhold documents from plaintiffs or federal courts. Could it be argued that the executive branch had ultimate, final control over agency documents, regardless of the need of defendants in court or investigations by Congress into agency corruption? Conceding such control to department heads challenged the American system of checks and balances and fair procedure in court.

Perhaps sensing this problem, the government looked to British precedents and the parliamentary model: "We believe that all controlling governmental and judicial material, here and in England, clearly supports the view that, in this type of case at least, disclosure by the head of an executive department cannot be coerced."[7] The analogy to Great Britain was misplaced because the U.S. Constitution recognizes values and principles that broke with British history and practice, including an independent judiciary capable of deciding against the executive branch, even in cases of national security. The American framers considered the British legal model, which placed all of external affairs, foreign policy, and the war power in the executive, and firmly rejected it.[8]

What deference should the district court have paid to the Finletter and Harmon statements? The government insisted that Finletter's assertion that disclosure would be contrary to the public interest "must at least constitute a factor worthy of great respect in measuring plaintiffs' real need for production."[9] Respect? Unquestionably. Controlling weight? Quite a different

5. Id. at 6.
6. Id.
7. Id.
8. Louis Fisher, Presidential War Power 1–16 (2004 ed.).
9. Government's Brief, at 7.

standard. To the government "there was no sufficient showing of good cause in this case by any standard. *A fortiori*, there was no showing of good cause sufficient to justify a coercive incursion into the internal affair of an executive department."[10] The executive branch insisted that its judgment be exclusive even in a tort claims case, after Congress had placed the government on a par with private plaintiffs. Where was the "coercion"? Was the judiciary acting in a coercive manner toward the executive branch, or were executive officials attempting to coerce the judiciary by deciding what evidence could be introduced in court?

The government analyzed what it considered to be inadequate power on the part of Judge Kirkpatrick to enter a judgment against the United States without requiring the plaintiffs to produce satisfactory evidence. It was the government's position that the Federal Rules of Civil Procedure prohibited the district court from acting as it did. Rule 55(e) provided that "no judgment by default shall be entered against the United States . . . unless the claimant establishes his claim or right to relief by evidence satisfactory to the court."[11] The purpose of the rule, said the government, was to protect the United States "against unmeritorious or collusive claims by requiring that the judge, as a matter of independent duty, have before him a public record on which a judgment requiring the payment of public revenues could be based."[12]

Having raised the issue of Rule 55(e), the government suggested that the case could be disposed of on other grounds: the failure of plaintiffs to show "good cause." However much uncertainty lay with the good-cause standard, it existed to protect parties from abuse during the discovery procedure.[13] According to Air Force regulations, the sole purpose of investigations into aircraft accidents was to determine the factors that led to the accident and to prevent a recurrence "in the interest of flying safety."[14] To encourage personnel to cooperate fully with the investigating board, Air Force regulations assured witnesses that the investigative report "will not be used in any manner in connection with any investigation or proceeding leading toward disciplinary action, determination of pecuniary liability or line-of-duty status, or reclassification."[15]

The government seemed to suggest that access to the accident report, by either plaintiffs or the district judge, might result in some type of disciplinary proceeding or sanction against witnesses. That was an understandable

10. Id.
11. Id. at 7–8.
12. Id. at 8.
13. Id. at 9.
14. Id. at 10.
15. Id. at 11.

and legitimate concern, but this executive interest had to be weighed against other interests, including the authority of courts to decide what evidence to admit, the intent of Congress in enacting the Federal Tort Claims Act, and the need of plaintiffs to gain access to agency documents to support their case. Moreover, any disciplinary proceeding against witnesses would be left to the executive branch. Why should that concern prevent private plaintiffs from obtaining the documents they requested?

As to plaintiffs' position that they knew of no other way to obtain information to prepare for trial other than by gaining access to the accident report and the survivor statements, the government's brief pointed to the availability of depositions of the survivors. To the extent that depositions would be burdensome, expensive, and inconvenient, the government offered to make the three witnesses available at government expense. However, as the brief notes, Judge Kirkpatrick had pointed to a different problem: the length of time since the accident "might tarnish the memory of the witnesses and the fact that they are subject to military authority would tend to make them biased."[16]

The government's brief faulted Judge Kirkpatrick's interpretation of the Supreme Court's decision in *Hickman v. Taylor* (1947), which placed a burden on litigants who sought the work product of a lawyer. In such cases, the government said, the individual seeking the work product must show that he has "invoked all of his available rights under the discovery rules to no avail before an adequate showing of good cause for the production of documents under Rule 34 is made."[17] The government said it was error on Kirkpatrick's part to limit *Hickman* to the narrow category of an attorney's work papers:

> It is hardly debatable that there are at least as many "considerations of policy" in the instant case, where a question of national interest is raised, as in a case involving a lawyer's work papers. If, in the latter case, "the party seeking discovery must show circumstances of an exceptional nature in order to establish good cause," surely he must also in a case where disclosure of the documents would have a detrimental effect on the interests of the Air Force and to flying safety. Plaintiffs have made no attempt to avail themselves of the right to take the depositions of the surviving witnesses.[18]

The issue of flying safety was flagged regularly by the government, without ever spelling out what role it should have, if any, regarding a plaintiff's access

16. Id. at 15.
17. Id. at 17 (citing Hickman v. Taylor, 329 U.S. 495 (1947)).
18. Id. at 18.

to agency documents. Finally, the government argued that the accident report and the statements of survivors were privileged and not subject to discovery. Rule 34 authorized a court to order the production of documents "not privileged." The power of a federal judge to compel production under this rule, "therefore, does not reach any matter which is privileged by statute, the Constitution, or common law."[19] The government had not analyzed the constitutional claim other than by referring generally to the doctrine of separation of powers. Mention of common law seemed to leave the door open to the state secrets privilege and perhaps reliance on English precedents.

Executive Immunity

To the government, executive immunity stood as "an independent barrier to the production of documents which the district judge ordered."[20] Other than Curtin's statement at the August 9, 1950, hearing before Judge Kirkpatrick, this was the first time that the government hinted at some type of executive immunity from a court order. Earlier government statements made no such explicit claim. The Zuckert letter of July 21, 1950, ended with what appeared to be deference to judicial judgment: "It is hoped that the extreme importance which the Department of the Air Force places upon the confidential nature of its official aircraft accident reports will be fully appreciated and understood by your Honorable Court." This language implied that the Air Force, after making its best case, would in the end submit to a court ruling. Did the government draft Zuckert's letter delicately to avoid needless offense to the court? The government now argued to the Third Circuit: "we urge that, in this case, the claim of privilege by the Secretary for Air [*sic*] should have been accepted as valid and binding by the district court."[21] Binding? No room for independent judgment by the court? No opportunity for a court to decide what evidence shall be introduced?

The Harmon affidavit of August 7, 1950, offered to make the three crew survivors available to the plaintiffs at government expense, and insisted that the accident report and the survivors' statements "cannot be furnished without seriously hampering national security, flying safety and the development of highly technical and secret military equipment." Moreover, disclosure of the survivor statements "would have a deterrent effect upon the much desired objective of encouraging uninhibited admissions in future inquiry proceed-

19. Id. at 19.
20. Id.
21. Id. at 20.

ings instituted primarily in the interest of flying safety." Such remarks seemed designed to alert the court to potential harmful consequences, not to announce an ironclad, unreviewable executive immunity.

The government offered this broad principle to the Third Circuit: "The independent decision of the head of an executive department, acting pursuant to his own constitutional and statutory powers, to decline to disclose records, can only be challenged by direct process which brings the validity of his action under adjudication."[22] An agency head has *statutory* powers, of course. But *constitutional* powers? Why should an agency head, created by statute, have a constitutional power to deny a federal court documents needed in a tort claims case? What did the government mean about challenges by "direct process"? Apparently Judge Kirkpatrick, if he wanted to see the documents in his chambers, would have to subpoena them, touching off a major executive-judicial collision.

For legal authority on the power of agency heads to block access to documents, the government cited *Touhy v. Ragen,* decided by the Supreme Court on February 16, 1951. The government said that the Court "held that a subordinate of the Attorney General could not be held in contempt for obeying the Department of Justice regulation which forbade him to comply with a *subpoena duces tecum* ordering production of departmental records in his possession."[23] That is all that the Court decided. A subordinate had no authority to release the records. That decision was reserved to the head of the department. As the government's brief explained, the Court "did not find it necessary" to decide the constitutionality of the Attorney General's exercise "of a statutory power, which it is assumed that he possessed, to refuse to produce departmental papers in response to a court order."[24] The statutory power was the Housekeeping Statute. In *Touhy,* the Court said that the determination of the Attorney General's refusal must await a later ruling because the Attorney General "was not before the trial court."[25]

How does *Touhy* relate to *Reynolds?* Roger Touhy, an inmate in the Illinois State penitentiary, initiated a habeas corpus proceeding in federal district court against the warden, alleging that the warden restrained him in violation of the Due Process Clause. In the course of that proceeding, a subpoena was issued and served upon an FBI agent, requiring the production of certain records that Touhy thought would establish that his conviction rested on fraud.

22. Id.
23. Id.
24. Id.
25. Id. at 21 (citing Touhy v. Ragen, 340 U.S. 462, 467 (1951)).

In court, the agent declined to produce the records in accordance with a Justice Department regulation issued by the Attorney General. The judge then held the agent in contempt.[26]

The potential issue before the Supreme Court in *Touhy* was "whether it is permissible for the Attorney General to make a conclusive determination not to produce records." The Court found it unnecessary to consider the "ultimate reach of the authority of the Attorney General to refuse to produce at a court's order the government papers in his possession, for the case as we understand it raises no question as to the power of the Attorney General himself to make such a refusal. The Attorney General was not before the trial court."[27]

In short, nothing in *Touhy* speaks to the authority of the Attorney General to make a conclusive determination to deny documents to a court. The government's brief overreached in finding in *Touhy* a basis for "executive immunity" and asserting that a decision by a department head not to release a document is "valid and binding" on courts. The Supreme Court specifically stated that it was not concerned with the effect of a refusal to produce a document "in a prosecution by the United States or with the right of a custodian of government papers to refuse to produce them on the ground that they are state secrets or that they would disclose the names of informants."[28] The Court did not concede a veto power by the Attorney General over access to documents. The constitutionality of the Attorney General's "exercise of determinative power as to whether or on what conditions or subject to what disadvantages to the Government he may refuse to produce government papers under his charge must await a factual situation that requires a ruling."[29]

In reaching the result it did in *Touhy,* the Court relied on *Boske v. Comingore,* a Court ruling from 1900.[30] Justice Frankfurter prepared a concurrence in *Touhy,* hoping to head off possible misunderstandings. He wrote: "There is not a hint in the *Boske* opinion that the Government can shut off an appropriate judicial demand for such papers."[31] In joining the Court's ruling in *Touhy,* Frankfurter assumed that the Attorney General "can be reached by legal process."[32]

The government drew two conclusions from these precedents. First, the attorneys in the Justice Department handling *Reynolds* "cannot dictate or even

26. Touhy v. Ragen, 340 U.S. at 465.
27. Id. at 467.
28. Id. at 467–68 (footnotes omitted).
29. Id. at 469.
30. Id.
31. Id. at 472.
32. Id.

participate" in the decision of the Secretary of the Air Force to withhold documents "and must abide by it."[33] The Housekeeping Statute placed authority in the secretary, not with someone from another department. The secretary would have to come before a court for a "final decision on the propriety of his action."[34] If the final decision depends on a court, why did the government argue that Judge Kirkpatrick should have accepted the Air Force claim as "valid and binding"?

The answer comes with the government's second conclusion. Having just argued that the agency head must await a court's a final decision, the government now maintained that the judgment of the Secretary of the Air Force to withhold a document is privileged under statutory authority and agency regulations. Here is the claim: "Revised Statutes, Section 161, and valid regulations thereunder, vest in the Secretary for Air [*sic*] the power and duty to determine the privileged character of the documents which the district court ordered to be produced."[35] R.S. § 161 is the Housekeeping Statute. According to the government: "*If* the Secretary's order is within the authority granted by R.S. 161 and *if* the section, as implemented by this order, is constitutional, the documents which the district court ordered produced were 'privileged' and Rule 34 did not permit an order requiring their promotion [production?]."[36]

There are several problems with the government's analysis. First, it rests on several big ifs. Second, it elevates one statute (the Housekeeping Statute) above all others, including the Federal Tort Claims Act and its requirement that the government be treated on a par with private litigants. Third, it gives superior rank to one statute over the constitutional obligation of federal courts to assure that documents needed by plaintiffs be made available. Why would a Secretary's judgment automatically override a contrary judgment by a federal judge? Nothing in the Housekeeping Statute dictates that result, even if the government's brief claims that the "privilege against disclosure which the Secretary for Air [*sic*] has here asserted has the direct support of statute."[37] The Housekeeping Statute does not state that and does not imply that.

The government insisted that *Boske v. Comingore* "directly establishes both that R.S. § 161 authorizes the Secretary's order and that this exercise of the authority granted by Congress is constitutional."[38] As the government

---

33. Government's Brief, at 22.
34. Id.
35. Id.
36. Id. at 23 (emphasis added).
37. Id.
38. Id.

explained in its brief, *Boske* involved the effort of the Commonwealth of Kentucky to determine the amount and value of whiskey in bonded warehouses owned by a private party. The U.S. Collector of Internal Revenue declined to provide copies of official records and was held in contempt by a state court. The Supreme Court ruled that the Collector properly refused to release the documents and acted with the full support of Treasury Department regulations that prohibited their disclosure.

There are two major differences between *Boske* and *Reynolds*. First, *Boske* involved the effort of a state court to obtain federal records, creating an issue of federalism. In *Reynolds,* the effort to seek documents from an executive agency involved a federal judge, raising questions of separation of powers. Second, whatever the motivation of the state court, the reason behind Judge Kirkpatrick's order was entirely different. It was his statutory duty, under the Federal Tort Claims Act, to obtain for the plaintiffs the documents they needed to prove government negligence. The heart of *Boske* was its determination that the Housekeeping Statute appropriately vests in the head of a department, and not a subordinate (a collector), the decision to release an agency document.[39]

Left undecided for the future was the question of what happens when the request for a document comes from a federal judge who seeks to protect a plaintiff's statutory rights under the Federal Tort Claims Act. It is the judge who runs the courtroom and makes rulings for the parties before it. On what grounds would a judge surrender to an agency head the ultimate decision to share or withhold documents requested by plaintiffs or the court?

The government offered an answer. It claimed that the Housekeeping Statute "reflects the constitutional independence of the Executive."[40] The government argued that the statute was "more than a provision for routine administration by agency heads in handling their internal housekeeping. Rather, it was intended to be a grant of independent authority, in accordance with and as part of the fabric of the constitutional plan of separation of powers."[41] The brief correctly states that the statute "stems directly from the original organic acts establishing the executive departments (1 Stat. 28, 49, 65, 68, 553)."[42] But those statutes reflected the independent authority of Congress, not the executive departments, and nothing in those statutes implied an overriding power by agency heads to withhold documents from courts or plaintiffs.

The government's brief compares Congress under the U.S. Constitution to the Continental Congress under the Articles of Confederation: "Under

39. Boske v. Comingore, 177 U.S. 459, 470 (1900).
40. Government's Brief, at 26.
41. Id.
42. Id.

the Continental Congress, the relationship between legislature and executive had been modeled on the British system. The executive departments were, in effect, answerable to the legislature, and could be called on for an accounting."[43] However, the Continental Congress was *not* modeled on the British system. It broke fundamentally with English precedents by placing all power in one branch: the Continental Congress, which passed legislation, handled administrative duties, and even adjudicated conflicts over admiralty matters.[44] Wholly absent were the independent powers exercised by the British king, the prime minister, or judicial bodies. The U.S. constitutional system that operated after 1789, with a separate and coequal Congress, was also divorced from the British model.

Wolkinson's Article

The government relied heavily on a three-part article published in 1949 by Herman Wolkinson, a Justice Department attorney who described the history of executive privilege. According to the government, executive privilege "has consistently and successfully been asserted in response to Congressional attempts to require production by the executive branch, often of the very type of documents involved in this case."[45] Generalizing about executive privilege is not helpful in analyzing the merits of the *Reynolds* litigation, unless one wants to assert that executive privilege prevails every time, which is not true.

Yet that was Wolkinson's position. He claimed that federal courts "have uniformly held that the President and the heads of departments have an uncontrolled discretion to withhold the information and papers in the public interest, and they will not interfere with the exercise of that discretion."[46] That statement was false when written and grows more false with time.[47] Similarly incorrect was Wolkinson's claim that "in every instance where a President has backed the refusal of a head of a department to divulge confidential information to either of the Houses of Congress, or their committees, the papers and the information requested were not furnished."[48] Presidents and executive officials had capitulated a number of times before Wolkinson's article appeared.[49]

---

43. Id.

44. Louis Fisher, President and Congress 6–17, 253–70 (1972).

45. Government's Brief, at 27, citing the three-part work of Herman Wolkinson, "Demands of Congressional Committees for Executive Papers," 10 Fed. Bar J. 103, 223, 319 (1949) (hereafter "Wolkinson").

46. Wolkinson, at 103.

47. Louis Fisher, The Politics of Executive Privilege (2004).

48. Wolkinson, at 104.

49. Fisher, The Politics of Executive Privilege.

Wolkinson asserted that Congress could not, "under the Constitution, compel heads of departments by law to give up papers and information, regardless of the public interest involved; and the President is the judge of that interest."[50] He seriously ignored the coercive powers of Congress by claiming that the heads of departments were "entirely unaffected by existing laws which prescribe penalties for failure to testify and produce papers before the House of Representatives or the Senate, or their committees."[51] Congress may hold executive officials in contempt and can use its constitutional powers over appropriations, appointments, and impeachment to flush out the documents it wants.[52]

The government's legal strategy was clear. First, it has an attorney in the Justice Department write a lengthy article for a law review, making it a convenient citation to support their agenda. There is nothing unique or original about that approach. Law firms and corporations frequently ask someone on staff to publish an article, book, or commission report, which can later be cited as an authority to support a legal claim, either in Congress, the agencies, or the courts.[53] The next step is for the government to wait for the right case to advance executive power, such as the state secrets privilege. The last step is to discover a case filed by three widows who are seeking damages resulting from the crash of a B-29 that was testing secret equipment.

The government's discussion of the Housekeeping Statute and Wolkinson's article was largely off the point. The question in *Reynolds* was not access to agency documents by Congress but by private plaintiffs and the courts. The brief acknowledged this distinction: "while there may very well be differences in the force of the [executive] privilege when it touches on the interest of parties to a judicial proceeding, the executive's relations with Congress, if not controlling, are certainly relevant."[54] The brief cites various opinions by Attorneys General for the proposition that the release of agency documents is one for the determination of the executive, not the judiciary.[55] This position was supposedly reinforced by precedents established at the state level, both in statute and court rulings,[56] but it is far too broad (and self-serving) to be accepted as American law or practice.

50. Wolkinson, at 107.
51. Id.
52. Fisher, The Politics of Executive Privilege.
53. Louis Fisher, American Constitutional Law 8 (6th ed. 2005).
54. Government's Brief, at 29.
55. Id. at 30–31.
56. Id. at 31–32.

British Precedents

The government looked to precedents outside the United States: "Nor can one ignore British judgments in the field of executive privilege."[57] There is no reason to ignore those judgments, but no reason to be controlled by them either. Congress and federal courts have much greater independence than their counterparts in England. Still, the government considered a decision by the House of Lords in *Duncan v. Cammell, Laird & Co.* (1942) to be particularly "authoritative."[58] The case, on appeal from the Court of Appeal, arose out of the sinking of a submarine and the efforts of the families of deceased seamen to bring an action against the builders. When the families sought the plans, contracts for construction, and other documents, the First Lord of the Admiralty in an affidavit claimed privilege from disclosure on the ground that it would be injurious to the public interest. After acknowledging that the rule in criminal cases might be different, the opinion held that it was the responsibility of the head of an executive department to read the disputed documents and decide whether release would damage the public interest. An executive determination that the document was privileged would then be conclusive on the court.[59] The public interest, said the British court, "must be preferred to any private consideration."[60] A footnote in the government's brief offers a lengthy quote from *Duncan.*[61] Just before the passage selected by the government, however, is a key passage the government conveniently omitted:

> Although an objection validly taken to production, on the ground that this would be injurious to the public interest, is conclusive, it is important to remember that the decision ruling out such documents is the decision of the judge. Thus, in the present case, the objection raised in the respondents' affidavit is properly expressed to be an objection to produce "except under the order of this honourable court." It is the judge who is in control of the trial, not the executive.[62]

What an omission! It is the judge, not an executive official, who controls the trial. It is the judge who decides whether a plaintiff has proper access to necessary documents and papers. An error that occurs in a trial court or appellate court, requiring reversal by a superior court, reflects the mistake of

---

57. Id. at 33.
58. Id.
59. Id. at 34–35.
60. Id. at 36.
61. Id. at 36 (Note 30).
62. Duncan v. Cammell, Laird & Co., Law Reports, A.C. (1942), at 642.

the judge, not the executive. *Duncan* took a grilling in 1968 by the House of Lords. One judge said that in many cases, "much dissatisfaction" had been expressed against it, "and I have not observed even one expression of whole-hearted approval."[63] Several judges pointed out that *Duncan* was clearly erroneous in describing Scottish law.[64]

The duty of a judge to decide questions of evidence was highlighted in a 1944 case by the Second Circuit interpreting the Housekeeping Statute. The court recognized that in earlier decisions, such as *Boske v. Comingore,* departmental regulations validly prohibited subordinates from releasing requested documents without the permission of the agency head. However, the Second Circuit stated that "none of these cases involved the prosecution of a crime consisting of the very matters recorded in the suppressed documents, or of matters nearly enough akin to make relevant the matters recorded."[65] The court disagreed that judicial deference to executive departments could allow the suppression of documents in a criminal proceeding that might "tend to exculpate."[66] In such situations the government must choose: "either it must leave the transactions in the obscurity from which a trial will draw them, or it must expose them fully."[67] If the government decides to prosecute someone, it must either release the documents that are exculpatory or drop the case.

The government's brief ends on an ambiguous note. It does not invoke the state secrets privilege, but perhaps something even broader. Throughout the brief, the government seemed to argue for judicial deference to executive documents about "privileged" documents and not merely documents in the field of national security: "we believe that the determination of what documents should not be disclosed in the public interest is a determination necessarily within the discretion and distinctive knowledge of the executive branch."[68] That sounds like total judicial (and legislative) deference to executive judgments. Yet a page later comes a different formulation: "In a government of separate powers, weight must be accorded to the judgment of the executive in a function primarily within his discretion, else his function is undermined."[69] Here the emphasis seems not to be on total or blind judicial deference, but on giving weight and respect to executive judgment. Depending on the case, a judge could agree with the determination of an agency head or treat it as less important than other competing values selected by the court. The gov-

---

63. Conway v. Rimmer, A.C. (1968), at 938.
64. Id. at 958, 960–61, 977.
65. United States v. Andolschek, 142 F.2d 503, 506 (2d Cir. 1944).
66. Id.
67. Id.
68. Government's Brief, at 38.
69. Id. at 39.

ernment may have drafted the language to show respect for the judiciary, knowing that it would be risky and imprudent to tell judges what they can and cannot do.

The Plaintiffs' Brief

Charles J. Biddle and Francis Hopkinson filed a brief that rebutted the government's argument that Judge Kirkpatrick had acted improperly by deciding in favor of the three widows "without requiring the production of evidence by the plaintiffs." They pointed out that once the government decided to disobey the court's order under Rule 34 (that the documents be given to the plaintiffs), or at least submit the documents to the court for in camera review, the case would be controlled by Rule 37. When a party refuses to comply with a court order for discovery, the rule provides that

> the court may make such orders in regard to the refusal as are just, and among others the following:
> (i) An order that the matters regarding which the questions were asked, . . . shall be taken to be established for the purposes of the action in accordance with the claim of the party obtaining the order;
> (ii) An order refusing to allow the disobedient party to support or oppose designated claims or defenses.[70]

When the government refused to comply with the court order, Judge Kirkpatrick entered an order "to the effect that the plaintiffs need produce no further proof of the facts that the plaintiffs' decedents were killed as a result of the crash of an airplane owned and operated by the defendant and that the crash was due to the negligence of the defendant, which facts were averred in the complaints, and, further, that the defendant should not be permitted to introduce evidence controverting these facts."[71]

The plaintiffs' brief reviewed Judge Kirkpatrick's decision in *O'Neill v. United States* (1948), which involved the government's refusal to produce statements taken by the FBI from witnesses to a shipping accident. Kirkpatrick had to apply Admiralty Rule 32(c), which is the counterpart for discovery of Rule 34 of the Federal Rules of Civil Procedure. When the government failed to produce the statements, he entered an order "refusing to allow it to

---

70. "Brief for Appellees," Reynolds v. United States, No. 10,483 (3d Cir. 1951), at 1 (hereafter "Appellee's Brief").
71. Id. at 2.

oppose the libellant's contention that his injury was due to negligence on the part of the personnel of the vessel in question."[72] Kirkpatrick warned that when the government refuses to make disclosure it "will incur certain procedural disadvantages by way of penalty and may lose its case."[73]

According to the plaintiffs' brief, the deaths "having occurred in Georgia, the case is governed by the law of that State," and judicial rulings in Georgia concluded that "mere proof of the happening of the accident affords satisfactory evidence of want of care."[74] A Georgia case in 1937 ruled that there must be reasonable evidence of negligence, "but where the thing is shown to be under the management of the defendant or his servants, and the accident is such as in the ordinary course of things does not happen if those who have the management use proper care, it affords reasonable evidence, in the absence of explanation by defendant, that the accident arose from want of care."[75]

The Good Cause Standard

The plaintiffs' brief acknowledged that under Rule 34 it was necessary for them to show good cause to be entitled to discovery, and that good cause had been demonstrated. They had no knowledge of the cause of the accident and no way to learn of the cause other than by obtaining the accident report and the statements of survivors.[76] As to making the survivors available at the convenience of the plaintiffs and at the expense of the government, depositions taken long after the accident were not an adequate substitute for statements taken at the time of the accident, when the recollections of the survivors were fresh.[77] Judge Kirkpatrick had also noted that the survivors, although not necessarily hostile to the plaintiffs, were employees of the government, "in military service and subject to military authority and it is not an unfair assumption that they will not be encouraged to disclose, voluntarily, any information that might fix responsibility upon the Air Force."[78]

Biddle and Hopkinson said it was their intention at the trial to call an aviation expert as a witness for the three widows. For such a witness "to be useful it is essential that he should be put in possession of all the facts and techni-

---

72. Id. at 3.
73. Id.
74. Id. at 4–5.
75. Id. (Citing Macon Coca-Cola Bottling Co. v. Crane, 55 Ga. App. 573, 190 S.E. 879 (1937), which relied on language from Chenall v. Palmer Brick Co., 117 Ga. 106, 43 S.E. 443 and 119 Ga. 837, 47 S.E. 329).
76. Id. at 7.
77. Id. at 9.
78. Id. at 10.

cal details having to do with the accident."[79] Without access to the accident report and the statements of survivors, the expert's testimony would be of little value. The government's answers to the interrogatories were insufficient. When the plaintiffs asked the government to describe "in detail the trouble experienced," the government answered: "At between 18,500 or 19,000 feet manifold pressure dropped to 23' on No. 1 engine."[80]

The plaintiffs' brief disputed the government's claim that a general privilege exists to prevent discovery of Air Force accident reports: "Briefly and baldly stated, the contention of the Government is that anything which any of its Departments sees fit to declare shall not be disclosed, shall be beyond the reach of the discovery provisions of the Federal Rules, and that the Government alone shall be the judge of what it will disclose."[81] The purpose of creating the Federal Rules was "to improve the administration of the law by making the facts in all cases available to both litigants and thus removing, so far as possible, the element of chance in legal trials."[82] The Federal Rules of Civil Procedure were adopted by the Supreme Court in response to legislation passed by Congress on June 19, 1934.[83] Such rules were to be applied fairly and evenly, without granting an advantage to a particular litigant: "Said rules shall neither abridge, enlarge, nor modify the substantive rights of any litigant."[84] An advisory committee appointed to draft the rules "believed and intended that the Rules should apply to the United States Government as a litigant, just as much as to any private party except, of course, where it was specifically provided otherwise."[85]

Executive Immunity

The plaintiffs' brief rejected the government's argument that the Justice Department had no power to require the Secretary of the Air Force to release the accident report and the survivor statements, and that it was necessary for the plaintiffs to bring the secretary before the court.[86] The secretary "obviously knows nothing about the facts of these cases and is already before the Court, as is demonstrated by the fact that he himself filed the Government's Claim

79. Id. at 11.
80. Id.
81. Id. at 14.
82. Id.
83. Id. (48 Stat. 1064).
84. 48 Stat. 1064, § 1 (1934).
85. Appellee's Brief, at 15.
86. Id. at 18.

of Privilege."[87] Although the federal government has many executive departments, "it is still one government."[88] The plaintiffs' brief quoted this language from a 1948 district court case: "The several departments are all agencies of one government, possessed, theoretically, at least, of a single will. When that will is exercised in favor of litigating its claims it is thereby exercised in favor of surrendering the conditional privilege of suppressing its housekeeping secrets when these are useful in the ascertainment of liability."[89]

As to the application of *Touhy v. Ragen,* the plaintiffs' brief said it stood only for the proposition that a subordinate in the Justice Department (an FBI agent) should not have been held in contempt for refusing to produce departmental papers, because the Housekeeping Statute assigned that determination to the head of the department: the Attorney General. The Supreme Court in *Touhy* had found it unnecessary to define the reach of the Attorney General's authority to refuse to produce government papers in response to a court order. The Court merely decided that the Attorney General "could forbid disclosure *by a subordinate* and hence the subordinate could not be held in contempt for merely doing what he was told by his superior."[90]

The plaintiffs' brief examined the general claim of privilege by executive departments, including not only the Housekeeping Statute but also other arguments that the courts and Congress should defer to executive judgments. The Secretary of the Air Force stated that under the Housekeeping Statute he was authorized to make regulations about the records under his control, and he had ruled that the accident report and other documents not be disclosed. Consequently, "that is the end of the matter."[91] Air Force Regulation No. 62 provided: "The report of investigations required herein . . . will not be used in any manner in connection with any investigation or proceeding leading toward disciplinary action, determination of pecuniary liability or line-of-duty status, or reclassification."[92] Investigative reports could not be disclosed without the specific approval of the secretary.

Why would a departmental regulation trump the request for documents needed by plaintiffs in a tort claims action, particularly when Congress in passing the tort claims statute provided that the government be treated on a par with other litigants? Why should a departmental regulation block the request of a federal judge that the disputed documents be given to him to read in camera? The plaintiffs' brief noted that the language in Air Force Regula-

87. Id. at 19.
88. Id.
89. Id. (citing Bank Line v. United States, 76 F.Supp. 801, 804 (1948)).
90. Id. at 20 (emphasis in original).
91. Id. at 21.
92. Id.

tion No. 62 prohibited disciplinary action, pecuniary liability or line-of-duty status, or reclassification *against the witnesses.*[93] To say that witnesses, because of their immunity, "will not tell the truth just because their statements may show that the Government should compensate the relatives of persons who have been carelessly killed, is a complete non sequitur."[94]

Agreeing that a privilege existed, plaintiffs asked whether it was absolute or qualified. If the latter, "then who is to decide whether the claim of privilege is well taken?"[95] The brief conceded that there "may be diplomatic secrets or highly confidential military information, of which disclosure might not be compelled under any circumstances."[96] But the historical examples of presidential privilege included in the government's brief did not support an absolute privilege. Federal courts asserted their authority "to determine whether an executive claim of privilege had merit."[97] In the *Reynolds* case, the government never expressly asserted the existence of diplomatic secrets or highly confidential military information in the accident report or the survivor statements. As Judge Kirkpatrick noted in his decision: "the Government does not here contend that this is a case involving the well recognized common law privilege protecting state secrets or facts which might seriously harm the Government in its diplomatic relations, military operations or measures for national security."[98]

Citing a case from the D.C. Circuit, decided May 18, 1951, the plaintiffs' brief drew attention to the need for an independent judiciary to determine whether a specific act is within the exclusive authority of the executive branch and thus immune from judicial interference. That determination should not be left to self-serving interpretations by the executive branch, and yet in this 1951 case, involving the Secretary of Commerce, the executive branch claimed authority to ignore a court order. The D.C. Circuit repudiated that position:

(The officials) say that, even though the courts determine that a specific action is not within the official capacity of an executive officer, he is immune from compulsion by the courts in respect to that action. That is to say that the executive can determine for himself whether the acts of his subordinate officials are within or without their official capacities.

93. Id. (emphasis in original).
94. Id. at 22.
95. Id.
96. Id.
97. Id. at 23.
98. Id.

That proposition asserts the impotency of the judiciary as an organ of government.[99]

Regarding the authority of a department head over agency documents, the plaintiffs' brief reviewed a federal district court decision in *Cresmer v. United States* (1949). The family of an individual killed in a Navy plane crash brought an action against the federal government for wrongful death under the Federal Tort Claims Act. The family asked for a copy of a report by the Navy Board of Investigation, but the government opposed the motion on the ground of privilege. The district judge asked for the report, examined it, and found no military or service secrets that would be detrimental to national security.[100] Similar rulings were handed down in *Bank Line, Ltd. v. United States* (1946) and *United States v. Cotton Valley Operators Committee* (1949).[101] The plaintiffs' brief quotes from Judge Kirkpatrick in *O'Neill:* "Certainly the right accorded to seamen to sue the government by the Suits in Admiralty Act would be of very little value if the government could in its character as sovereign refuse to comply with any order of the Court in procedural matters without incurring any penalty or disadvantages."[102]

The government depended on *Boske v. Comingore,* but that case differs fundamentally from *Reynolds.* In both *Boske* and *Touhy,* the courts recognized that the Housekeeping Statute gave a department head control over the decisions of a subordinate to release an agency document. Nothing in either decision, however, suggested that the government can block an appropriate judicial demand for documents.[103] Applied to *Reynolds,* the Secretary of the Air Force had every right to prohibit the release of an accident report without his approval, but he did not have an overriding and unreviewable authority to deny the document to the plaintiffs or the judge.[104]

The government's reliance on the English case of *Duncan v. Cammell, Laird & Co.* was not persuasive. First, the objection of the admiralty was subject to the order of the court. The judge controlled the trial, not the executive.[105] Second, whatever the rule in England, the law of the United States does not make the judgment of an agency head conclusive on the courts. Third, En-

99. Id. at 25 (citing Land v. Dollar Line [Sawyer v. Dollar], 190 F.2d 623, 639 (D.C. Cir. 1951)).
100. Id. at 27–28.
101. Id. at 28–31.
102. Id. at 32.
103. Id. at 34–36.
104. Id. at 36.
105. Id. at 36–37.

gland did not have a tort claims act that made the government liable under the same circumstances as a private individual.[106] Fourth, five years after the decision in *Duncan,* England passed the Crown Proceedings Act, authorizing discovery against the crown for the first time, but the statute specifically exempted any document that a Minister determined would be injurious to the public interest to disclose.[107]

If a case arose concerning documents of such "vital importance and secret character that for the good of the nation disclosure should be made to no one," even to a federal judge, the burden nevertheless remained on the executive branch to explain why the order to produce the documents must be refused. All that Secretary Finletter argued in *Reynolds* was that "in his opinion it is for the good of the Service not to tell what went wrong with the crew or mechanical equipment of an obsolete plane."[108] No danger to the national security would have resulted had Finletter or one of his assistants met with the trial judge to explain why the documents could not be examined in camera, or to allow the judge to examine them in his chambers to decide what portions to withhold from plaintiffs. If the judge decided to make public items that Finletter decided would be dangerous, the dispute could be appealed to a higher court.[109]

The Third Circuit Decides

On December 11, 1951, the Third Circuit upheld Judge Kirkpatrick's decision that good cause had been shown by the plaintiffs for the production of the accident report and the statements of survivors, and that the documents were not privileged.[110] Writing for the court, Judge Maris said that "considerations of justice may well demand that the plaintiffs should have had access to the facts, thus within the exclusive control of their opponent, upon which they were required to rely to establish their right of recovery."[111] The alternative offered by the government (for the plaintiffs to depose the three survivors) was not "a sufficient answer."[112] Nor did depositions have anything to do with the request for the accident report.

106. Id. at 37.
107. Id. at 37–38.
108. Id. at 38.
109. Id.
110. Reynolds v. United States, 192 F.2d 987 (3d Cir. 1951).
111. Id. at 992.
112. Id.

Executive Immunity

On the question of privilege, the government relied "primarily on Section 161 of the Revised Statutes" (the Housekeeping Statute).[113] The government argued that this statute gave the Secretary of the Air Force authority to prescribe regulations for the custody of records within the department, and "necessarily confers upon him full discretionary power in the public interest to refuse to produce any such records for examination and use in a judicial proceeding and that such records thereby become 'privileged.'"[114] The government's reading of separation of powers, Judge Maris said, placed its discretionary power "wholly beyond judicial review."[115]

Judge Maris did not dispute the validity of the regulations issued by the Secretary of the Air Force, including the secretary's full control over subordinates in releasing documents and records. For that reason, the cases of *Boske* and *Touhy* were "not in point."[116] Nor was there any issue about gaining access to the documents by directing a subpoena to the secretary or holding him in contempt for failing to comply. No such action had "been asked for or taken."[117] The sole issue was the legal duty of the secretary under the Federal Tort Claims Act and the action of the district court when he refused to release the documents requested during discovery.

Maris noted that the Federal Tort Claims Act provides that the United States "shall be liable . . . in the same manner and to the same extent as a private individual under like circumstances."[118] By the express terms of the statute, Congress had "divested the United States of its normal sovereign immunity to the extent of making it liable in actions such as those now before us in the same manner as if it were a private individual."[119] At the same time, Congress made the Federal Rules of Civil Procedure, including the discovery provisions, applicable to tort actions against the United States. From those statutory provisions, Maris concluded: "We think that by so doing Congress has withdrawn the right of the executive departments of the Government in tort claims cases, even if under other circumstances such right exists, to determine without judicial review the extent of the privilege against disclosure of Government documents sought to be produced for use in the litigation."[120]

113. Id.
114. Id.
115. Id.
116. Id. at 992–93.
117. Id. at 993.
118. Id.
119. Id.
120. Id.

Turning to the claim of privilege, Maris examined the government's arguments that release of the requested documents would not be in the public interest and would interfere with the capacity of the Air Force to investigate aircraft accidents.[121] He examined Air Force Regulation No. 62-7, which prohibited the use of aircraft accident information in connection with "any investigation or proceeding toward disciplinary action, determination of pecuniary liability, or line-of-duty status or reclassification," and concluded that the regulation had "no bearing on the problem before us since it merely imposes restrictions upon the subsequent use within the department for disciplinary and other purposes of statements of Air Force personnel with respect to aircraft accidents."[122]

Judge Maris also rejected the position of the government, in tort claims cases, that the Housekeeping Statute entitled the Air Force to an absolute privilege in withholding statements or reports relating to the airplane accident "regardless of their contents."[123] However convenient or efficient it might be for the Air Force to withhold all documents, private persons "do not ordinarily enjoy that privilege."[124] In such cases as *Reynolds,* where the government had consented to be sued as a private person, whatever claims of public interest might exist in withholding accident reports "must yield to what Congress evidently regarded as the greater public interest involved in seeing that justice is done to persons injured by governmental operations whom it has authorized to enforce their claims by suit against the United States."[125]

If Congress wanted to prohibit the admission into evidence of airplane accident reports, it knew how to do it. Maris pointed to a section in the Civil Aeronautics Act of 1938 as a model. Not only did the statute direct the Air Safety Board of the Civil Aeronautics Authority to preserve custody of records and reports, it stated that "no part of any report or reports of the Board or the Authority relating to any accident, or the investigation thereof, shall be admitted as evidence or used in any suit or action for damages growing out of any matter mentioned in such report or reports."[126] Congress knew how to grant department heads with discretionary authority to refuse to produce records in suits brought against the United States. In earlier legislation, it had authorized the Court of Claims to call upon any department or agency for papers and reports, but added this qualification: "The head of any department or agency may refuse to comply when, in his opinion, compliance will be injurious to

121. Id. at 993–94.
122. Id. at 994.
123. Id.
124. Id.
125. Id.
126. Id. at 994–95 (citing 52 Stat. 1013).

the public interest."[127] In the type of suits brought under the Federal Tort
Claims Act, Congress chose to withhold those conditions.

In addition to these matters of public law, Judge Maris considered the case
from the standpoint of public policy. To grant the government the "sweeping
privilege" it claimed would be contrary to "a sound public policy." It would
be a small step, he said, "to assert a privilege against any disclosure of records
merely because they might prove embarrassing to government officers."[128]
Maris reached into history to warn about perfunctory and mechanical deference to secrecy claims. Edward Livingston, a contemporary of James Madison,
wrote: "No nation ever yet found any inconvenience from too close an inspection into the conduct of its officers, but many have been brought to ruin, and
reduced to slavery, by suffering gradual imposition and abuses, which were
imperceptible, only because the means of publicity had not been secured."[129]
At the Virginia ratifying convention, Patrick Henry said that "to cover with
the veil of secrecy the common routine of business, is an abomination in the
eyes of every intelligent man and every friend to his country."[130]

Judge Maris reviewed the choices available to government when it decides
not to release information. In a criminal case, if the government does not
want to reveal all the evidence within its control (such as the identity of an
informer), it can drop the charges. To Maris, the Federal Tort Claims Act "offers the Government an analogous choice" in civil cases.[131] It could produce
relevant documents under Rule 34 and allow the case to move forward, or
it could withhold the records at the risk of losing the case under Rule 37. In
Reynolds, the government chose the latter.

Maris rejected the government's argument that the proper procedure would
be for the court to order Secretary Finletter to come before it to answer the
plaintiffs' demands for the documents. He said that the original order in district court was directed not to the Attorney General or to a particular officer,
but to "defendant, the United States of America, its agents and attorneys."
The Secretary of the Air Force "is the agent of the United States concerned
with the documents here ordered to be produced," and it "seems quite clear
that the order is directed to and binding upon him just as much as upon
the Attorney General who in these cases is merely attorney for the United
States."[132] Moreover, Finletter was already before the court when he presented
his claim of privilege.[133]

127. Id. at 995 (citing 28 U.S.C. § 2507).
128. Id. at 995.
129. Id. (citing 1 Edward Livingston, Works 15).
130. Id. (citing 3 Elliot's Debates 170).
131. Id. at 995.
132. Id. at 996.
133. Id.

State Secrets

Next was the claim of state secrets, or something close to it. Finletter stated on August 9, 1950: "The defendant further objects to the production of this report, together with the statements of witnesses, for the reason that the aircraft in question, together with the personnel on board, were engaged in a confidential mission of the Air Force. The airplane likewise carried confidential equipment on board and any disclosure of its mission or information concerning its operation or performance would be prejudicial to this Department and would not be in the public interest."[134]

The qualifier "something close to it" is appropriate because of Finletter's language, which did not seem to assert an absolute privilege. In seeking to persuade the district court to accept his judgment, he appeared to acknowledge that the final decision on access to the document was one for the court, not the executive branch. His statement is quite ambiguous. After stating that the B-29 was engaged in a "confidential mission" and carried "confidential equipment," he said that "any *disclosure* of its mission or information" would be prejudicial to the Air Force and "would not be in the public interest." Giving the documents to the plaintiffs would have been disclosure, unless the court imposed a protective order. Giving them to the district judge, to be read in chambers, is not "disclosure," or certainly not public disclosure. To insist that it was would require the government to argue (not advisable) that giving confidential documents to a judge is equivalent to making them public.

Finletter also said: "The furnishing of such information to claimants or litigants" was not contemplated by Air Force regulations. He said nothing about furnishing the information to a federal judge. True, he asserted "the privileged status of reports here involved" and "respectfully decline[s] to permit their production."[135] Perhaps that counts as the state secrets privilege, but the government did not incorporate that doctrine in its briefs, and Finletter's statement did not explain what happens when a district court orders that the documents be shared at least with the judge. Finally, his remarks fudged the issue. Yes, the aircraft was on a confidential mission and carried confidential equipment, but why would release of the accident report and the survivor statements jeopardize confidentiality?[136] The purpose of the mission need not be reflected in the contents of those documents. Reading the declassified documents today reveals no state secrets.

Judge Maris analyzed Finletter's statement in this manner: "It asserts in effect that the documents sought to be produced contain state secrets of a

134. Id.
135. Claim of Privilege by the Secretary of the Air Force, Brauner and Palya v. United States, Civil Action No. 9793 (E.D. Pa. 1950), at 5.
136. Reynolds v. United States, 192 F.2d at 996.

military character. State secrets of a diplomatic or military nature have always been privileged from disclosure in any proceeding and unquestionably come within the class of privileged matters referred to in Rule 34." It was for that reason, Maris said, that the district court had directed that the documents be produced for the judge's personal examination in camera "so that he might determine whether all or any part of the documents contain, to use the words of his order, 'matters of a confidential nature, discovery of which would violate the Government's privilege against disclosure of matters involving the national or public interest.'" Through that process, the district court "adequately protected" the government from the disclosure of any privileged matter.[137]

Although Maris seemed satisfied that Finletter had claimed that the documents contained "state secrets of a military character," Finletter never said that. Instead, Finletter mixed apples and oranges. Maris could have cut through the confusion by defining state secrets as the disclosure of information about the "confidential mission" and the "confidential equipment," and then point out that the plaintiffs and the district court had not asked for that. The state secrets privilege was thus not at issue. However, the muddled nature of Finletter's statement was not analyzed and clarified, and it created a major problem when the dispute reached the Supreme Court and when it returned to federal courts a half century later.

Who Decides on Evidence?

The key question remained: Who has the final say on disclosure? A court or the executive branch? Judge Maris summarized the government's position this way: "it is within the sole province of the Secretary of the Air Force to determine whether any privileged material is contained in the documents and . . . his determination of this question must be accepted by the district court without any independent consideration of the matter by it. We cannot accede to this proposition."[138] The government's position had been more cloudy. No doubt the government argued that the Housekeeping Statute gave an agency head final say on the release of a document, but it never unequivocally said that an agency head could refuse a court order. Curtin had made that argument on August 9, 1950, but did not repeat it in his October 10 petition for a rehearing. By declining to give Judge Kirkpatrick the documents to be read in his chamber, the government was put on notice that such a move would trigger a win for the plaintiffs.

137. Id.
138. Id. at 996–97.

Judge Maris announced that a claim of privilege against disclosing evidence "involves a justiciable question, traditionally within the competence of the courts, which is to be determined in accordance with the appropriate rules of evidence, upon the submission of the documents in question to the judge for his examination *in camera.*"[139] To hold that an agency head in a suit to which the government is a part "may conclusively determine the Government's claim of privilege is to abdicate the judicial function and permit the executive branch of the Government to infringe the independent province of the judiciary as laid down by the Constitution."[140] Maris rejected the government's reliance on the decision by the British House of Lords in *Duncan.* First, it involved the plans of the submarine *Thetis* and military secrets. Second, it was a suit between private parties. Third, "whatever may be true in Great Britain the Government of the United States is one of checks and balances."[141] An independent judiciary is part of those checks, he said, and neither Congress nor the executive branch "may constitutionally encroach upon the field which the Constitution has reserved for the judiciary by transferring to itself the power to decide justiciable questions which arise in cases or controversies submitted to the judicial branch for decision."[142]

What of the risks of sharing confidential documents with a federal judge? Judge Maris found no danger in allowing judges to review sensitive or classified materials: "The judges of the United States are public officers whose responsibility under the Constitution is just as great as that of the heads of the executive departments."[143] Judges may be depended upon to protect against disclosure matters which would do damage to the public interest.[144] If, as the government argued, "a knowledge of background facts is necessary to enable one properly to pass on the claim of privilege those facts also may be presented to the judge *in camera.*"[145]

Burden on Plaintiffs

A few issues remained. The government pointed to Civil Procedure Rule 55(e), which provides that "No judgment by default shall be entered against the United States . . . unless the claimant establishes his claim or right to relief

139. Id. at 997.
140. Id.
141. Id.
142. Id.
143. Id.
144. Id.
145. Id. at 998.

by evidence satisfactory to the court." To the government, Judge Kirkpatrick's order in favor of the plaintiffs on the issue of negligence, taken as established because of the government's refusal to release the documents, amounted to the entry of judgment against the United States by default in violation of Rule 55. Maris disagreed. Paragraph (a) of Rule 55 "in effect defines judgment by default as the judgment which the clerk enters when a party against whom a judgment for affirmative relief is sought has failed to plead or otherwise defend as provided by the rules." In *Reynolds*, the government had filed answers and defended its actions. There were no grounds for default.

The district court decided against the government because of Rule 37(b)(2), which defines the relief a court may grant when a party refuses to produce evidence after having been directed to do so by the court:

> (i) An order that the matters regarding which the questions were asked, or the character or description of the thing or land, or the contents of the paper, or the physical or mental condition of the party, or any other designated facts shall be taken to be established for the purposes of the action in accordance with the claim of the party obtaining the order;
>
> (ii) An order refusing to allow the disobedient party to support or oppose designated claims or defenses, or prohibiting him from introducing in evidence designated documents or things or items of testimony, or from introducing evidence of physical or mental condition;
>
> (iii) An order striking out pleadings or parts thereof, or staying further proceedings until the order is obeyed, or dismissing the action or proceeding or any part thereof, or rendering a judgment by default against the disobedient party.

Judge Maris ruled that the district court's order depended on (i) and (ii), not (iii). He concluded that Judge Kirkpatrick (1) "did not err" in holding that the plaintiffs had shown good cause for the production of the accident report and the statements, (2) the district court "rightly rejected the broad claim of privilege" made by the government, (3) the district court's order for the production of documents "rightly provided" for the court's determination on the government's claim of privilege as to particular parts of the documents, and (4) upon the government's decision not to produce the documents, the court's order directing that certain facts be taken as established against the government was authorized by Rule 37(b)(2) (i) and (ii) "and was accordingly not erroneous."[146] The Third Circuit affirmed the trial court's judgments on the issue of damages.

146. Id.

Academic Responses

The Third Circuit's decision provoked a number of short comments in law reviews. A note in the *Harvard Law Review* observed that a private party's inability to obtain government accident reports "might result in particular injustice, since the plaintiffs would have little opportunity otherwise to ascertain the facts. The result in many cases would be that the Government's consent to suit would be to no avail if its executives had the uncontrolled power to withhold information in their sole possession."[147] The note recommended that "a clear distinction should be drawn between alleged state secrets and other information as to which there is a less pervasive need for secrecy." A clear distinction? What is "clear" about "alleged state secrets"?

Another judgment in the *Harvard Law Review:* "the magnitude of the security risk involved in state secrets may often preclude full disclosure even at *in camera* proceedings."[148] Why? What support exists for that conclusion other than executive claims? The note appeared to concede that in the case of "state secrets" there would be no review and no check by an independent judiciary. Retreating somewhat from that position, the note suggests: "Probably something more than a blanket allegation of secrecy should always be required, but beyond this the court's discretion should be tempered by a great deference to the administration determination."[149]

Great deference to executive assertions means the absence of an independent judiciary and the inability of a private plaintiff to effectively sue the government. "Something more" is required? The note offers this procedure: "Perhaps a certification from the highest official of the department in question that this revelation would be prejudicial to national security should be controlling."[150] That is hardly something more. It is merely "a blanket allegation of secrecy" accompanied by a certification.

The Harvard note suggests a remedy if certifications became so routine as to prevent any chance of a plaintiff's recovery: "it may be that special statutory alleviation in the form of reimbursement would be justified on the theory that the cost of maintaining security is a burden properly to be borne by the Government."[151] Congress had already provided for that result in the Federal Tort Claims Act (FTCA) by consciously putting the government on a par with a private litigant, including the discovery process. When the government

---

147. Note, "Federal Courts—Rules of Civil Procedure—Secretary of Air Force Subject to Discovery in Suit Under Federal Tort Claims Act," 65 Harv. L. Rev. 1445, 1446 (1952).
148. Id. at 1447.
149. Id.
150. Id.
151. Id.

in *Reynolds* refused to let Judge Kirkpatrick see the documents, he decided in favor of the plaintiffs and awarded them a monetary benefit.

A note in the *Texas Law Review* correctly summarized the results of the decisions by the district court and the Third Circuit: "the government was adequately protected from the disclosure of privileged matter by the submission of the documents to the district judge for his examination and determination of the question of privilege." It had the choice of either producing the documents "or to have the facts to which the documents were applicable taken against it."[152] The article recognized the appropriate review by judges in camera and the legislative purpose of Congress in the FTCA to assure fairness of discovery. The government's position that an agency head's claim of privilege should be conclusive "fails to recognize the capability of federal trial judges to determine for themselves, with a view to all the factors involved, the existence of any information the disclosure of which would be prejudicial to the interests of the United States."[153] The ruling by the Third Circuit "rightfully places" in the hands of the federal trial judge the balancing of interests, including those of national security, "against the effectiveness of the remedy given by the Federal Tort Claims Act and the discovery process itself."[154]

Similarly, a note in the *Minnesota Law Review* recognized that in a lawsuit under the FTCA, the government's privilege against discovery "does not extend to all the records of accident investigations, regardless of their contents."[155] The statute withdrew from the executive branch the right to determine the privilege against discovery "without judicial review."[156] By passing the FTCA and the Suits in Admiralty Act, Congress had not only given the government's consent to be sued but placed it "on a par with private litigants."[157]

The political context of the case was explored in the *University of Pennsylvania Law Review,* which noted the growth of "the very real need in the current world situation to guard against any unnecessary security risk. Today the overwhelming bulk of all federal activity is directed at national defense, where the argument against disclosure of official documents is strongest." Despite those "impelling factors there exists no clear, authoritative policy—at least none devised with a view to present necessities—for the judicial treatment of the opposed social interests of the government in protecting its defense secrets

---

152. Note, "Federal Courts—Discovery—Requiring Production of Documents by the Government," 30 Tex. L. Rev. 889 (1952).
153. Id. at 891.
154. Id.
155. Note, "Practice and Procedure—Discovery—Governmental Priviledge [*sic*] in Litigation Under the Federal Tort Claims Act," 36 Minn. L. Rev. 546, 546–47 (1952).
156. Id. at 547.
157. Id. at 548–49.

and the courts in deciding litigation on the basis of all available facts."[158] The note regarded reliance on the Housekeeping Statute as "questionable at best" and stated that the district court and the Third Circuit "wisely refused to expand the doctrine in the instant case."[159] It also warned against indiscriminate acceptance of the state secrets privilege: "national security has become a pervasive concept susceptible to abuse in its name, and to allow the assertion of military secrecy to serve as a complete defense to a bona fide claim against the government would place many injured persons at an unfair disadvantage."[160]

A note in the *Miami Law Quarterly* accurately described the FTCA as making the government liable for tort claims "in the same manner and in the same extent as a private individual under like circumstances," and dismissed the government's reliance on English cases to support the contention that agency heads have exclusive authority to determine whether documents should be released to a private litigant. The British government "is not one of checks and balances or separation of powers as is that of the United States."[161]

A longer analysis in the *Northwestern University Law Review* examined the district court and Third Circuit rulings in *Reynolds* in terms of the government's authority to withhold evidence in suits brought under the FTCA. Like the *Harvard Law Review*, it endorsed the theory that once the government describes a document as a state secret its judgment is binding on other branches, including the judiciary: "Should the records contain state, military, or diplomatic secrets they would unquestionably be privileged and not subject to discovery. There the interest of the individual litigant must bow to the superior interest of the public welfare."[162] What makes the possibly self-serving (and possibly erroneous) decision of an agency head necessarily and inevitably in the "interest of the public welfare"? The article offered a solution that would not "bow" entirely to the executive branch:

Air force accident reports, stating testimony as to circumstances surrounding the accident and containing data gleaned from examination of the wreckage, are not likely to contain such confidential information. Faced by a claim of secrecy in the public interest, the courts could adequately protect the national security by making an independent personal

---

158. Note, "Procedure—Discovery Against the Government—Privilege for State Secrets," 100 U. Pa. L. Rev. 917, 918 (1952).

159. Id. at 921.

160. Id.

161. Note, "Evidence—Government Agencies—Right to Determine Privilege of Non-Disclosure of Records," 6 Miami L. Q. 509, 510–11 (1952).

162. Note, "The Executive Evidential Privilege in Suits Against the Government," 47 Nw. U. L. Rev. 259, 262–63 (1952).

in camera examination of the documents in question. In that manner the court would not abdicate to an executive department official its function of determining the admissibility of evidence in a law suit.[163]

The article stated that circumstances might develop where the judge, "faced with a wealth of material of a complicated and technical nature, would not be competent to decide whether such matter need be classified as secret."[164] A footnote singles out the area of atomic energy and explains that the judge, "not a scientist," could not adequately determine what information should be withheld from the public.[165] Of course agency heads may not be scientists either. The article suggested that a special court be created to handle questions of privilege related to national security, and that judges on this court would develop a special competence.[166] However, judges on a special court dedicated to national security issues may begin to think like executive officials and lose their independence. As to *Reynolds,* the article accepts the outcome of a district court giving the executive official "a choice to comply or to refuse to submit the department records. Should he decline, . . . [the court] orders a decree establishing the issues in favor of the plaintiff opponent."[167]

The Northwestern article develops another point. The government in *Reynolds* argued that treating Air Force investigations of plane accidents as privileged serves the important purpose of "encouraging uninhibited statements in future inquiry proceedings instituted primarily in the interest of flying safety." The article agreed that the promotion of flying safety is an important objective, but giving an injured party access to agency records, in order to establish negligence on the part of the government, also promotes flying safety: "Liability is an effective antidote to continued carelessness, as much or more so than information gleaned from military investigations. That factor, when coupled with a basic interest in the dispensation of justice to litigants, suggests that the approach taken in the *Reynolds* case is proper."[168]

The government's reliance on the Housekeeping Statute, the British case of *Duncan,* the American cases of *Boske* and *Touhy,* the Wolkinson study, and precedents taken from American history had failed to convince the lower courts that the executive branch had exclusive control over the release of

163. Id. at 263.
164. Id.
165. Id. (Note 18).
166. Id.
167. Id. at 266–67.
168. Id. at 269.

agency documents. Judge Kirkpatrick and the Third Circuit insisted on independent judicial review of the documents as a procedural means to assure that the Air Force claim of privilege was properly based. If the government objected to that procedure, it would lose the case. A number of statutory and constitutional issues, well honed in the lower courts, were now ready for the Supreme Court.

4

THE SUPREME COURT DECIDES

The district court and the Third Circuit carefully examined the law of military accidents and the purpose of Congress in passing the Federal Tort Claims Act (FTCA). The government chose to withhold the requested documents, even from in camera inspection, with full knowledge that its decision would strengthen the plaintiffs' case. After two losses in a row, the government may have been hoping that the Justices of the Supreme Court would defer to national security claims. That judgment was not unreasonable, given the record of the Court. Nevertheless, the timing of the case was not ideal for the government. *Reynolds* reached the Court in 1952 when broad claims of presidential power by the Truman administration, in the middle of the Korean War, suffered a stinging judicial defeat.

The Constitutional Climate

The government's strategy to press national security was somewhat of a gamble, particularly in light of the judicial reception to President Harry Truman's claim that he possessed emergency power to seize steel mills. He acted on the eve of a nationwide strike that threatened to cripple his ability to prosecute the war in Korea. Instead of following the statutory procedure set forth by Congress in the Taft-Hartley Act, including an 80-day cooling-off period, Truman issued an executive order on April 8, 1952, stating that "American fighting men and fighting men of the United Nations are now engaged in deadly combat with the forces of aggression in Korea."[1] In the face of strong public opposition to the two-year-old war, Truman's standing in public opinion had plummeted. The Korean issue, "not crooks or Communists," resonated deeply with the voters in an election year.[2]

Truman defended the steel seizure by unveiling an ambitious theory of unlimited and unchecked presidential power. One week after the seizure, at a news conference, a reporter asked: "Mr. President, if you can seize the steel

1. 17 Fed. Reg. 3139 (1952).
2. 1 Stephen E. Ambrose, Eisenhower: Soldier, General of the Army, President-Elect 1890–1952, at 569 (1983).

92

mills under your inherent powers, can you, in your opinion, also seize the newspapers and/or the radio stations?" Truman never flinched: "Under similar circumstances the President has to act for whatever is for the best of the country. That's the answer to your question."[3] Three days later, when asked if he recognized the danger to civil liberties by substituting inherent presidential power for the written law, he responded: "Well, of course I do. . . . But when you meet an emergency in an emergency, you have to meet it."[4]

Newspapers around the country denounced this sweeping interpretation of executive power. An editorial in the *New York Times* rebuked Truman for creating "a new regime of government by executive decree," a system of government that was inconsistent "with our own democratic principle of government by laws and not by men."[5] The *Washington Post* predicted that Truman's action "will probably go down in history as one of the most high-handed acts committed by an American President."[6] Other newspapers excoriated Truman for exercising "dictatorial powers."[7]

When the Steel Seizure Case was heard in district court, Assistant Attorney General Holmes Baldridge told District Judge David Pine that there were only two limitations on executive power: "One is the ballot box and the other is impeachment." Pine asked whether the government was arguing that when a "sovereign people" granted powers to the federal government, it limited Congress and the judiciary but not the executive. Baldridge replied: "That's our conception, Your Honor." Pine pressed for clarification. If the President determined that an emergency existed, "the Courts cannot even review whether it is an emergency." Baldridge: "That is correct."[8]

Judge Pine lost little time in jettisoning this theory of "unlimited and unrestrained Executive power."[9] In striking down Truman's executive order, he set about to demolish the theory of an emergency power that is not subject to judicial control: "To my mind this [theory] spells a form of government alien to our Constitutional government of limited powers," and consequently, to recognize it "would undermine public confidence in the very edifice of government as it is known under the Constitution."[10] In a blistering opinion, Pine concluded that the "awful results" of a nationwide strike "would be

3. Public Papers of the Presidents, 1952–53, at 272–73.
4. Id. at 294.
5. "The Seizure Order" (editorial), New York Times, April 10, 1952, at 28.
6. 98 Cong. Rec. 4035 (1952).
7. See Neal Devins and Louis Fisher, "The Steel Seizure Case: One of a Kind?," 19 Const. Comm. 63, 68 (2002).
8. H. Doc. No. 534 (Part I), 82d Cong., 2d Sess. 371–72 (1952).
9. Youngstown Co. v. Sawyer, 103 F.Supp. 569, 577 (D.D.C. 1952).
10. Id. at 576–77.

less injurious to the public" than recognition of the President's claim of unbounded power.[11] The Supreme Court affirmed Judge Pine's decision.[12]

Chief Justice Vinson, who would write for the majority a year later in *Reynolds,* prepared a lengthy dissent that defended Truman's actions. He was joined by Justices Reed and Minton. The tenor of Vinson's dissent placed him in the camp of those who are willing to suspend judicial independence to advance what the executive branch claimed to be in the interest of national security. He specifically rejected the position of Justices who "are of the view that the President is without power to act in time of crisis in the absence of express statutory authorization."[13] Vinson believed that presidential emergency power deserved a broader and more generous interpretation, going beyond express powers granted by Congress. For those who suggested that the case involved extraordinary powers, he reminded them "that these are extraordinary times. A world not yet recovered from the devastation of World War II had been forced to face the threat of another and more terrifying global conflict."[14] To successfully handle national and international emergencies, he wanted Presidents free to draw upon a mix of express and implied powers. The same type of national security theory would flavor his *Reynolds* opinion.

William H. Rehnquist, destined to fill the seat of Chief Justice, served as a law clerk in 1952 for Justice Robert H. Jackson. Rehnquist, who expected Truman to win the case, was puzzled at the outcome. The Court was composed of Roosevelt and Truman appointees, and "the entire decisional trend for fifteen years [1937–1952] had been in the direction of the aggrandizement of the powers of the president and Congress."[15] To have the Justices turn against presidential power in the middle of a war surprised many seasoned observers. In later years Rehnquist came to appreciate the impact of public opinion on the judiciary: "I think that this is one of those celebrated constitutional cases where what might be called the tide of public opinion suddenly began to run against the government, for a number of reasons, and that this tide of public opinion had a considerable influence on the Court."[16]

The timing of the Steel Seizure Case overlapped with *Reynolds.* Compare these dates in 1952. Judge Pine issued his ruling on April 29, and the Supreme Court affirmed it on June 2. On April 7 the Supreme Court agreed to hear the *Reynolds* case from the Third Circuit. If federal courts could reject a President's claim that his emergency order was not subject to judicial con-

11. Id. at 577.
12. Youngstown Co. v. Sawyer, 343 U.S. 579 (1952).
13. Id. at 667.
14. Id. at 668.
15. William H. Rehnquist, The Supreme Court 171 (2001 ed.)
16. Id. at 189.

trol, could they also challenge the determination of the Secretary of the Air Force that certain documents were privileged and could not be shared with the courts? For a variety of reasons, a claim brought by three widows did not carry the same political or legal weight as the steel companies whose property had been seized.

Both cases involved fundamental questions of national security. Both implicated the capacity of the judiciary to check executive power. Yet the two cases differed in many ways. The war in Korea had soured by June 1952, fueling opposition in the general public and the media. The impact of the steel seizure on the domestic economy, combined with Truman's personal involvement in promoting unchecked power, added prominence to the constitutional dispute. The B-29 case seemed to have the ingredients needed to arouse broad public interest: a midair explosion of a plane testing confidential equipment, the government asserting a new "state secrets" doctrine, and three widows suing the government for negligence. Yet the story never took hold. Newspaper coverage of lower court activity, the Supreme Court granting cert, the Court holding oral argument, and the Court finally deciding the case was meager or nonexistent.

Moreover, the government's insistence that it had a right to protect military secrets came at the height of investigations into Americans charged with leaking sensitive and classified information to the Soviet Union. This period featured the spectacular trial of Julius and Ethel Rosenberg, who were prosecuted for sending atomic bomb secrets to Russia. They were arrested in 1950, indicted and convicted in 1951, and pursued an appeal to the Second Circuit in 1952. After a failed effort to have the Supreme Court hear their case, they were executed on June 19, 1953.

The political climate of the early 1950s no doubt strengthened the government's argument in *Reynolds* that it had a right and a duty to protect state secrets, withholding them not only from litigants but from federal judges. The period after World War II was dominated by congressional hearings into communist activities, the Attorney General's list of subversive organizations, loyalty oaths, security indexes, reports of espionage, and counterintelligence efforts. The national security state had arrived, held together by claims of state secrets. Alger Hiss, convicted of perjury in 1950 concerning his dealing with the Community Party, served three and a half years in prison. The government pursued J. Robert Oppenheimer for possible espionage, which led to the loss of his security clearance in 1954.[17]

17. Katherine A. S. Sibley, Red Spies in America: Stolen Secrets and the Dawn of the Cold War (2004).

The Government's Brief

Having lost in the Third Circuit, the government in March 1952 petitioned for a writ of certiorari, asking the Supreme Court to call up the papers from the Third Circuit and determine whether the case had been properly decided. The government highlighted three issues: (1) whether the determination of Secretary of the Air Force Finletter that documents are privileged "can, consistently with R.S. § 161 [the Housekeeping Statute] and the doctrine of separation of powers, be reviewed by the judiciary," (2) whether Congress in the FTCA "could or intended to force" the executive to submit his determination to judicial review "or suffer judgment to be entered against the United States," and (3) whether the validity of Finletter's determination "can be tested in this case in the absence of the issuance of direct process against him."[18] Again, it looked like the government wanted the district court to subpoena the documents to set up a major clash between the judicial and executive powers.

The government's language had changed somewhat but was not materially different from the questions raised in the lower courts. At the stage of petitioning for certiorari, the case was still largely a matter of statutory construction (the Housekeeping Statute and the FTCA), with suggestions of a constitutional dimension involving separation of powers. The government questioned whether the judiciary had the power "to order production of documents which the executive chooses to withhold, or to substitute its judgment for the judgment of the executive as to whether certain documents can be disclosed consistently with the public interest."[19]

After the Court agreed to hear the case, the government submitted its brief in September 1952. In addition to the three questions stated above, the government added another: "Whether respondents have shown good cause for discovery, as required by Rule 34, Federal Rules of Civil Procedure."[20] The government's arguments about exclusive executive power, over which courts have no control, seemed identical to what it had presented in the Steel Seizure Case. It was the government's position in *Reynolds* that (1) the courts "lack power to compel disclosure by means of a direct demand on the department head" and (2) that "the same result may not be achieved by the indirect method of an order against the United States, resulting in judgment when compliance is not forthcoming."[21]

18. "Petition for a Writ of Certiorari to the United States Court of Appeals for the Third Circuit," United States v. Reynolds, No. 21, October Term, 1952, at 2–3.
19. Id. at 10.
20. "Brief for the United States," United States v. Reynolds, No. 21, October Term, 1952, at 3 (hereafter "Government's Brief").
21. Id. at 9.

To support this contention, the government interpreted the Housekeeping Statute in a manner that precluded judicial review. The government regarded the legislation "as a statutory affirmation of a constitutional privilege against disclosure," and one that "protects the executive against direct court orders for disclosure by giving the department heads sole power to determine to what extent withholding of particular documents is required by the public interest."[22] Congress had never provided that authority, and earlier judicial rulings specifically rejected that interpretation. After looking to history, practices in the states, and British rulings, the government for the first time pressed the state secrets privilege in a brief: "There are well settled privileges for state secrets and for communications of informers, both of which are applicable here, the first because the airplane which crashed was alleged by the Secretary to be carrying secret equipment, and the second because the secrecy necessary to encourage full disclosure by informants is also necessary in order to encourage the freest possible discussion by survivors before Accident Investigation Boards."[23]

The government had made these points before, but not as crisply or as dramatically. What was new? The fact that the plane was carrying secret equipment was known by newspaper readers the day after the crash. The fundamental issue, which the government repeatedly muddled, was whether the accident report and the survivor statements contained secret information. The second point, regarding the process used to investigate airplane accidents, had been discussed many times before. The government opened the door slightly to judicial review: "The courts should not interfere in such policy determinations without, at least, a showing that the executive determination is plainly arbitrary. No such reasons exist here, for, as noted, the Secretary's determination was clearly founded on adequate considerations."[24] How would a court, or a plaintiff, know that an official's determination was adequately founded or plainly arbitrary unless the judge at least examined the documents in camera?

Some of the government's arguments were contradictory. For example, the brief conceded that during the Revolutionary War, the Continental Congress had full access to agency documents because the "executive departments were, in effect, answerable to the legislature, and could be called on for an accounting." That is true. Next claim: Under the Continental Congress, "the relationship between legislature and executive had been modeled on the British system." Not true. The Continental Congress was a unique and temporary experiment of placing all legislative, executive, and judicial powers in a single

22. Id. at 9–10.
23. Id. at 11.
24. Id. at 12.

branch. The brief then states that this model ended when the Constitution created three separate branches.[25] The lesson drawn, apparently, was the inapplicability of the British parliamentary system. Yet later in the brief, the government argues that "great weight should also be given to the decision in *Duncan v. Cammell, Laird & Co.,* [1942] A.C. 624, in which the House of Lords reached the result urged by the Government here."[26] Here the British parliamentary model is championed.

Toward the end of the brief, the government returned to "the so-called 'state secrets' privilege."[27] The claim of privilege by Secretary Finletter "falls squarely" under that privilege for these reasons:

He based his claim, in part, on the fact that the aircraft was engaged "in a highly secret military mission" and, again, on the "reason that the aircraft in question, together with the personnel on board, were engaged in a highly secret mission of the Air Force. The airplane likewise carried confidential equipment on board and any disclosure of its mission or information concerning its operation or performance would be prejudicial to this Department and would not be in the public interest."[28]

Not a word of this has anything to do with the *contents* of the accident report or the survivors' statements. Had those documents been made available to Judge Kirkpatrick, he would have seen nothing in them that related to military secrets or confidential equipment. He could have passed them on to the plaintiffs. The three wives would have received $225,000 instead of what they later settled for: $170,000. Did the government fight this battle to save $55,000? No. It fought the way it did because it wanted to permanently establish an exclusive presidential power: a determination that would be final and conclusive on the legislative and judicial branches. The *Reynolds* case became the vehicle for promoting and entrenching that doctrine. The executive branch had never possessed an unreviewable power to withhold documents, either before *Reynolds* or after it. Presidents and executive agencies would lose confrontations with Congress and the courts over access to information, such as in the Watergate Tapes Case, covered in the next chapter.

At various places in the brief the government misled the Court on the contents of the accident report. It asserted: "to the extent that the report reveals military secrets concerning the structure or performance of the plane that crashed or deals with these factors in relation to projected or suggested

25. Id. at 23.
26. Id. at 38.
27. Id. at 42.
28. Id. at 42–43.

secret improvements it falls within the judicially recognized 'state secrets' privilege."[29] "To the extent"? In the case of the accident report the extent was zero. The report contained nothing about military secrets or military improvements. Nor did the survivor statements. The government seemed to be holding a strong hand even if it had few cards to play. In the area of national security, shadows may seem more threatening than substance. Fear and threats can trump facts.

The Plaintiffs' Brief

The reply brief by the plaintiffs was half the size of the government's: 42 pages compared with 81. The government had turned a corner and was now pressing the state secrets privilege to the fullest, amassing 81 pages that repeated over and over its key positions. The plaintiffs did not need to produce a brief of equivalent size, but it was not enough to merely summarize points made in earlier briefs. It had to attack the government head-on with clarity and intensity.

The plaintiffs began by stating that the claim of privilege "is a justiciable question for the Court and the Secretary for Air [sic] may not successfully assert that he alone shall be the judge of whether his own claim is well founded." That was especially so, said the brief, "where there is no showing that the documents in question contain any military secret and the claim is based merely upon the assertion that in the opinion of the Secretary it would be for the best interests of the management and morale of the Air Force that the documents should be kept secret."[30]

That was part of the government's argument, but only part. In several places the government insisted that the Secretary of the Air Force was not merely looking out for the interests of the Air Force but for the plaintiffs as well: "In the absence of compelling evidence to the contrary, it can be presumed that the Secretary has given full consideration to the problems involved in civil litigation, has weighed the possible hardships to plaintiffs, and has made a responsible decision in the light of the adverse effects of nondisclosure."[31] Again: "Once it is recognized that the duty of appraising all relevant considerations resides in the Secretary, and not in the court."[32] Once more: "As we have pointed out, . . . the Secretary must weigh not only the

29. Id. at 45.

30. "Brief for Respondents," United States v. Reynolds, No. 21, October Term, 1952, at 2 (hereafter "Plaintiffs' Brief").

31. Government's Brief, at 51.

32. Id. at 54.

public's interest in maintaining security but also its great interest in assuring litigants full information."[33]

What the government argued in these passages is that the traditional role of the courts in considering the interests of opposing sides can be dispensed with because the government has already done that. The executive branch, in its great wisdom, becomes the adjudicator of national security disputes, carefully and judiciously weighing the competing merits of both sides before arriving at a just and balanced verdict. The Secretary of the Air Force had "great interest in assuring litigants full information." That assertion was pretentious, risible, and preposterous, calling for a spirited riposte by the plaintiffs. The institution responsible for assuring fairness in the courtroom and access to documents is the judiciary, not the executive branch. The riposte never came.

The plaintiffs' response was instead more muted. Their brief summarized the government's position as saying, in so many words, "we will tell you only what *we* think it is in the public interest that you should know."[34] If the government were to prevail with its argument that Secretary Finletter's determination was final and binding, "clearly it would be the end of any efficient discovery in any case in which the United States was involved."[35] The government's brief created "a great deal of confusion . . . by mixing together a number of different principles each of which, though sound in the abstract, is wholly inapplicable in the present cases."[36] Yes, the government's brief managed to generate substantial confusion, but some of its principles were not sound in the abstract. They gave short shrift to an independent judiciary, separation of powers, and the rights of litigants under the FTCA.

The plaintiffs' brief unnecessarily gave ground on the state secrets privilege. After enumerating a number of positions, including the "privilege against the disclosure of important diplomatic or military secrets," the brief stated: "No one questions that these statements are correct in themselves."[37] Why concede so much? The brief attempted to limit the damage of this admission by saying that Secretary Finletter should not have the "uncontrolled discretion to refuse a departmental report in toto, not only without any attempt to show that it contains military secrets, but where, as here, the actual proof contained in the interrogatories and the answers thereto showed that the information requested had nothing to do with any military secret."[38] Still, the government's brief to the Supreme Court, in surreptitious fashion, had strongly hinted

33. Id. at 65.
34. Plaintiffs' Brief, at 3 (emphasis in original).
35. Id. at 4.
36. Id.
37. Id.
38. Id.

that the accident report and the statements of survivors *did* contain military secrets, and it would take an alert Justice to see that this claim was wholly lacking in evidence. Without close scrutiny and independent analysis, the government's assertion is easily taken to be factual.

The plaintiffs' brief fundamentally erred by suggesting that the President is immune from judicial control. It argued that most of the congressional demands for papers and documents in the past "were made on the President, which explains why they went no further, for although Congress can impeach the President, he cannot as a practical matter be hailed into Court."[39] Why make that admission? The plaintiffs filed their brief with the Court in October 1952. Just months earlier, on June 2, the Supreme Court had thoroughly repudiated President Truman's theory of emergency power in the Steel Seizure Case. Although the case is styled *Youngstown Co. v. Sawyer,* with Charles Sawyer the Secretary of Commerce, there was never any doubt that it was *Truman* who was hailed into Court, and it was his view of presidential power that had been excoriated, flayed, and denounced.

The plaintiffs' brief endorsed the state secrets privilege if used properly: "No one doubts that there is at least a qualified privilege in the case of some highly important military and diplomatic secrets."[40] An example, it said, might be the plans of the atomic bomb: "not even the Judge should be allowed to see them."[41] Having conceded that point, the brief proceeds to backtrack: "On the other hand, some representatives of the Government must hold the secret and there is certainly no reason why the members of the Federal Judiciary should not be considered as trustworthy as the representatives of any other branch of the Government." Why concede the point in the first place? "But be that as it may, it is self-evident that before any privilege can be sustained based on an important military secret, there must at least be some specific showing that the disclosure of such a secret is involved."[42] How is the "showing" to be done? If the head of a department says that an accident report has secrets, either one accepts that judgment as final and conclusive, or else a neutral party, outside the executive branch, must look at the report. That is the procedure Judge Kirkpatrick and the Third Circuit required: Give the report to the trial judge to inspect in camera.

On that crucial point the plaintiffs' brief waffled. It said that Judge Kirkpatrick's order to have the documents referred to him for inspection "was the correct procedure."[43] Two pages later comes a conflicting position: "Even

39. Id. at 6.
40. Id.
41. Id.
42. Id.
43. Id. at 7.

should we assume that there may be some information so confidential that not even a Federal Judge may be permitted to see it."[44] That sentence continues: "at least the burden is upon the Government to explain to the Judge the nature of such information and to offer to supply the non-secret portion." All the Air Force had to do, according to the plaintiffs, was to say to Judge Kirkpatrick, "if such was the fact, that its report gave the details of a secret weapon which it did not feel justified in showing to anyone." Had the Air Force done that, Judge Kirkpatrick "would undoubtedly have told them to take that part out and give him the rest."[45]

How would that process work? Judge Kirkpatrick would receive an edited report with presumably secret material removed, but without knowing whether the deletion of material also eliminated passages showing negligence on the part of the government. A doctored report has no credibility, either in the hands of a judge or anyone else. It offers too great an opportunity for manipulation and deceit. Does that observation cast doubt on the integrity, honesty, and motivations of executive officials? Yes, and properly so. President Nixon wanted to present edited versions of the Watergate tapes to Congress and the courts, a procedure those branches wisely rejected. Through its suggested remedy, the plaintiffs in *Reynolds* endorsed the state secrets privilege, gave the Supreme Court ammunition to side with the government, and proposed a procedure that Chief Justice Vinson would happily adopt.

The plaintiffs' brief tried to return to solid ground by questioning the need to rely on "some sort of a common law special privilege in the Government which was not possessed by private individuals."[46] The government had referred to common law, such as the state secrets privilege, and certainly the plaintiffs' brief had discoursed about state secrets and the President's supposed freedom from congressional and judicial requests for documents. Now the brief properly asked: "why talk about what the common law used to be when we now have a statute [the FTCA] changing it?" Congress, it said, had the right "to pass a law doing away with any such special privilege, just as it had the right to do away with the Government's immunity from suit, and when the Chief Executive approved such a law, that ended the privilege both for himself and all minor executives."[47]

A strong and well-placed point, but the plaintiffs' brief had already given away too much and continued to give ground and muddy the waters. Later it stated: "It is indeed a hollow gesture for the United States to waive its immunity from suit, if it may then suppress the evidence necessary for the proof of

44. Id. at 9.
45. Id.
46. Id. at 18–19.
47. Id. at 19.

the plaintiff's case."[48] Hollow indeed, but the brief had previously consented to the trial judge receiving an edited report, with unrestricted authority on the part of the executive branch to delete whatever it wanted to. The brief insisted: "It is clear that any power claimed for the Executive Branch of the Government must be based upon an Act of Congress or a provision of the United States Constitution."[49] Yet the brief had already endorsed the state secrets privilege as created by the common law. It even cited the Steel Seizure Case of 1952,[50] without ever drawing from it the fundamental right to haul a President into court and hold him accountable there.

The last half of the plaintiffs' brief marched dutifully through familiar territory: *Boske* and *Touhy,* the Housekeeping Statute, historical precedents, *Duncan,* Rule 37, and "good cause" under Rule 34, with long quotes dropped in from various court rulings.[51] The brief concluded with the proposal that Secretary Finletter or one of his assistants meet with Judge Kirkpatrick to either deliver the documents or explain why they are "so vital to security that they must not be shown."[52] That marked a clear victory for the state secrets privilege and offered a procedure ready-made for the Supreme Court. What were Biddle's priorities? At this point was he primarily trying to win a tort case for his clients, with the maximum financial package, and not necessarily thinking about the larger policy issue of the state secrets privilege and its impact on presidential power? He suggested that if Judge Kirkpatrick was allowed to see the unedited documents and decided that some items must be disclosed that Finletter and the government deemed dangerous, the Third Circuit would review the trial judge's decision. The brief closed with a tired, confused passage:

If both the District Court and the Circuit Court and this Court are clear that no jeopardy to the national security will result from the disclosure ordered, we may be entirely sure that the position of the Government is based on its natural, although arbitrary, desire to be in no way supervised or interfered with, irrespective of the rights of innocent parties. We may also perhaps be not far wrong in assuming what we believe to be the conclusion in the present case, that the Government has no sound defense on the merits, and that no injustice will result if the Government chooses, in order to avoid the objectionable disclosure, to be subjected to the procedural disadvantage here directed.[53]

48. Id. at 21.
49. Id.
50. Id. at 22.
51. Id. at 23–41.
52. Id. at 41.
53. Id. at 41–42.

Even had the government agreed to the plaintiffs' proposed procedure, it would have posed few disadvantages to the executive branch. A department head or an assistant merely needed to tell the trial judge that the documents are "so vital to security" they must not be shown. The documents needed by the plaintiffs for their case would be permanently withdrawn on the government's say-so.

The Justices Accept the Case

Other than the briefs filed by both sides, few documents are available to help understand why the Justices decided *Reynolds* as they did. The transcript of the oral argument does not exist, even though oral arguments before 1953 are often available.[54] A search of such institutions as the Supreme Court, the Justice Department, National Archives, and the Library of Congress uncovered no oral argument. The papers of Justices, located in various archives, can yield rich and illuminating insights into how the Court debates and decides principal issues. The papers of the nine Justices who sat on the *Reynolds* Court reveal little. The records of Justice Sherman Minton at the Indiana University contain no documents on the case. Some materials on *Reynolds* appear in the collections of the other Justices, but not much. Newspaper coverage can highlight significant developments when a lawsuit reaches the Supreme Court.[55] Press reports on *Reynolds* are remarkably skimpy. For Supreme Court cases, perceptive and detailed articles usually dissect how the Justices made their way toward a decision.[56] No such scholarly studies are available on *Reynolds*. The case reached the Supreme Court with little fanfare and received cursory public attention once there.

On April 7, 1952, the Court announced its decision to take the case from the Third Circuit.[57] Five Justices voted to grant certiorari, the procedural step that orders papers called up from a lower court. The five included Sherman Minton ("general subpoena should be denied"), Tom Clark ("wrong below"),

---

54. For example, the nine hours of oral argument, over a two-day period, in the Nazi Saboteur Case of 1942 (*Ex parte Quirin*) are published; 39 Landmark Briefs and Arguments of the Supreme Court of the United States: Constitutional Law 495–666 (1975). For an analysis of that oral argument, see Louis Fisher, Nazi Saboteurs on Trial: A Military Tribunal and American Law 95–108 (2003).

55. Fisher, Nazi Saboteurs on Trial, at 49, 55, 64, 78–84, 87, 127–29 (newspaper stories on *Ex parte Quirin*).

56. Id. at 137–38 (articles by Alpheus Thomas Mason, Michal Belknap, and David J. Danelski on *Ex parte Quirin*).

57. "Court to Act on Secrets," New York Times, April 8, 1952, at 15.

Harold Burton ("right below"), Robert H. Jackson, and the Chief Justice, Fred Vinson. The parenthetical comments appear in the papers of Justice Burton, explaining why the five voted as they did. Interestingly, Clark and Burton gave opposite reasons for granting cert. Voting to deny cert were William O. Douglas, Felix Frankfurter, Stanley Reed, and Hugo Black.[58]

These votes merit close attention. Minton's remark relates to the possibility of the district court issuing a subpoena for the disputed documents. If one takes the four Justices who voted to deny cert, assume that they were satisfied with the way the case was decided by the district court and the Third Circuit, and add the name of Burton ("right below"), there appeared to be five votes against the government. However, one cannot always understand why a Justice grants or denies cert. Douglas and Reed voted to deny cert, yet later voted with the majority to reverse the Third Circuit. As finally decided, only three Justices voted against the government (Black, Frankfurter, and Jackson). They merely said in their dissent that it was "substantially for the reasons set forth in the opinion of Judge Maris below."[59] What does that mean? Agreement with some but not all? Why didn't they express in their own words their disagreement with the majority? In addition to three dissents, Douglas and Reed voted to deny cert. Did that imply acceptance with the Third Circuit ruling or merely a judgment that the case was not worth bringing up? Burton's comment ("right below") seemed to have the makings of a dissent. Why did Jackson vote to call up the case, apparently to question the Third Circuit's ruling, but then state his agreement with it? Why did Reed vote to deny cert (letting the Third Circuit ruling stand) and later join with the majority to reverse? Many questions; few answers.

58. Papers of Harold H. Burton, Library of Congress, Container 222, Folder No. 10 (United States v. Reynolds, No. 21).

59. United States v. Reynolds, 345 U.S. 1, 12 (1953). In a note to Chief Justice Vinson on February 24, 1953, Justice Jackson wrote: "I took the other view in this case, but do not intend to write. Unless someone else does, I would like you to note 'Mr. Justice Jackson would affirm on the opinion of the Court of Appeals, 192 F. 2d 987.'" Papers of Robert H. Jackson, Library of Congress, Container 178, Legal File No. 21, United States v. Reynolds. Justice Frankfurter sent a similar note to the Chief Justice on March 3, 1953: "Will you please put at the foot of your opinion in No. 21, *United States* v. *Reynolds,* the following: 'Mr. Justice Frankfurter would affirm, substantially for the reasons set forth in Judge Maris's opinion for the Court of Appeals. 192 F. 2d 987.' Of course, if one of the other dissenters will write what I can join, I shall do so." The Papers of Fred Vinson, University of Kentucky, Supreme Court Subject File, Box 224, folder "Reporter Opinions, 1952–1953." On the back of the page proofs of *United States* v. *Reynolds,* which circulated on February 20, 1953, Justice Black wrote to Vinson: "Dear Fred—Please note that I agree with the district court & the Court of Appeals & would affirm their judgment" (dated February 23, 1953). The Papers of Fred Vinson, University of Kentucky, Supreme Court Subject File, Box 224, folder "Reporter Opinions, 1952–1953."

Judicial Deliberation

After granting cert, the Justices and their law clerks began to analyze the issues decided by the Third Circuit. The Justices received briefs from the opposing parties and had their clerks write bench memos to guide the discussion. Some Justices, like Douglas, had their clerk write a cert memo at the earlier stage. The Court heard oral argument on October 21, 1952, and met in conference a few days later, on October 25, to discuss the case. Justice Burton's notes in conference reveal an interesting discrepancy. When the Justices met in conference to discuss *Reynolds,* there were five votes to reverse the Third Circuit (Minton, Clark, Burton, Reed, and Vinson) and four to affirm (Jackson, Douglas, Frankfurter, and Black). That pattern held firm by the time the Court issued its decision, except for Douglas, who by that time joined the majority to support the government. Why did he change sides? Available documents provide no explanation.

Douglas's notes taken at the conference help explain why some Justices voted as they did. He summarizes Vinson's position: "should judges have the power to make an inspection? If so, counsel could claim to see it & so eventually you would have a complete disclosure—Judiciary can't enter into it without taking away a privilege from the Executive—not convinced that U.S. can be forced to pay for exercising its privilege—reverses."[60] He seemed to have no confidence that district judges could read sensitive documents in their chambers without sharing them with private counsel. Seeing no role for the judiciary in reviewing claims of state secrets, Vinson was willing to accept the finality of executive branch judgments. His comment about having to pay to exercise a privilege refers to the position of Judge Kirkpatrick and the Third Circuit. If the government refused to show the documents to the trial judge, it would lose the case and plaintiffs would receive a full monetary award from the government.

Black's remarks at conference are captured this way by Douglas: "Tort Act placed U.S. in same position as other defs [defendants]—U.S. can decline to permit [produce?] papers—but if so it must pay the consequences—affirms." Black agreed that the government had to pay a price for exercising the state secrets privilege. He held to this position with his dissent. Douglas wrote about Reed's position: "U.S. can protect itself against disclosure of secret intelligence." Every citizen, he said, had the privilege of not releasing some information, such as incriminating evidence, confidences of a wife, and confessions made to a priest. Believing that the United States should have the same privilege, Reed voted to reverse.

---

60. Papers of William O. Douglas, Library of Congress, Container 223, File "Nos. 1–24 Argued Cases" (No. 21, U.S v. Reynolds, Conference, 10-25-52).

In Douglas's notes, Frankfurter expressed his concern that no "body of law" existed on the secrets of the sovereign. He referred to the British cases and added: "document here has no secrets that are claimed—objection of Sec. of War was merely that disclosure would hurt future investigations." Frankfurter voted to affirm and held to that position. Douglas recorded his own position: "affirms" (the Third Circuit ruling), which is how Burton's notes at the conference show Douglas. Somewhere between voting at conference and in the release of the opinion, Douglas switched sides. When Chief Justice Vinson circulated to the Justices the page proofs of the decision on February 20, 1953, Douglas merely wrote on the back: "I voted the other way but will go along. It's a nice opinion."[61] What a lackadaisical way to handle the legal issues of a case! Douglas's note was not received in Vinson's chambers until March 6, three days before the decision was released. According to Douglas's notes, Jackson said that the district court did not deny the U.S. privilege, but wanted to look at the document in camera to determine whether it was privileged: "here there is an accident the cause of which is not known without the report." Jackson voted to affirm, which is consistent with his dissent from the Court's decision to reverse the Third Circuit. Douglas briefly describes the statements by Burton and Clark in conference and notes that Minton voted to reverse, which reflects his vote in the reported decision.

A March 30, 1952, memo to Justice Douglas from his law clerk, Marshall Small, may explain why Douglas voted to deny cert. He told Douglas that the case "poses important problems deserving of review by this Court. . . . But you may not wish to review here if you consider the [Third Circuit] decision correct—since a majority of the Court might not agree with the CA's [Court of Appeal's] view of the executive privilege."[62] From his knowledge of the Justices, Small concluded that the Court was unlikely to affirm the Third Circuit.

Justice Burton received an eight-page bench memo from one of his law clerks, James Ryan, who explored the issues in the case. Burton voted to grant cert, finding that the Third Circuit was "right below," and yet later voted to reverse. After summarizing the main features of the case, Ryan remarked: "The Government's best point to me is that the federal rules do not call for disclosure of documents which are privileged and this must include the historical privilege of the Executive not to disclose matters he deems in the national interest should be secret."[63] He added: "the Executive's privilege has historically been asserted in a different manner than a private party's claim of privilege."[64]

61. The Papers of Fred Vinson, University of Kentucky, Supreme Court Subject File, Box 224, folder "Reporter Opinions, 1952–1953."
62. Id. (Memo to Douglas from his law clerk, "MLS"), March 30, 1952, at 2.
63. Papers of Harold H. Burton, Library of Congress, Container 223, Folder No. 8, "Bench Memo," No. 21, 1952 Term, U.S. v. Reynolds, at 1.
64. Id. at 2.

Swallowing whole what the government claimed in its brief, Ryan refers to "the long history of Congressional and Executive differences about Executive privilege in which the Executive has always won."[65] This "history" was based on the self-serving study prepared by a Justice Department attorney, Herman Wolkinson, who wildly exaggerated the success of the executive branch in document disputes. Ryan ended with this recommendation: "I would reverse either on the narrow ground that good cause had not been shown for requiring such disclosure or reverse on the ground that Congress did not express any intention in the Tort Claims Act to waive the Executive privilege the Presidents have historically claimed in battles with Congress. In the absence of clearer language on the point by Congress, it should not be assumed that it intended this broad a result."[66]

At the bottom of the memo, Burton registered agreement with part of Ryan's analysis: "Congress & Executive by legislation could waive this [privilege] in varying degrees—and it is claimed that Tort Claims Act does so. I think it does not—while the act permits suit against U.S. as against a private party—this covers the liability & waiver of immunity but is not specific enough to cover collateral questions of executive authority." Burton was willing to acquiesce to the state secrets privilege and let Congress later consider and enact specific limitations on the executive branch.

Justice Burton's other law clerk, John Douglas, also prepared a memo. He regarded the Third Circuit's decision as "quite sensible, balancing as it does considerations of national security as against the desirability of not blocking adequate disclosure in Tort Claims cases. Examination by the judge *in camera* prior to revelation to plaintiffs appears to be a happy resolution of the competing equities. Nevertheless, the issue is novel and important."[67]

Justice Jackson's law clerk, Cornelius G. Niebank Jr., remarked "that the problem presented here is that left open in *Touhy*," where the Court ruled that release of an agency document had to be decided by a department head, not a subordinate. "The question here relates to the power of the Secretary of the Air Force himself to make such a refusal."[68] Niebank concluded: "Somehow I am inclined to think that the courts below here went too far, in view of the govt's offer to produce the witnesses at govt expense. But then, on the other hand, it would seem that the DC [District Court] request to submit the accident report for examination *in camera* was also reasonable. The problem

65. Id.

66. Id. at 8.

67. Papers of Harold H. Burton, Library of Congress, Container 223, Folder No. 8, #638–1951 Term, U.S. v. Reynolds et al., cert to CA 3, at 3.

68. Papers of Robert H. Jackson, Library of Congress, Container 178, Legal File No. 21, bench memo from CGN to Jackson, No. 21, United States v. Reynolds, at 1–2.

will require some unraveling."[69] In what appears to be Jackson's handwriting, at the bottom of the memo, is this remark: "Affirm but not touch privilege. Court should not try to pass on matter. Can't tell what protecting—can't know what nations already have—i.e., respect privilege." These conflicting comments may explain why Jackson decided not to articulate his views in a dissenting opinion. On the form he filled out in conference, Jackson records the same breakdown as Burton on the votes for cert and the votes in conference on the merits (with Jackson, Douglas, Frankfurter, and Black ready to affirm the Third Circuit).[70]

Justice Clark received a memo from his law clerk, Stuart Taylor, who recommended that "this case is probably important enough to warrant granting cert." On the merits, Taylor felt "quite strongly that in this situation the conflicting interests of the parties—the govt and private litigants—are best accomodated [*sic*] by the procedure adopted by the DC here, *i.e.,* a submission of the documents to the judge for his examination *in camera* and a ruling by him as to whether the nat'l interest precludes disclosure."[71] Clark did not follow that advice.

To Justice Reed's law clerk, John Calhoun, *Reynolds* raised problems "akin to those you treated in *Touhy* v. *Ragen*," which Reed had authored. Calhoun explained how the Third Circuit distinguished *Touhy* and *Boske* from the B-29 case. In the earlier cases, the courts were asked to pass on whether regulations adopted pursuant to the Housekeeping Statute "might vest in the Secretary sole discretion viz e viz [*sic*] subordinates to him on the release of documents." Those cases, Calhoun noted, merely decided "it was possible to strip all authority to produce from the subordinates of a Department head and to vest the authority in the head." In *Reynolds,* however, the Third Circuit "points out that here the order to produce did not run against a subordinate of a Department head but rather ran against the US. It is argued that even an Executive Department head has to respond to such an order or at least permit the court to see the documents *in camera* to determine the veracity of the privilege claimed."[72]

Reed wrote on the second page of his clerk's memo: "Perhaps the statute protecting a departmental head would be a dead letter if U.S. should be compelled to produce." The Housekeeping Statute would not have been a dead

---

69. Id. at 2.
70. Papers of Robert H. Jackson, Library of Congress, Container 178, Legal File No. 21 (No. 21, United States v. Reynolds, Conference, 10-25-52).
71. Papers of Tom C. Clark, Tarlton Law Library, University of Texas at Austin, Box No. B149, Folder No. 3.
72. Papers of Stanley Reed, University of Kentucky, Certiorari Memos, Box 40, Folder "October Term, 1952: Argued Cases," bench memo from JDC to Reed, at 1–2.

letter. It merely placed responsibility in the head of a department to take custody of agency records. It did not attempt to resolve court-agency collisions. As to the process governing in camera inspection, Reed remarked: "Touhy shows this is not too good for plaintiff—may want to cross examine. It is best, however, if there is doubt of the judge, U.S. protection is to pay price of judgment for release." Relying on the British case of *Duncan,* Reed concluded that the "proper rule is for the head of department or agency himself [to] assert privilege in diplomatic negotiations or safety of the Nation & submit himself to cross-examination as to his *personal* examination of the privilege."[73]

What type of "cross-examination" would the head of a department possibly undergo if the federal judge had not seen the document? What questions could an uninformed judge ask? Reed also jotted down what Clark said at conference in objecting to the handling of the case in district court: "Judge K [Kirkpatrick] did not exhaust evidence of witnesses. Must exhaust all other avenues. U.S. has privilege."[74] Reed wanted the plaintiffs to depose the surviving crew members. The Court's decision would incorporate that point.

The Court's Decision

On March 9, 1953, Chief Justice Vinson ruled that the government had presented a valid claim of privilege. He also determined that the district court's judgment, issued after the government refused to produce the documents, subjected the United States to liability that Congress had not consented to when it passed the FTCA.[75] The Court divided 6 to 3, with Vinson, Burton, Clark, Douglas, Minton, and Reed in the majority, and Black, Frankfurter, and Jackson dissenting. Their dissent reads: "MR. JUSTICE BLACK, MR. JUSTICE FRANKFURTER, and MR. JUSTICE JACKSON dissent, substantially for the reasons set forth in the opinion of Judge Maris below. 192 F. 2d 987."[76] What a vague way for Justices to record their disagreement! What parts of Maris's decision did they accept? What parts did they not? We will never know.

Chief Justice Vinson reviewed the issues litigated below and identified two "broad propositions pressed upon us for decision." The government "urged that the executive department heads have power to withhold any documents in their custody from judicial review if they deem it to be in the public interest." From the plaintiffs' side came the assertion that "the executive's power to withhold documents was waived by the Tort Claims Act." Vinson found that

73. Reed's handwritten notes at bottom of bench memo (emphasis in original).
74. Id.
75. United States v. Reynolds, 345 U.S. 1 (1953).
76. Id. at 12.

both positions "have constitutional overtones which we find it unnecessary to pass upon, there being a narrower ground for decision."[77] His implication that the Court would discover some middle ground, giving something to both sides, is misleading. The decision marked a solid win for the government.

Rule 34 compelled production only of documents "not privileged." The term "not privileged" referred to privileges "as that term is understood in the law of evidence," and here Vinson cited various court decisions, law journal articles, and treatises on evidence, including Wigmore.[78] The Finletter statement invoked a privilege against revealing military secrets, and that privilege was "well established in the law of evidence."[79] Vinson missed Wigmore's point that the institution to decide what evidence to submit in a state secrets case is the judiciary, not the executive.

Vinson associated certain qualities and procedures with the state secrets privilege: it "belongs to the Government and must be asserted by it; it can neither be claimed nor waived by a private party. It is not to be lightly invoked. There must be a formal claim of privilege, lodged by the head of the department which has control over the matter, after actual personal consideration by that officer."[80] He described this level of judicial supervision: "The court itself must determine whether the circumstances are appropriate for the claim of privilege, and yet do so without forcing a disclosure of the very thing the privilege is designed to protect."[81]

This latter point is confused. If the government can keep the actual document from the judge, even for in camera inspection, how can the judge "determine whether the circumstances are appropriate for the claim of privilege"? There is no reason to regard in camera inspection as "disclosure." How can a court be assured that the head of a department conducted a "personal consideration" of the claim? It is implausible to think that Finletter and Harmon actually examined the lengthy accident report and survivor statements and reached a personal judgment on whether the contents of those documents, if released, would be prejudicial to national security. It is more likely that government attorneys drafted the statements and presented them to Finletter and Harmon, who signed them without personal knowledge of what the accident reports and statements contained.

Vinson attempted to draw an analogy between the question of privilege over documents and the privilege against self-incrimination. The argument is difficult to follow. He warned that "too much judicial inquiry into the

77. Id. at 6.
78. Id. and Note 11.
79. Id. at 6–7.
80. Id. at 7–8.
81. Id. at 8.

claim of privilege would force disclosure of the thing the privilege was meant to protect, while a complete abandonment of judicial control would lead to intolerable abuses."[82] In the case of self-incrimination, judges can probe a witness's reliance on the privilege, provided they do not compel the witness to surrender this constitutional protection.[83] Vinson said that in the case of the privilege against disclosing documents, the court "must be satisfied from all the evidence and circumstances," after which the claim of the privilege "will be accepted without requiring further disclosure."[84] Denied the actual document, what "evidence" could a judge rely on other than claims and assertions by executive officials? Disclosure to the court in camera cannot be equated with disclosure to the public or to the private plaintiffs. In his opinion, Vinson urged the adoption of "some like formula of compromise," stating that judicial control "over the evidence of a case cannot be abdicated to the caprice of executive officers."[85]

If an executive officer acted capriciously and arbitrarily, how would the judge know under the procedure urged by Vinson? He said that the Court "will not go so far as to say that the court may automatically require a complete disclosure to the judge before the claim of privilege will be accepted in any case."[86] Under some circumstances there would be no opportunity for in camera inspection: "the court should not jeopardize the security which the privilege is meant to protect by insisting upon an examination of the evidence, even by the judge alone, in chambers."[87] Why would in camera inspection jeopardize national security? Without access to the disputed document, the judge necessarily rules in the dark.

The shadow of national security settled over Vinson's decision: "we cannot escape judicial notice that this is a time of vigorous preparation for national defense." Air power was "one of the most potent weapons" in that defense, and it was necessary to keep secret newly developing electronic devices. "On the record before the trial court it appeared that this accident occurred to a military plane which had gone aloft to test secret electronic equipment." That much had been known by newspaper readers, without any damage to national security. Vinson concluded that there was a "reasonable danger" that the accident report "would contain references to the secret electronic equipment which was the primary concern of the mission."[88] Reasonable danger?

82. Id.
83. Id. (Note 22).
84. Id. at 9.
85. Id. at 9–10.
86. Id. at 10.
87. Id.
88. Id.

On the basis of what information? The government never submitted any evidence that the documents sought by plaintiffs contained anything about the secret equipment or secret mission—hints and intimations, to be sure, but never evidence. Without access to evidence, federal courts necessarily rely on vapors and allusions. Through that process, judicial control was "abdicated to the caprice of executive officers."

Finletter's statement is a model of exquisite ambiguity, susceptible of conflicting readings. The interpretation of that document became the key issue in 1953. It was the key issue a half century later, when the *Reynolds* case returned after the accident report had been declassified and made available on the Internet. Both the district court and the Third Circuit, in 2004 and 2005, parsed and plumbed the statement to determine whether the government had misled the judiciary and committed fraud upon the court. In the Third Circuit, the significance of the Finletter statement turned decisively on the meaning of the word "its" (Chapter 6).

Instead of insisting on the accident report and survivor statements, the Court in 1953 viewed the depositions offered by the government as "an available alternative" that might have given the plaintiffs "the evidence to make out their case without forcing a showdown on the claim of privilege." Plaintiffs were given "a reasonable opportunity" to depose the surviving crew members and a majority of the Justices thought "that offer should have been accepted."[89] The Court faulted the plaintiffs for citing cases in the criminal field, where the government at times is forced to invoke its evidentiary privileges "only at the price of letting the defendant go free." The Court concluded from these criminal cases that it would be unconscionable for the government, when seeking to prosecute someone, to invoke a governmental privilege that deprived the accused of material needed for his defense. "Such rationale," said the Court, "has no application in a civil forum, where the Government is not the moving party, but is a defendant only on terms to which it has consented."[90]

Chief Justice Vinson's solution was to allow the government to withhold documents from a federal judge, even in chambers, simply by having a government official sit down with the judge and explain why certain documents could not be seen. The same approach had been recommended by Charles Biddle in the brief for plaintiffs. Vinson did not need Biddle or anyone else to think up this remedy. Vinson already had a strong position on national security and presidential power, as evident from his dissent in the Steel Seizure Case. Reed and Minton had joined him in that dissent, and he could be

89. Id. at 11.
90. Id. at 12.

confident that they would be with him on the *Reynolds* case. Vinson needed just two other Justices to prevail. He had good reason to believe that Tom Clark, on national security grounds, would join him, especially after what Clark had said in conference. One more vote was needed. Vinson got two: Burton and Douglas.

Some insight into the Court's decision in *Reynolds* comes from another tort claims case decided three months later, *Dalehite v. United States.*[91] Both cases involved the military. In *Dalehite,* the Court considered personal and property claims resulting from a disastrous accident at Texas City, Tex. A massive explosion led to 560 deaths, 3,000 injuries, and the leveling of the surrounding area. Some 1,850 tons of fertilizer-grade ammonium nitrate (FGAN) had been loaded on the steamship *Grandcamp,* with another 1,000 tons on the *High Flyer* docked nearby. The *Grandcamp* also carried a substantial cargo of explosives, and the *High Flyer* carried 2,000 tons of sulfur.

Plant facilities used to produce FGAN had been used during World War II to make ammonium nitrate for explosives. The fertilizer was produced and distributed according to the specifications and under the control of the U.S. government. The shipment of FGAN abroad was part of the government's effort to feed the populations of Germany, Japan, and Korea after the war, to prevent possible insurgent attacks against the U.S. occupation. The Court, divided 4–3, held that the government was not liable under the FTCA, which contained an exception for a "discretionary function or duty on the part of a federal agency or an employee of the Government."

Justices Douglas and Clark took no part in the decision. Justice Reed wrote for the majority. As with *Reynolds,* Jackson, Black, and Frankfurter dissented. But instead of dissenting for reasons "substantially" the same as a lower court, as they did in *Reynolds,* Jackson wrote a dissent explaining why the majority's opinion was deficient. He called the Texas City explosion "a man-made disaster; it was in no sense an 'act of God.'"[92] The fertilizer had been manufactured in government-owned plants, at the government's order and specifications, and was shipped as part of the government's foreign aid program. Congress "has defined the tort liability of the Government as analogous to that of a private person." One function of civil liability for negligence, Jackson said, "is to supply a sanction to enforce the degree of care suitable to the conditions of contemporary society and appropriate to the circumstances of the case."[93] To Jackson, "whoever puts into circulation in commerce a product that is known or even suspected of being potentially inflammable or explosive is under an

91. 346 U.S. 15 (1953).
92. Id. at 48 (Jackson dissenting, joined by Black and Frankfurter).
93. Id. at 49.

obligation to know his own product and to ascertain what forces he is turning loose."[94] The government had an obligation to follow each step of the distribution of a hazardous substance, "with warning of its dangers and with information and directions to keep those dangers at a minimum."[95]

Jackson denied that the catastrophe resulted from a "discretionary function" of the government, or that finding negligence in this case would make executive officials "timid and restrained" for fear that their decisions would be liable in court.[96] The government's negligence "was not in policy decisions of a regulatory or governmental nature, but involved actions akin to those of a private manufacturer, contractor, or shipper."[97] As for the reach of the FTCA, Jackson said that "surely a statute so long debated was meant to embrace more than traffic accidents." He expressed concern that "the ancient and discredited doctrine that 'The King can do no wrong' has not been uprooted; it has merely been amended to read, 'The King can do only little wrongs.'"[98]

When the King does big wrongs, Congress can pass legislation to settle private claims. In 1955, Congress did precisely that, stating that it "recognizes and assumes the compassionate responsibility of the United States for the losses sustained by reason of the explosions and fires at Texas City, Texas, and hereby provides the procedure by which the amounts shall be determined and paid."[99] An early stage of the legislative history of this bill acknowledged that the federal government "was responsible for the explosions and the resulting catastrophe at Texas City; that the disaster was caused by forces set in motion by the Government, completely controlled or controllable by it."[100] Conferees, however, decided not to acknowledge legal responsibility or negligence on the part of the government, but to recognize "compassionate responsibility."[101]

Settlement

The Supreme Court reversed the Third Circuit in *Reynolds* and remanded the case to the district court "for further proceedings consistent with the views expressed in this opinion."[102] On March 27, 1953, Charles Biddle issued a

94. Id. at 53.
95. Id.
96. Id. at 58.
97. Id. at 60.
98. Id. For more on the Texas City disaster, see William G. Weaver and Thomas Longoria, "Bureaucracy that Kills: Federal Sovereign Immunity and the Discretionary Function Exception," 96 Am. Pol. Sci. Rev. 335 (2002).
99. 69 Stat. 707 (1955).
100. S. Rept. No. 684, 84th Cong., 1st Sess. 4 (1955).
101. H. Rept. No. 1623, 84th Cong., 1st Sess. 4 (1955).
102. 345 U.S. at 10.

notice of depositions, requesting the government to produce Moore, Peny, and Murrhee "for oral depositions" at his office in Philadelphia on April 10, 1953.[103] He wrote to Phyllis Brauner on April 29, telling her that "we went ahead and took the depositions of the three surviving members of the crew." As he anticipated, "they made it quite clear that the secret equipment on board the plane had absolutely nothing to do with the accident and had not even been put into operation."[104] A half century later, when the case returned to district court in 2004, the plaintiffs maintained that Biddle took depositions before settling, although copies of the transcripts are not available and may never have been transcribed.[105]

Biddle seemed inclined to take the issue back to district court, using the depositions as evidence that access to the accident report was needed. He told Phyllis Brauner that he was getting an aviation expert as a witness "through one of the Airlines" and hoped "to try the case in June, or if not then, certainly during the summer." He expected to show "not only that the accident was caused by the negligence of the Air Force but that we can do this without getting ourselves in any further legal problems, which might result in further appeals by the Government and delays."[106] At some point in April or May, Biddle and the three women decided against another round of litigation.

Some reasons against returning to district court are included in a letter from Theodore Mattern, the family attorney for Phyllis Brauner. He wrote to her on March 16, a week after the Supreme Court's decision, expressing his "doubts now, as we are deprived of most essential proof to make out a case." The accident report was "of official character and carries in it the determinable cause of the failure in the plane which precipitated the tragedy." Statements by the surviving crew members "might and might not spell out negligence sufficient to base a judgment in your favor thereon; but inasmuch as these are all that is left to us to proceed on, Biddle will have to make the best of them on the trial."[107]

Mattern summed up the discouraging legal and political climate. He told Phyllis Brauner that the Court's decision "is very much in line with the present hysterical trend in the Government and in peaceful times is almost un-

103. Notice of Depositions, Brauner and Palya v. United States, Civil Action No. 9793, and Reynolds v. United States, Civil Action No. 10142 (E.D. Pa. 1953).

104. Letter from Charles J. Biddle to Mrs. William Brauner, April 29, 1953; http://www.wbur.org/photogallery/news%5Fbrauner/default.asp?counter=5.

105. Plaintiffs' Memorandum in Opposition to Defendant's Motion to Dismiss, Herring v. United States, Civil Action No. 03-5500 (LDD) (E.D. Pa. 2004), at 24 (Note 9).

106. Letter from Biddle to Brauner, April 29, 1953.

107. Letter from Theodore Mattern to Mrs. Phyllis Brauner, March 16, 1953; http://www.wbur.org/photogallery/news%5Fbrauner/default.asp?counter=6.

thinkable." The three dissenters "went even so far as to vote against it even in our troubled times when disclosures of any sort are so deeply dreaded." Mattern thought that Judge Kirkpatrick's "sympathies will lie with the plaintiffs when he will have to decide the final outcome of this prolonged litigation." Whether those sympathies "will be able to overcome the emaciated proof available is, in my opinion, more than doubtful." He advised Brauner that she "not count on a positive decision and make no plans based on a favorable one." He closed with warm words of support: "You work too hard to permit yourself the luxury of daydreams or wishful thinking. You have carried on so far [*sic*] and you will continue successfully without the expected windfall. Your strength will not falter."[108]

In a stipulation dated June 22, 1953, the three women and the U.S. government agreed to settle their differences under Section 413 of the FTCA, which authorized the Attorney General, with "a view to doing substantial justice," to arbitrate, compromise, or settle claims under the statute.[109] The parties reached a compromise settlement. Under this section of the law, the government did not have to concede any negligence on its part for the accident. The widows settled for less money than they had been previously awarded by Judge Kirkpatrick. Instead of $225,000, they accepted $170,000: $49,855.55 to Phyllis Brauner, $48,355.55 to Elizabeth Palya (now Elizabeth Sacker), and $39,288.90 to Patricia J. Reynolds (now Patricia J. Herring). Deducted from the $170,000 was $32,500 for counsel fees for Charles J. Biddle.[110]

These amounts were awarded to the women "in full settlement and discharge of any and all of [their] several claims, demands, or causes of action" on behalf of themselves individually, and their heirs, executors, administrators, or assigns against the United States for damages on account of the deaths of their husbands.[111] Under the stipulation, the women agreed to execute and deliver to the United States "a full and final release" of their claims against the United States and agree "that no further suit will be instituted for the same cause of action."[112] The Franklin Institute and the Radio Corporation of America also agreed not to bring any further legal action against the government for the accident.[113] On June 22, 1953, Judge Kirkpatrick issued an order putting into

---

108. Id.

109. 60 Stat. 845, § 413 (1946).

110. Stipulation, Brauner and Palya v. United States, Civil Action No. 9793, and Reynolds v. United States, Civil Action No. 10,142 (E.D. Pa. June 22, 1953), at 5. (The stipulation is not paginated.)

111. Id. at 2–3.

112. Id. at 3–4.

113. Id. at 4–5.

effect the compromise detailed in the stipulation.[114] In a separate order of August 5, 1953, the two cases were dismissed.[115]

Several of the families received less than their allocation of $170,000 because they had to forgo funds from the companies the men worked for. After the death of Albert Palya, his wife received workers' compensation from RCA in the following amounts. She received $25.00 per week for 300 weeks, or $7,500. Each child received $25.00 per week until they reached age 18. That meant $3,025 for Robert ($25 times 121 weeks), $3,796.43 for William ($25 times 151 weeks), and $7,971.43 for Judith ($25 times 318 weeks). When Elizabeth Palya remarried, she lost the compensation for herself. When the case was settled, she lost the compensation for her children.[116]

The check to Phyllis Brauner of $49,855.55 was similarly reduced. Charles Biddle wrote to her on August 3, 1953, explaining that Maryland Casualty Co. was "legally entitled to get back the amount of compensation payments which it has paid to you."[117] On August 8, Biddle wrote to her again, giving her the precise figures. The amount that Maryland Casualty had paid to her over a period of 250 weeks came to $4,687.71. Also, Phyllis Brauner owed the law firm $389.38 for some "out-of-pocket expenses."[118] The balance she received was therefore $44,778.46. She sent a portion of that to William Brauner's mother.[119]

The financial settlement for Patricia Reynolds (Herring) was different. She had no children and her husband had not been employed very long. RCA gave her a modest cash settlement and there was no workers' compensation, but she did get a job with the company.[120]

Reaction to the Decision

The Court's decision did not hang together. It declared, as a constitutional principle, that judicial control "over the evidence in a case cannot be abdi-

114. Order, Brauner and Palya v. United States, Civil Action No. 9793, and Reynolds v. United States, Civil Action No. 10,142 (E.D. Pa. June 22, 1953).

115. Order to Dismiss, Brauner and Palya v. United States, Civil Action No. 9793, and Reynolds v. United States, Civil Action No. 10,142 (E.D. Pa. Aug. 5, 1953).

116. E-mail to author from Judy Loether.

117. Letter from Charles J. Biddle to Mrs. William H. Brauner, August 3, 1953. Copy sent to author by Cathy Brauner.

118. Letter from Charles J. Biddle to Mrs. William H. Brauner, August 10, 1953. Copy sent to author by Cathy Brauner.

119. Letter from Cathy Brauner to author, November 15, 2005.

120. E-mail to author from Pat Herring.

cated to the caprice of executive officers."[121] It then created a procedure that did precisely that. The district judge would never see evidence that an executive department considered privileged. The judge was entitled only to what a department head or an assistant might tell the judge about the evidence and why it could not be disclosed. The court "should not jeopardize the security which the privilege is meant to protect by insisting upon an examination of the evidence, even by the judge alone, in chambers."[122] That procedure reduced a federal court to subordinate status, kept at arm's length from evidence and therefore unable to function as a neutral referee between a private plaintiff and the government.

In a conversation with Professor Walter Murphy on December 18, 1962, Justice Douglas explained some of the factors that make it difficult for a court majority to produce a coherent opinion:

One of the reasons that judicial opinions are sometimes so opaque or irrational perhaps, in the sense of not being logical development structurally, is because of the patchwork that goes into their creation, satisfying this judge, getting a majority by putting in a footnote, striking out a sentence that would have made a paragraph lucid, and it becomes opaque. This is also one of the reasons why judicial opinions, except dissents, are usually very poor literature.[123]

In the case of *Reynolds,* even the dissent was opaque and very poor literature. As for the majority opinion by Chief Justice Vinson, it seemed to have little to do with the briefs, the merits, the law, or the facts. It reads more like a decision designed to meet institutional and political needs. Those considerations are always present and important, but not at the cost of constitutional principles or the right of litigants. Vinson presented the decision as a judicious and balanced search for middle ground, even by urging the plaintiffs to return to district court and depose the surviving crew members. Yet he was with the government on all essential points. Through his language and logic, he gave a green light to the state secrets privilege, and it has been so used consistently by the Justice Department over the years.

121. United States v. Reynolds, 345 U.S., at 9–10.
122. Id. at 10.
123. Transcriptions of Conversations Between Justice William O. Douglas and Professor Walter F. Murphy, December 18, 1962, Cassette No. 12, at 2; Seeley G. Mudd Manuscript Library, Princeton University; http://infoshare1.princeton.edu/libraries/firestone/rbsc/finding_aids/douglas/douglas12.html.

When issued, the Court's ruling caused barely a ripple in the press. The *New York Times* devoted four short paragraphs to the story, stating that "judges were no more entitled to learn real military secrets than any other parties to a lawsuit."[124] Although brief, the *Times* certainly made short work of the Court's pretension that judges were not abdicating their powers. At the same time, the story falsely implied the existence of "real military secrets." Without access to documents, the Court could not know whether there were secrets or not. The most it knew is that the government said so—or appeared to say so. The *Philadelphia Inquirer,* given its location in the city where the trial court and the Third Circuit did their work, might have been expected to run a longer story. It did not. It interpreted the ruling as saying that federal judges "hearing damage suits against the Government are not entitled to scan documents revealing military secrets."[125] In fact, Judge Kirkpatrick was not allowed to scan the documents even if no military secrets were present.

The *Washington Post,* plying its trade in the same city as the Supreme Court, did not even bother to run a separate story on the decision. On the day after the ruling, an article summed up 13 decisions issued by the Court, with the *Reynolds* decision placed next to last: "Refused, 6 to 3, to uphold a Federal judge in Philadelphia who ordered the Secretary of the Air Force to produce secret reports made after a B-29 crash to settle a damage suit by three widows of civilians involved. The Air Force's contention that disclosure of the reports might damage the public interest was upheld by Chief Justice Vinson. Justices Black, Frankfurter and Jackson dissented."[126] Short and sweet. The *Post* promoted the same misconception as the *New York Times* and the *Philadelphia Inquirer* by assuming that the government was ordered to produce "secret reports."

Strangely, law reviews gave less attention to the Supreme Court's decision than they did to the Third Circuit ruling. A note in the *George Washington Law Review* correctly observed that the decision "prevents examination by the court, and in such a case no penalty can be attached to the withholding of the documents."[127] The district court and the Third Circuit attached a penalty; the Supreme Court did not. The note reasoned: "No one could logically argue that the judiciary would be less mindful of the national security or public interest than would members of the executive branch. Nevertheless, the exper-

124. "High Court Denies Right of Judges to Arms Secrets," New York Times, March 10, 1953, at 2.
125. "High Court Bars Secret Evidence," Philadelphia Inquirer, March 10, 1953, at 5.
126. "Supreme Court Upholds 'Featherbedding' by Printers, Musicians in T-H Law Decision," Washington Post, March 10, 1953, at 15.
127. Note, "Discovery Under Federal Tort Claims Act—Privilege for Defense Secrets Upheld Without Requiring Disclosure," 21 G.W. L. Rev. 792, 792 (1953).

tise of many of the administrative departments makes them better qualified to decide technical questions."[128] Executive officers might be better qualified to decide technical questions, but their work within an agency and under the control of the White House invites bias and deception when it comes to withholding and characterizing public documents. That is why scrutiny by an independent judiciary is so vital.

The only other student note appeared in the *New York University Law Review,* which found unpersuasive the Court's analogy to the privilege against self-incrimination: "Whereas with incriminating matter there is the danger that a judge might feel impelled to disclose information regarding the commission of a crime, with state secrets he would be motivated by the welfare of the nation as well as by duty to remain mute."[129] Unless the Supreme Court considered judges less trustworthy than executive officials, "there is no reason why the judge cannot examine the documents *ex parte.*"[130] This article shoots a hole through Vinson's claim that the judiciary would not be abdicating its powers to the executive branch: "The Court by this decision has, in practical effect, relinquished to an executive officer discretion to determine whether Government documents shall be produced in the courts."[131] With judges denied documents and spoon-fed whatever executive officials want to share, the process blessed by the Court "makes possible the suppression of material merely because it is unflattering to important officials."[132]

An article published in the *Vanderbilt Law Review* spoke critically of recent court decisions on the scope of discovery against the United States. Included among the decisions that misapplied the privilege of executive officials was the Supreme Court's opinion in *Reynolds.* The claim of the executive branch that it possessed "an all inclusive privilege" that executive officers "alone can apply" had done much to undermine the ability of private plaintiffs to obtain documents during the discovery phase.[133]

The article began with the fundamental premise that the application of a privilege "is a question of the admissibility of evidence," and "it is usually unquestioned that at a trial the judge determines whether a privilege exists."[134] In *Reynolds,* the government had objected that the judiciary was violating the separation of powers by attempting to determine for itself whether a

128. Id. at 794.
129. Note, "Evidence—State Secrets Privilege—Discovery Under Federal Tort Claims Act," 28 N.Y.U. L. Rev. 1188, 1190 (1953).
130. Id.
131. Id.
132. Id. at 1190–91.
133. Mac Asbill and Willis B. Snell, "Scope of Discovery Against the United States," 7 Vand. L. Rev. 582, 582 (1954).
134. Id. at 593.

document judged privileged was actually so. The article argued that this analysis turned the separation of powers doctrine upside down: "The judiciary is not attempting to impinge on the executive function, since the only question is the admissibility of evidence, a question purely judicial in nature."[135] It was the executive that was impinging on the judiciary.

The government in *Reynolds* relied on several historical precedents to bolster its case, but the article concluded that "none of them is controlling."[136] The examples of the President refusing to disclose information to Congress "has nothing to do with the power of the courts to impose sanctions in proceedings before them."[137] The article faulted the Court for showing "too little faith in the ability and loyalty of judges"[138] and for surrendering a judicial function by "accept[ing] as final a determination by an administration official."[139]

A short note in the *Washington Law Review* expressed satisfaction with the Court's ruling. The decision offered a "proper solution," it rested upon "sound policy considerations," and it provided "adequate safeguards" against the abuse of privilege by executive officials.[140] Courts "must consider all the evidence, circumstances and implications of the question or request before it."[141] Yet under the procedures established by the Court in *Reynolds,* federal judges had no assurance of considering all the evidence. Depending on the case, they might have to rely entirely on explanations offered by executive officials, who were at liberty to abuse the privilege. No judicial safeguards existed to limit or prevent the abuse.

Two law review articles in 1955 discussed *Reynolds,* one of them only in passing and at a high level of generality.[142] The other found unconvincing the majority's analogy between the privilege against self-incrimination and the privilege not to disclose a document. With incriminating matter, a judge might feel obliged to disclose information regarding a crime, but with state secrets, he would place a higher priority on the national interest and the need to remain silent.[143] In *Reynolds,* the Court agreed to relinquish to an execu-

135. Id. at 595.
136. Id. at 596.
137. Id.
138. Id. at 600.
139. Id. at 602.
140. Robert F. Brachtenbach, "The Privilege Against Revealing Military Secrets," 29 Wash. L. Rev. 59, 62 (1954).
141. Id.
142. Wilbur Branch King, "Military Secrets as an Evidentiary Problem in Civil Litigation," 4 J. Pub. L. 196 (1955).
143. Charles R. Gromley, "Discovery Against the Government of Military and Other Confidential Matters," 43 Ky. L. J. 343, 349 (1955). The language here is identical to the student note in the *New York University Law Review* article published in 1953, presumably written by Gromley.

tive officer the judgment on whether to produce government documents in court.[144] Notwithstanding the Court's claim to find a middle ground between the interests of the plaintiffs and those of the government, it failed to protect a basic constitutional value: "The courts are the agency best fitted to determine issues of executive privilege."[145]

After the Court's decision in *Reynolds,* Congress took a number of steps to give private citizens and federal judges greater access to documents held by executive departments. As explained in the next chapter, the Freedom of Information Act and its amendments helped open agency files, and other statutes entrusted to the judiciary a duty over sensitive national security information. Several Supreme Court cases (particularly the Pentagon Papers Case and the Watergate Tapes Case) served to explode shibboleths about national security secrets and the motivations that lead executive officials to withhold documents. But the very first initiative by Congress was to address the executive branch's chronic abuse of the Housekeeping Statute.

144. Id.
145. Id. at 355.

5

OPENING UP GOVERNMENT

A number of legislative and judicial actions after *Reynolds* began to place limits on the authority of executive officials to keep documents from congressional committees, federal judges, and private citizens. The Freedom of Information Act of 1966 marked the first of many initiatives. In 1974 it was
amended to authorize federal judges to conduct in camera inspections of classified documents. The Foreign Intelligence Surveillance Act (FISA) of 1978
created a special court to review applications by government attorneys for
national security wiretaps. The Classified Information Procedures Act (CIPA)
of 1980 authorized federal judges to look at classified documents in camera to
determine what evidence can be used in open court. High-profile decisions by
the Supreme Court, including the Pentagon Papers Case and the Watergate
Tapes Case, spotlighted the capacity and willingness of top executive officials
to abuse their powers. Leading the way in this string of reforms was an amendment to the Housekeeping Statute.

Fixing the Housekeeping Statute

Continued misuse of the Housekeeping Statute by executive departments
prompted Congress in 1958 to amend it. Its original purpose, dating back to
the First Congress, was to make department heads responsible for the documents in their custody. Gradually it evolved into an instrument for withholding agency documents from outside parties, even Congress and the courts.
Members of Congress discovered "bizarre examples" and "some pure slapstick
comedy illustrations of confused secrecy."[1] In one example, an Air Force telephone recording (offering weather forecasts to anyone who dialed a publicly
listed phone number) closed with the warning that the information was classified. In another case, the Pentagon refused to permit publication of a book
on military tactics used during the American Revolutionary War.[2]

The purpose of the 1958 amendment was modest. It would not affect
some 78 separate statutes that protected the secrecy of government records,

---

1. 104 Cong. Rec. 6564 (1958) (statement by Rep. Wright).
2. Id.

ranging from atomic energy information to income tax returns.[3] A statute could not, by itself, take from the President or the executive branch authorities and powers they believed are implicit in the Constitution. The amendment merely added a sentence at the end of the Housekeeping Statute: "This section does not authorize withholding information from the public or limiting the availability of records to the public."[4]

Interestingly, the amendment said nothing about withholding information from the courts, unless that is implied in members of the public who become litigants. The *Reynolds* case was referred to only a few times in the legislative history of the 1958 amendment.[5] Most of the citations to court cases focused on two decisions that did not relate at all to the state secrets privilege (*Boske v. Comingore* and *Touhy v. Ragen*), but those cases were nonetheless frequently cited in state secrets litigation.[6] Political support for the amendment seemed to come largely from the press. Several reporters worked on the House committee that reported the amendment.[7]

When Deputy Attorney General William P. Rogers expressed his views on the pending amendment on June 13, 1957, there had been no committee reports or floor debates to explain the bill's purpose. Without that guidance, he believed that the amendment "would not clarify the present law." However, he offered these comments:

Insofar as the purpose of this legislation is to assure the full and free flow of information to the public not inconsistent with the national interest, the Department of Justice is in full accord. We believe that within limits the executive and legislative branches should keep the public informed as to their activities, and should make available information, papers, and records. Without doubt the legislative and executive branches are in agreement with this fundamental principle.[8]

When the bill reached President Dwight D. Eisenhower, he described its purpose as "to make clear the intent of the Congress that Section 161 of the Revised Statutes shall not be cited as a justification for failing to disclose

3. Id. at 6548 (statement by Rep. Brown) and 6550 (statement by Rep. Moss).
4. H. Rept. No. 1461, 85th Cong., 2d Sess. 3 (1958).
5. Id. at 23; 104 Cong. Rec. 6554 (statement of Rep. Hoffman).
6. S. Rept. No. 1621, 85th Cong., 2d Sess. 2, 8–9, 14 (1958); 104 Cong. Rec. 15689 (1958) (letter to Senator Richard Russell from Senator Thomas C. Hennings Jr.); id. at 15690–95 (statement by Senator Hruska).
7. H. Rept. No. 1461, at 11–12, 24–28 (1958); 104 Cong. Rec. 6550 (1958) (statement by Rep. Hoffman).
8. S. Rept. No. 1621, at 15.

information which should be made public."[9] He said that Congress, in considering the legislation, "has recognized that the decision-making and investigative processes must be protected." To Eisenhower, the legislative history of the bill revealed that "it is not intended to, and indeed could not, alter the existing power of the head of an Executive department to keep appropriate information or papers confidential in the public interest. This power in the Executive Branch is inherent under the Constitution."[10] Did this imply that the head of a department could keep information only from the public or also from Congress and the courts? The bill became law on August 12, 1958.[11]

What impact would the 1958 amendment have on the *Touhy* doctrine, which had upheld the authority of a department head to prevent a subordinate from releasing agency documents? As one article noted, the amendment should have "knocked the judicially sanctioned prop out from under the bureaucratic privilege claims," and yet the *Touhy* doctrine retained some of its force.[12] Many of the cases that involve *Touhy* originate in state courts.[13] The Justice Department argues in state court that federal agencies "have unlimited discretion in deciding whether to comply with discovery requests," and state courts agree.[14] Federal courts, however, "have never supposed that sovereign immunity could prevent them from reviewing agency decisions to refuse disclosure."[15] The *Touhy* doctrine is not based on sovereign immunity. When raised in state court it relies on principles of federalism and the Supremacy Clause.[16] The survival of *Touhy* at the state level should not interfere with access to agency documents by Congress, federal courts, or private litigants.

9. Public Papers of the Presidents, 1958, at 601.

10. Id.

11. 72 Stat. 547 (1958). For floor debate, see 104 Cong. Rec. 6547–75, 15688–99 (1958).

12. Gregory S. Coleman, "*Touhy* and the Housekeeping Privilege: Dead but Not Buried?," 70 Tex. L. Rev. 685, 688 (1992). The quote comes from EEOC v. Los Alamos Constructors, Inc., 382 F.Supp. 1373, 1378 (D. N.M. 1974).

13. Coleman, "*Touhy* and the Housekeeping Privilege," at 689.

14. Id. at 695.

15. Id. at 699.

16. Id. at 702. The Supremacy Clause (Art. VI of the U.S. Constitution) provides: "This Constitution, and the Laws of the United States which shall be made in Pursuance thereof; and all Treaties made, or which shall be made, under the Authority of the United States, shall be the supreme Law of the Land; and the Judges in every State shall be bound thereby, any Thing in the Constitution or Laws of any State to the Contrary notwithstanding." For other studies on the Housekeeping Statute, see John J. Mitchell, "Government Secrecy in Theory and Practice: 'Rules and Regulations' as an Autonomous Screen," 58 Colum. L. Rev. 199 (1958); and Don Lively, "Government Housekeeping Authority: Bureaucratic Privileges Without a Bureaucratic Privilege," 16 Harv. C.R-C.L. L. Rev. 495 (1981).

Freedom of Information Act

The 1958 amendment to the Housekeeping Statute marked the first step toward a more general statute on freedom of information. During debate in 1958, one lawmaker referred to the amendment as "the freedom-of-information bill, or amendment."[17] Starting with John F. Kennedy, Presidents began to remove from agency officials far down the line the capacity or authority to claim "executive privilege" over documents. In 1962, Kennedy informed Congress that he—and not an agency official—would invoke the privilege. President Lyndon B. Johnson affirmed that policy on April 2, 1965.[18]

Following the 1958 amendment, agencies began to rely on Section 3 of the Administrative Procedure Act as a handy source of authority to withhold records and documents from the public.[19] Congress had passed it in 1946 to establish procedures to be followed by agencies when they issued regulations and engaged in adjudication. Section 3, governing public information, provided: "Except to the extent that there is involved (1) any function of the United States requiring secrecy in the public interest or (2) any matter relating solely to the internal management of an agency," every agency was required to publish in the *Federal Register* information about their organizations, formal and informal procedures, substantive rules adopted, and statements of general policy or interpretations.[20]

The phrase "secrecy in the public interest" was significant. Agencies were not authorized to withhold information merely on some general ground of secrecy or to hide executive wrongdoing. There was no carte blanche to engage in secrecy for the sake of secrecy. It had to be secrecy "in the public interest." But neither did Congress require agencies to demonstrate how secrecy in a particular area would serve the public interest. Executive officials had ample opportunity to manipulate the language to serve not "the public interest" but rather their internal agency needs. In 1962, the National Science Foundation decided it would not be "in the public interest" to release cost estimates submitted by unsuccessful contractors for a multimillion-dollar deep-sea study. It was later learned, after the agency was pressured to disclose the estimates, that the winning firm had not submitted the lowest bid.[21]

Section 3 also withheld agency records from the public if the information was classified "confidential for good cause found."[22] Apparently agency

17. 104 Cong. Rec. 6548 (1958) (statement by Rep. Brown).
18. H. Rept. No. 1497, 89th Cong., 2d Sess. 3 (1966).
19. Id.
20. 60 Stat. 238, § 3 (1946).
21. H. Rept. No. 1497, at 5.
22. 60 Stat. 238, § 3(c).

actions needed to be reasoned and substantive, but no remedy existed if the agency wrongfully denied someone access to public records. A House report explained that Section 3 was never intended to be "a general public records law in that it does not afford to the public at large access to official records generally."[23]

In 1966, Congress passed what is known as the Freedom of Information Act (FOIA). One objective was to eliminate Section 3 as a vehicle for agency nondisclosure and to provide some remedies for improper denials. In reporting the bill, the Senate Judiciary Committee said that "the theory of an informed electorate is vital to the proper operation of a democracy," but that witnesses before the committee had objected that Section 3 "has been used more as an excuse for withholding than as a disclosure statute."[24] "Innumerable times it appears that information is withheld only to cover up embarrassing mistakes or irregularities," and that Section 3 "was being used as an excuse for secrecy."[25] The committee offered these general conclusions:

> A government by secrecy benefits no one.
> It injures the people it seeks to serve; it injures its own integrity and operation.
> It breeds mistrust, dampers the fervor of its citizens, and mocks their loyalty.[26]

The 1966 legislation required each executive agency to publish in the *Federal Register* the "places at which, the officers from whom, and the methods whereby, the public may secure information, make submittals or requests, or obtain decisions." Each agency shall, in accordance with published rules, make available for public inspection and copying all final agency opinions, all orders made in the adjudication of agency cases, and statements of policy and interpretations adopted by the agency yet not published in the *Federal Register*.[27] In addition, "any person" (not just U.S. citizens) would have access to agency records and could go to court to challenge agency noncompliance. In these cases "the court shall determine the matter de novo [anew or afresh] and the burden shall be upon the agency to sustain its action."[28] As explained in the Senate report, the de novo proceeding was considered essential to assure that the "ultimate decision as to the propriety of the agency's action is made

23. H. Rept. No. 1497, at 1.
24. S. Rept. No. 813, 89th Cong., 1st Sess. 3 (1965).
25. Id.
26. Id. at 10.
27. 80 Stat. 250 (1966).
28. Id. at 251, § 3 (c).

by the court."[29] If an agency failed to comply with the court's order, the court "may punish the responsible officers for contempt."[30]

The statute carved out nine areas exempt from disclosure. Exemption 1 stated that the provisions for access to agency records "shall not be applicable to matters that are (1) specifically required by Executive order to be kept secret in the interest of the national defense or foreign policy."[31] After a collision between the executive branch and Congress, this national security exemption was amended in 1974. Other exemptions cover matters:

(2) related solely to the internal personnel rules and practices of any agency;

(3) specifically exempted from disclosure by statute;

(4) trade secrets and commercial or financial information obtained from any person and privileged or confidential;

(5) inter-agency or intra-agency memorandums or letters which would not be available by law to a private party in litigation with the agency;

(6) personnel and medical files and similar files the disclosure of which would constitute a clearly unwarranted invasion of personal privacy;

(7) investigatory files compiled for law enforcement purposes except to the extent available by law to a private party;[32]

(8) contained in or related to examination, operating, or condition reports prepared by, on behalf of, or for the use of any agency responsible for the regulation or supervision of financial institutions; and

(9) geological and geophysical information and data (including maps) concerning wells.

FOIA covered *public* access. It deleted language in Section 3 that had made matters of official record available only to persons "properly and directly concerned." The statute made agency records available to "any person." Moreover, it was not meant to limit in any way the ability of Congress and its committees to request and receive agency documents. FOIA specifically stated: "Nothing in this section authorizes withholding of information or limiting the availability of records to the public except as specifically stated in this section, nor shall this section be authority to withhold information from Congress."[33]

29. S. Rept. No. 813, 89th Cong., 1st Sess. 8 (1965).

30. 80 Stat. 251, § 3(c).

31. Id. at § 3(e)(1).

32. Exemption 7 was later amended to require that the records satisfy one of six subsections; 5 U.S.C. § 552(b)(7) (2000).

33. 80 Stat. 251, § 3(f).

Amchitka Nuclear Tests

In the early 1970s, the Nixon administration refused to release data to Congress on a scheduled 1971 nuclear test in Amchitka, an island part of the Aleutian chain off Alaska. Just as in *Reynolds,* federal officials argued that they had the exclusive right to determine what records to release, in this case to determine what information fell within the exemptions of FOIA. When federal courts, including the Supreme Court, failed to give members of Congress access to the documents, Congress amended FOIA in 1974 to authorize federal judges to examine classified agency records in their chambers.

In 1966, the Atomic Energy Commission (AEC) decided that its Nevada test grounds were not suitable for a planned nuclear blast having 250 times the explosive force of the atomic bomb dropped on Hiroshima. An executive order issued by President William Howard Taft in 1913, creating the Aleutian Wildlife Refuge, provided that the establishment of the reservation "shall not interfere with the use of the islands for . . . military . . . purposes." The AEC concluded that the planned nuclear test in Amchitka was "fully in accord" with the executive order because the purpose was to test a warhead for the Antiballistic Missile system. The Interior Department, responsible for administering the wildlife area, agreed with that assessment. The test received the code name "Cannikin."[34]

An international treaty against nuclear tests did not cover underground explosions. Engineers were brought into Amchitka to dig a hole more than a mile into the earth. The government maintained that a one-megaton explosion, four thousand feet down, proved that the five-times-larger Cannikin test could be conducted safely at Amchitka. Environmentalists and other nations protested that the test would threaten Amchitka's wildlife, including sea otters and bald eagles. There was also concern about radioactive contamination of commercial fishing interests, and the governments of Canada and Japan feared that the venting of radiation would endanger nearby populations. Moreover, Amchitka was located near an earthquake zone, with a major fault line running along the Pacific coast to California and posing a threat to Hawaii both from an earthquake and a resulting tsunami.[35]

Representative Patsy T. Mink, Democrat of Hawaii, tried to prevent the test by offering an amendment on July 29, 1971, to a public works appropriations bill that included funds for the AEC. Her amendment read: "None of the funds appropriated by this Act shall be obligated or expended, directly

34. This background on the Amchitka nuclear test comes from Representative Patsy T. Mink, "The Cannikin Papers: A Case Study in Freedom of Information," in Secrecy and Foreign Policy, edited by Thomas M. Franck and Edward Weisband (1974) (hereafter "Mink").
35. Id. at 116–17.

or indirectly, to pay any part of the cost of the testing by detonation of any nuclear bomb, warhead, or other similar device on, or in the vicinity of, the Aleutian Island of Amchitka, Alaska."[36] Opponents pointed out that both Houses had voted to support the test and that her earlier amendment to delete funds from the AEC authorization bill had been rejected by the House. The Senate had also rejected two amendments to the authorization bill to delay the test.[37] During debate on the Mink amendment, lawmakers discussed documents held by the executive branch concerning the test that had been classified as secret and kept from members of Congress.[38] Mink's amendment failed, 108 to 275.[39]

EPA v. Mink

Three days before the House vote on the Mink amendment, the Washington *Evening Star* reported that two agencies (the Defense Department and the AEC) supported the test, whereas five others (the State Department, Office of Science and Technology, U.S. Information Agency, Environmental Protection Agency, and the Council on Environmental Quality) recommended that Cannikin either be canceled or postponed.[40] Mink contacted each of the five agencies to obtain copies of their evaluations but received nothing. The State Department told her that "it would not be appropriate for the Department of State or any other agency to make available to anyone outside the Executive Branch an internal study that was prepared for the President."[41] When she appealed directly to President Nixon for the studies, she was advised by White House Counsel John Dean that the agency recommendations were prepared for the advice of the President "and involve highly sensitive matter that is vital to our national defense and foreign policy." They were not, he said, available for release.[42]

Having exhausted all administrative remedies, Mink and several of her colleagues went to court to seek what became known as the Cannikin Papers. On August 11, 1971, 33 members of Congress filed a suit in federal district court to compel four executive agencies (the U.S. Information Agency and part of the State Department not included) to release the papers. They requested the documents both under FOIA procedures—as ordinary members of the

36. 117 Cong. Rec. 28080 (1971).
37. Id. at 28081.
38. Id. at 28082.
39. Id. at 28089–90.
40. Mink, at 118.
41. Id. at 119.
42. Id. at 120.

public—and in their official capacity as lawmakers. They argued that, as members of Congress, they were entitled to disclosure of the Cannikin data without regard to the exemptions concerning national security or other grounds. The Justice Department maintained that the requested materials were covered by Exemptions 1 and 5 of FOIA.[43] The district court, without conducting an in camera inspection of the disputed documents, ruled that the records were covered by the two exemptions. It granted the government's motion for summary judgment and dismissed the action.[44]

On October 15, 1971, the D.C. Circuit reversed the district court, concluding that summary disposition of the issue was inappropriate. It remanded the case with directions to the district court to inspect the documents in camera. With regard to one of the documents—an unclassified memo from the Council on Environmental Quality—the D.C. Circuit found no reason for it to be withheld on national security grounds simply because it was attached to a classified report. To the extent that an executive order issued by President Eisenhower in 1953 conflicted with FOIA, the D.C. Circuit sided with FOIA because it came later in time.[45] "Secrecy by association," it said, "is not favored."[46] If nonsecret components can be separated from secret documents "and may be read separately without distortion of meaning, they too should be disclosed."[47]

An affidavit by Undersecretary of State John Irwin, identifying certain documents as "separately classified," was not accepted as final and conclusive by the D.C. Circuit: "we do not think that a matter as important as this is to be determined on the basis of Undersecretary Irwin's affidavit as it stands."[48] In the midst of this litigation, the administration conducted the nuclear test of the five-megaton device on November 6, 1971.

The D.C. Circuit, in the *Mink* case, did not rely on *Reynolds,* but the Supreme Court did. On January 22, 1973, the Court reversed the D.C. Circuit, holding that Exemption 1 (national defense) did not permit "compelled disclosure of documents" or in camera inspection to sift out "nonsecret components."[49] The Court also held that Exemption 5 (agency memos) did not require that otherwise confidential documents be made available for district court inspection. As in *Reynolds,* the Court ruled that the government should be given an opportunity to demonstrate by means short of in camera inspec-

43. Id. at 121.
44. Id. at 122.
45. Mink v. EPA, 464 F.2d 742, 745 (D.C. Cir. 1972).
46. Id. at 746.
47. Id.
48. Id.
49. EPA v. Mink, 410 U.S. 73, 81 (1973).

tion that the documents sought by the lawmakers were beyond the range of material that would be available to a private party in litigation with a federal agency.[50] The Court treated the lawmakers as purely private persons litigating a FOIA suit, rather than as members of Congress who had sued also in their official capacities.

Once again, as with *Reynolds,* the Court was content to remain arm's length from evidence. It spoke about eight documents, later reduced to six, that "were said to involve highly sensitive matter vital to the national defense and foreign policy and were described as having been classified Top Secret or Secret pursuant to Executive Order 10501."[51] "Were said to." "Were described as." The government was at liberty to say what it liked, and the Court declined to put itself in a position where it could make an informed and independent judgment about the documents. The Court seemed satisfied to operate as a subordinate agency of the White House, accepting the word of an undersecretary. The Court said that on "the strength of this showing" the district court had granted summary judgment in the government's favor.[52] There had been no "showing." The government had made an assertion—nothing more. The traditional depiction of Justice with her eyes covered seemed quite apt. How can one respect the judgment of a court that knows nothing and does not want to?

The Supreme Court stated that the nine exemptions in FOIA "are explicitly made exclusive."[53] Exclusive? That seems to imply a superior, overriding status for an executive assertion. However, as the Court noted, FOIA allowed aggrieved citizens (1) a speedy remedy in district court, (2) directed trial courts to "determine the matter de novo," and (3) placed the burden "on the agency to sustain its action."[54] The nine exemptions represented a general claim to be tested in court—if judges were determined to exercise the authority vested in them.

The Supreme Court acknowledged that FOIA sought "to permit access to official information long shielded unnecessarily from public law."[55] In *Mink,* information would remain shielded, necessarily or not. The Court would never know and did not want to. FOIA, admitted the Court, created "a judicially enforceable public right to secure such information from possibly unwilling official hands."[56] As interpreted by the Court, however, the judicially

50. Id. at 93–94.
51. Id. at 77.
52. Id. at 78.
53. Id. at 79.
54. Id.
55. Id. at 80.
56. Id.

enforceable public right was empty. A governmental claim about national security would always prevail.

The Court regarded Exemption 1 as "intended to dispel uncertainty with respect to public access to material affecting 'national defense or foreign policy.'" The test was "to be simply whether the President by Executive Order [directed] that particular documents are to be kept secret."[57] The language of FOIA and its legislative history convinced the Court that Congress never intended "to subject executive security classifications to judicial review at the insistence of anyone who might seek to question them."[58] What is the purpose of judicial review if federal courts have no right to independently examine executive claims?

Relying on *Reynolds,* the Court stated that Congress "could certainly have provided that the Executive Branch adopt new procedures or it could have established its own procedures—subject only to whatever limitations the Executive privilege may be held to impose upon such congressional ordering."[59] To the Court, Exemption 1 placed the determination entirely with the President, with no opportunity for courts to examine and override executive judgments: "What has been said thus far makes wholly untenable any claim that the Act intended to subject the soundness of executive security classifications to judicial review at the insistence of any objecting citizen."[60] How about an objecting court? Exemption 1 did not authorize or permit in camera inspection "of a contested document bearing a single classification so that the court may separate the secret from the supposedly nonsecret and order disclosure of the latter."[61] Why not? The D.C. Circuit was "in error" to suggest such a procedure. The Court said that the classifications and Undersecretary Irwin's characterizations of the documents "have never been disputed" by the members of Congress bringing the suit.[62] How could they possibly dispute characterizations about documents they had never seen? In the words of the Senate committee that reported the bill that became FOIA, Congress put the burden of proof on the agency for a basic reason: "The private party can hardly be asked to prove that an agency has improperly withheld public information because he will not know the reasons for the agency action."[63]

As for Exemption 5 on agency memos, the Court said it was "beyond question" that the Irwin affidavit, "standing alone, is sufficient" to establish that

57. Id. at 82.
58. Id.
59. Id. at 83.
60. Id. at 84.
61. Id.
62. Id.
63. S. Rept. No. 813, at 8.

all of the documents at issue in the litigation are interagency or intra-agency memos or letters used in the executive decision-making processes.[64] Without actually seeing the documents, the Court accepted an affidavit signed by an executive official as "beyond question . . . sufficient." Taking its cue from *Reynolds,* the Court held that in camera inspection was not a necessary tool in every case, and that the government should be given an opportunity to demonstrate to the district court the propriety of withholding documents without showing them to the judge.[65]

Justice Rehnquist did not take part in the consideration or decision of the case. Justice Stewart, concurring, denied that the Court was acquiescing to executive judgment. Congress, not the Court, had "ordained unquestioning deference to the Executive's use of the 'secret' stamp."[66] Exemption 1 required the nondisclosure of matters "specifically required by Executive order to be kept secret in the interest of the national defense or foreign policy." To Stewart, the statutory language of FOIA prohibited courts to question an executive's decision to mark a document "Secret," no matter how "cynical, myopic, or even corrupt that decision might have been."[67] He agreed with the majority that Congress could rewrite Exemption 1 to establish new procedures for the handling of documents marked "Secret," at which point the President might attempt to invoke what he considered to be his constitutional powers under "executive privilege."[68]

Justices Brennan and Marshall concurred in part and dissented in part. They agreed with the majority's assessment of Exemption 5 but concluded that those same procedures—leaving open the possibility of in camera inspection—should also govern Exemption 1. FOIA's mandate to the courts to determine a matter de novo and to put on the agency the burden of sustaining its action should apply with equal force to both exemptions.[69] They pointed out that executive orders governing classification recognized that documents for which there was no need for secrecy "in the interest of the national defense or foreign policy" had been "indiscriminately classified" and mixed with materials that are legitimately classified as secret.[70]

Brennan and Marshall agreed with the D.C. Circuit that the district court, through in camera inspection, should read the documents to determine whether some nonsecret components were separable from the secret

64. 410 U.S. at 85.
65. Id. at 93.
66. Id. at 94.
67. Id. at 95.
68. Id.
69. Id. at 96.
70. Id. at 97.

and should be disclosed.[71] They insisted that the judiciary, through this process, would not be second-guessing executive determinations about what is secret or not. That judgment was left "exclusively" to the agency head or the President.[72] Then what room was left for independent judicial judgment? The suggestion by Brennan and Marshall would likely encourage agencies to mark everything remotely related to secret documents as secret. They thought that in camera review of Exemption 1 materials would fulfill the congressional intent for de novo proceedings. A Senate report called de novo review essential "in order that the ultimate decision as to the propriety of the agency's action is made by the court and prevent it from becoming meaningless judicial sanctioning of agency discretion."[73]

A dissent by Justice Douglas focused on President Nixon's action on March 8, 1972, two days after the Court agreed to hear the Mink case. Nixon revoked the previous executive order on classification and issued a new one, stating in the first paragraph: "The interests of the United States and its citizens are best served by making information regarding the affairs of Government readily available to the public. This concept of an informed citizenry is reflected in the Freedom of Information Act and in the current public information policies of the Executive branch."[74] To Douglas, unless trust can be placed in federal judges "the Executive will hold complete sway and by *ipse dixit* [because he said so] make even the time of day 'Top Secret.'"[75]

The 1974 Amendments

Congress reacted to *EPA v. Mink* by amending FOIA to authorize federal judges, as part of their de novo determination, to examine documents covered by Exemption 1 in their chambers.[76] The purpose was to authorize a federal judge "to go behind the official notice of classification and examine the contents of the records themselves."[77] Also, instead of FOIA's language for Exemption 1 ("specifically required by Executive order to be kept secret"), the new language deleted "required" and adopted this language: "authorized under the criteria established by an Executive order to be kept secret." The purpose was to allow federal judges in their chambers to "look at the reason-

---

71. Id. at 99.
72. Id.
73. Id. at 100 (quoting from S. Rept. No. 813, at 8).
74. Id. at 106 (quoting from Executive Order 11652).
75. Id. at 109–10.
76. H. Rept. No. 93-876, 93d Cong., 2d Sess. 2 (1974).
77. Id. at 7.

ableness or propriety of the determination to classify the records under the terms of the Executive order."[78] The statutory provision for in camera review was "permissive and not mandatory."[79]

The Justice Department did not object to in camera inspection of documents covered by Exemptions 2 through 9. However, it opposed any attempt by Congress "to overrule the Supreme Court's decision in *Mink* with respect to classified (exemption 1) documents."[80] The department regarded federal courts as "not equipped to subject to judicial scrutiny Executive determinations that certain documents if disclosed would injure our foreign relations or national defense."[81] What gives attorneys in the Justice Department the ability to decide what is in the interest of foreign relations and national security? The Defense Department also expressed misgivings about allowing federal judges to examine Exemption 1 materials in camera.[82] Under this theory, employees at quite low levels in the Pentagon are entitled to see the documents, but not federal judges.

The FOIA amendments unanimously cleared the House Committee on Government Operations and was agreed to by the House, 383 to 8.[83] The bill, with additional amendments, passed the Senate 64 to 17, emerged from conference committee, and was submitted to President Gerald Ford, who vetoed it.[84] He expressed concern "that our military or intelligence secrets and diplomatic relations could be adversely affected by this bill." He was prepared to accept provisions that enabled courts to "inspect classified documents and review the justification for their classification," but wanted a different procedure: "where classified documents are requested the courts could review the classification, but would have to uphold the classification if there is a reasonable basis to support it. In determining the reasonableness of the classification, the courts would consider all attendant evidence prior to resorting to an *in camera* examination of the document."[85] Offering to submit substitute language, he called the bill "unconstitutional and unworkable."[86] Ford's suggestion mirrored *Reynolds*. Federal judges, without actually seeing the document in camera, would somehow have to decide whether the classification was "reasonable."

78. Id.
79. Id. at 8.
80. Id. at 18.
81. Id.
82. Id. at 23–24.
83. 120 Cong. Rec. 6806, 6819–20 (1974).
84. S. Rept. No. 93-854, 93d Cong., 2d Sess. (1974); 120 Cong. Rec. 17047 (1974); H. Rept. No. 93-1380, 93d Cong., 2d Sess. (1974); S. Rept. No. 93-1200, 93d Cong., 2d Sess. (1974).
85. Public Papers of the Presidents, 1974, at 375.
86. Id. at 376.

Ford's veto message took Congress by surprise. House and Senate conferees had met four times to resolve differences between the chambers and to address concerns raised by the White House. President Ford had written to the conference managers to spell out his objections, and the conferees had modified the bill to accommodate his views.[87] The Senate approved the conference product by voice vote, and it was sustained in the House by the overwhelming margin of 349 to 2. Clearly the votes were there to override a veto, and that is what Congress did. The House voted 371 to 31 for the override, the Senate 65 to 27.[88] With each chamber satisfying the two-thirds margin, the bill became law.

The 1974 legislation changed a number of provisions in FOIA, ranging from the fees charged by agencies for duplicating documents to procedures for law enforcement records. Two sections responded to *EPA v. Mink:* in camera review and the language of Exemption 1. In camera proceedings were authorized but not mandated:

On complaint, the district court of the United States in the district in which the complainant resides, or has his principal place of business, or in which the agency records are situated, or in the District of Columbia, has jurisdiction to enjoin the agency from withholding agency records and to order the production of any agency records improperly withheld from the complainant. In such a case the court shall determine the matter de novo, and may examine the contents of such agency records in camera to determine whether such records or any part thereof shall be withheld under any of the exemptions set forth in subsection (b) of this section, and the burden is on the agency to sustain its action.[89]

Congress redefined Exemption 1 by eliminating the word "required." It now read: "(1) (A) specifically authorized under criteria established by an Executive order to be kept secret in the interest of national defense or foreign policy and (B) are in fact properly classified pursuant to such Executive order."[90] The second part—entirely new—was designed to allow judicial scrutiny of careless and heavy-handed agency classification that is inconsistent with or contrary to the President's executive order. A stamp of "Secret" or some other highly sensitive classification would not automatically block judicial review.

87. 120 Cong. Rec. 34162–64 (1974).
88. Id. at 36633, 36882.
89. 88 Stat. 1562 (1974).
90. Id. at 1562, § 2(a).

In Camera in Practice

Congressional authority for federal courts to conduct in camera review does not mean that in camera proceedings are conducted. It depends on what a trial judge wants to do. For various reasons, courts may decide not to conduct in camera review of Exemption 1 materials. First, district judges might decide that an agency affidavit makes in camera examination unnecessary. Second, in camera review conflicts with the presumption that favors the adversary process. Plaintiff's counsel is excluded from in camera proceedings.[91] Third, court personnel handling classified materials submitted in camera for an Exemption 1 case may need security clearances, even though the trial judge alone reviews the disputed documents.[92] Fourth, the court reporter who transcribes in camera proceedings also needs a security clearance. For these and other complications, a trial judge may decide to forgo in camera review.[93]

To take the burden off courts and place it on agencies (FOIA's express intent), appellate courts have challenged agencies that use broad grounds to withhold documents. An entire document should not be exempt "merely because an isolated portion need not be disclosed."[94] It is "quite possible that part of a document should be kept secret while part should be disclosed."[95] One remedy against overbroad agency claims is to require it to "specify in detail which portions of the document are disclosable and which are allegedly exempt. This could be achieved by formulating a system of itemizing and indexing that would correlate statements made in the Government's refusal justification with the actual portions of the document."[96] To assist the trial judge in analyzing this "Vaughn Index," courts can appoint a special master to examine the documents, in camera if necessary.[97]

This procedure can be used to separate the secret from the nonsecret.[98] It applies as well to Exemption 1 materials that involve the field of national

---

91. U.S. Department of Justice, Freedom of Information Act Guide & Private Act Overview 158 (2004).

92. Id. For some early assessments on in camera inspections under FOIA, see Ronald M. Levin, "In Camera Inspections Under the Freedom of Information Act," 41 U. Chi. L. Rev. 557 (1974); Note, "National Security and the Public's Right to Know: A New Role for the Courts Under the Freedom of Information Act," 123 U. Pa. L. Rev. 1438 (1975); and Note, "*In Camera* Inspection of National Security Files Under the Freedom of Information Act," 26 Kans. L. Rev. 617 (1978).

93. 1 James T. O'Reilly, Federal Information Disclosure 532–35 (2000).

94. Vaughn v. Rosen, 484 F.2d 820, 825 (D.C. Cir. 1973).

95. Id.

96. Id. at 827.

97. Id. at 828.

98. Cuneo v. Schlesinger, 484 F.2d 1086, 1091–92 (D.C. Cir. 1973).

security.[99] Some courts decline to use in camera inspection unless the agency's record is too vague or too sweeping, or has demonstrated a record that shows bad faith.[100]

Rejected Rule 509

Various efforts have been made over the years to define "state secrets." Experts with long experience in the legal profession, in private practice and on the bench, have tried their hand at discovering the right mix and sequence of words. Proposed definitions are drafted, circulated, and voted on. Repeatedly they are rejected as circular, vague, and open-ended, offering little in the way of helpful standards. Definitions invariably fail because they rely on inherently ambiguous and subjective words, such as "secret" and "national defense."

An Advisory Committee on Rules of Evidence, appointed by Chief Justice Warren in March 1965, held its initial meeting and began work three months later. The committee consisted of 15 members, including eight trial attorneys, the head of the Criminal Appeals Division of the Justice Department, law professors, and federal judges. They met four to five times a year at meetings that lasted three to five days. After its last meeting in December 1968, the committee completed a preliminary draft of proposed rules of evidence and submitted them to Judge Albert B. Maris, who chaired the Standing Committee on Rules of Practice and Procedure. Among the many proposals was Rule 5-09, covering "secret of state." It began with this definition: "A 'secret of state' is information not open or theretofore officially disclosed to the public concerning the national defense or the international relations of the United States."[101]

Duties of a Judge

The definition clearly applied only to *public* access, not to the right of Congress or the judiciary to see confidential documents. The committee recognized that the government "has a privilege to refuse to give evidence and to prevent any person from giving evidence upon a showing of substantial danger that the evidence will disclose a secret of state."[102] Picking up language and ideas from *Reynolds,* the committee said that the privilege may be claimed

99. Ray v. Turner, 587 F.2d 1187 (D.C. Cir. 1978).
100. Weissman v. Central Intelligence Agency, 565 F.2d 692, 698 (D.C. Cir. 1977).
101. 46 F.R.D. 272 (1969).
102. Id. at 273.

only by the chief officer of the department administering the subject matter that the secret concerned. The chief officer would be required to make a showing to the judge, "in whole or in part in the form of a written statement." The trial judge "may hear the matter in chambers, but all counsel are entitled to inspect the claim and showing and to be heard thereon."[103] The judge "may take any protective measure which the interests of the government and the furtherance of justice may require."[104]

If a judge sustained a claim of privilege for a state secret in a case involving the government as a party, the court would have several options. If sustaining the claim deprived a private party of "material evidence," the judge could make "any further orders which the interests of justice require, including striking the testimony of a witness, declaring a mistrial, finding against the government upon an issue as to which the evidence is relevant, or dismissing the action."[105] Finding against the government was the path taken by Judge Kirkpatrick and the Third Circuit. The Supreme Court in *Reynolds* supported the government.

A note prepared by the advisory committee explained that the showing needed by the government to claim the privilege "represents a compromise between the complete abdication of judicial control which would result from accepting as final the decision of a departmental officer and the infringement upon security which would attend a requirement of complete disclosure to the judge, even though it be *in camera*."[106] Left unexplained was what would happen if a judge countermanded the judgment of a departmental official. Apparently the document could be read in chambers and perhaps even shared with plaintiff's attorney, but "all counsel are entitled to inspect the claim," and the information in the document would therefore not be made public. The draft placed final control with the judge, not the agency head.

A Second Draft

Because of that feature and others, the Justice Department strongly opposed the draft. It wanted the proposed rule changed to recognize that the executive's classification of information as a state secret was final and binding on judges.[107] In March 1971, Judge Maris released a revised draft, which renumbered the rule from 5-09 to 509 and eliminated the definition of "a secret of

103. Id.
104. Id.
105. Id. at 273–74.
106. Id. at 274.
107. 26 Federal Practice and Procedure 423 (Wright and Graham eds. 1992) (hereafter Federal Practice and Procedure).

state." It was therefore necessary to strike "secret" from various places in the rule. The new draft rewrote the general rule of privilege to prevent any person from giving evidence upon a showing of "reasonable likelihood of danger that the disclosure of the evidence will be detrimental or injurious to the national defense or the international relations of the United States."[108] Final control remained with the judge.

The Justice Department had wanted to add a qualified privilege for "official information," defined as "information within the custody or control of a governmental department or agency, either initiated within the department or agency or acquired by it in the exercise of its official responsibilities."[109] This concept, which seemed a throwback to executive interpretations of the Housekeeping Statute, was rejected by the advisory committee, which reviewed a number of statutory changes following *Reynolds,* including the 1958 amendment to the Housekeeping Statute and passage of the Freedom of Information Act of 1966.[110] Also, "official information" seemed wholly out of place in a rule designed for state secrets.

In addition to opposition from the Justice Department, several prominent members of Congress voiced their objections, partly because of the procedure used to adopt rules of evidence for the courts (giving Congress only 90 days to disapprove). Objections were also aimed at Rule 509, which some lawmakers thought weakened the Court's decision in *Reynolds.*[111] Senator John McClellan, a senior member of the Judiciary Committee, wrote to Judge Maris on August 12, 1971, offering a detailed critique of 17 rules. One was 509.[112] A few days earlier, Deputy Attorney General Richard Kleindienst forwarded his views on the proposed rules of evidence, identifying 30 areas of concern. He highlighted three in a cover letter to Judge Maris. The first was Rule 509. Kleindienst wanted the rule rewritten to recognize that the government had a privilege not to disclose "official information if such disclosure would be contrary to the public interest."[113] The Justice Department insisted that once a departmental official, pursuant to executive order, decided to classify information affecting national security, that judgment must be regarded as having "conclusive weight" in determining state secrets unless the classification was "clearly arbitrary and capricious."[114]

---

108. 51 F.R.D. 375 (1971).
109. 26 Federal Practice and Procedure 423 (Note 10).
110. 51 F.R.D. 377 (1971).
111. 117 Cong. Rec. 29894–96 (1971).
112. Id. at 33644.
113. Id. at 33648.
114. Id. at 33652–53.

How would that procedure actually function? Who would decide that the classification was clearly arbitrary and capricious, and on what grounds? Apparently a judge. Otherwise the check against arbitrariness and capriciousness would remain entirely within the executive branch. But a judge could not intelligently reach a conclusion without examining the document.

A Final Try

The Supreme Court sent the proposed rules of evidence to Congress on February 5, 1973, to take effect on July 1, 1973. New language for Rule 509 included a redrafted definition of secret of state: "A 'secret of state' is a governmental secret relating to the national defense or the international relations of the United States."[115] The Justice Department recommendation for "official information" was piggybacked to this new version of Rule 509. The rule defined "official information" as information within the custody of an executive department "the disclosure of which is shown to be contrary to the public interest."[116] Official information consisted of:

(A) intragovernmental opinions or recommendations submitted for consideration in the performance of decisional or policymaking functions, or (B) subject to the provisions of 18 U.S.C. § 3500 [regarding witness statements], investigatory files compiled for law enforcement purposes and not otherwise available, or (C) information within the custody or control of a governmental department or agency whether initiated within the department or agency or acquired by it in its exercise of its official responsibilities and not otherwise available to the public pursuant to 5 U.S.C. § 552 [FOIA].[117]

Section (C) was basically an effort by the Justice Department to revive the original Housekeeping Statute and executive interpretations attached to it. This section would modify, if not reverse, the 1958 amendment. The three sections had little to do with state secrets. Section (A) contained elements that are usually included in assertions of executive privilege. The Justice Department decided to take the three sections and shoehorn them into a rule designed for state secrets.

As for the remainder of the new Rule 509, the words "secret of state" and "secret information" were inserted in Sections (B) and (C). The privilege for

115. 56 F.R.D. 251 (1973).
116. Id.
117. Id.

state secrets would have to be claimed by the chief officer of a government agency or department, whereas the privilege for "official information" could be asserted "by an attorney representing the government."[118] Contrary to earlier precedents where the President would have to invoke executive privilege, that step could now be taken by any attorney representing the government.

Congress concluded that it lacked time to review all of the proposed rules of evidence within 90 days and vote to disapprove particular ones. Under stringent time constraints, it decided to reverse the burden from legislative disapproval to approval. On February 7, 1973, the Senate passed by voice vote a bill to provide that the proposed rules "shall have no force or effect" prior to the adjournment of the first session of the 93d Congress (end of 1973) unless expressly approved by Congress before that time.[119] Approval never came. The House debated the Senate bill on March 14. Clearly the proposed rules contained lots of provisions that alienated Democrats and Republicans, liberals and conservatives. On a roll call vote, the House passed the Senate bill 399 to 1. Among the rejected rules was Rule 509.[120]

Action in 1975

Congress passed the rules of evidence in 1975, including Rule 501 on privileges. It comes down squarely on the side of authorizing courts to decide the scope of a privilege. The rule covers all parties to a case, including the government. Rule 501 does not recognize any authority on the part of the executive branch to dictate the scope of a privilege. There is no acknowledgment of state secrets or "official information." The only exception in Rule 501 concerns civil actions at the state level:

> Except as otherwise required by the Constitution of the United States or provided by Act of Congress or in rules prescribed by the Supreme Court pursuant to statutory authority, the privilege of a witness, person, government, State, or political subdivision thereof shall be governed by the principles of the common law as they *may be interpreted by the courts* of the United States in the light of reason and experience. However, in civil actions and proceedings, with respect to an element of a claim or defense as to which State law supplies the rule of decision, the privilege

118. Id. at 251–52.
119. 119 Cong. Rec. 3755 (1973).
120. Id. at 7651–52. For a review of the legislative defeat of the proposed rules of evidence, including Rule 509, see 26 Federal Practice and Procedure 415–58.

of a witness, person, government, State, or political subdivision thereof shall be determined in accordance with State law.[121]

The legislative history of Rule 501 explains how and why the provisions on state secrets and "official information" were deleted.[122] When the bill reached the House floor, it came with a closed rule that prohibited amendments to it. The privileges covered by the rule (including government secrets, husband and wife, and physician and patient) were considered "matters of substantive law" rather than rules of evidence: "we were so divided on that subject ourselves, let alone what the House would be, that we would never get a bill if we got bogged down in that subject matter which really ought to be taken up separately in separate legislation."[123] The Senate Judiciary Committee also reported on the fractious nature of the rule on privileges: "Critics attacked, and proponents defended, the secrets of state and official information privileges," the husband-wife privilege "drew fire," the doctor-patient privilege "seemed to satisfy no one," the attorney-client privilege "came in for its share of criticism," and many objections were voiced over the failure to include a newsman's privilege.[124] Under these cross-pressures, Congress abandoned Rule 509.

FISA Court

Before 1978, Congress had never enacted legislation to regulate the government's use of electronic surveillance within the United States for foreign intelligence purposes. With reports in the early 1970s of executive branch abuse of electronic eavesdropping justified on the ground of "national security"—without ever seeking or obtaining a court warrant—Congress felt compelled to act. The Supreme Court had consistently ducked the issue. The FISA statute of 1978 brought federal judges into close contact with national security intelligence. It required approval from a special court before the executive branch could engage in electronic surveillance within the United States for purposes of obtaining foreign intelligence information. Judges on the court, the Foreign Intelligence Surveillance Court (FISC), are appointed by the Chief Justice to review applications submitted by government attorneys.[125]

121. 88 Stat. 1933–34 (1975) (emphasis added).
122. H. Rept. No. 93-650, 93d Cong., 1st Sess. 8 (1973).
123. 120 Cong. Rec. 1409 (1974) (statement by Rep. Dennis).
124. S. Rept. No. 93-1277, 93d Cong., 2d Sess 6 (1974).
125. 92 Stat. 1788, § 103 (1978).

FISA grew out of a long-standing practice of the executive branch engaging in electronic surveillance without first obtaining a court warrant. The Fourth Amendment of the U.S. Constitution provides: "The right of the people to be secure in their persons, houses, papers, and effects, against unreasonable searches and seizures, shall not be violated, and no Warrants shall issue, but upon probable cause, supported by Oath or affirmation, and particularly describing the place to be searched, and the persons or things to be seized." The Fourth Amendment has never required warrants for every search and seizure to make them reasonable. There are too many exceptions to the warrant requirement to accept that interpretation.

An early (and continuing) exception to the warrant requirement are the border searches that take place at ports of entry to prevent the introduction of contraband into the country.[126] Warrantless searches are also allowed when an individual grants consent, for "hot pursuit" and no-knock entry, the "plain view" doctrine, "stop and frisk," and many other exceptions that have developed outside the warrant requirement.[127] The government practice that has raised the greatest concern was electronic eavesdropping done in the name of national security.

Early Practices

The Supreme Court first confronted electronic eavesdropping when it reviewed the use of wiretaps by Prohibition agents in the 1920s to monitor and intercept telephone calls. In the 1928 *Olmstead* case, the Court reasoned that there was no violation of the Fourth Amendment because the taps did not enter the premises of a home or business. Hence there was neither "search" nor "seizure."[128] Congress, finding that interpretation inadequate, passed Section 605 of the Federal Communications Act of 1934 to make it a crime to intercept or to use any wire or radio communication for surveillance. That statute prevented the government from introducing at trial any information obtained from a wiretap.[129]

In the 1930s, the executive branch followed a divided policy on wiretapping. The Bureau of Investigation (later the Federal Bureau of Investigation) regarded wiretapping as unethical and impermissible under the regulations issued by the Attorney General. The Bureau of Prohibition, located with the Department of the Treasury, freely engaged in wiretapping. Congress consid-

126. Fisher, American Constitutional Law, at 703–4.
127. Id. at 704–17.
128. Olmstead v. United States, 277 U.S. 438 (1928).
129. Nardone v. United States, 302 U.S. 379 (1937); Weiss v. United States, 308 U.S. 321 (1939); Nardone v. United States, 308 U.S. 338 (1939).

ered, but never passed, statutory prohibitions on wiretapping by the Bureau of Prohibition. The agency was abolished after the states ratified the 21st Amendment in 1933, repealing the constitutional prohibition on liquor.

In the early 1940s, committee reports from the House of Representatives recommended that certain federal agencies be authorized to wiretap for purposes of national security, including investigations into sabotage, treason, seditious conspiracy, espionage, and violations of the neutrality law. The House passed such a bill in 1940 but the Senate took no action. After the attack on Pearl Harbor on December 7, 1941, the House passed legislation to authorize wiretapping for national security purposes. Once again, the Senate did not act.

Denied statutory authority for wiretapping, Attorney General Robert H. Jackson issued this order to the Bureau of Investigation: "Wire tapping: Telephone or telegraph wires shall not be tapped unless prior authorization of the Director of the Bureau has been secured."[130] On May 21, 1940, President Franklin D. Roosevelt sent a confidential memo to Jackson that permitted wiretapping in selected areas. Bureau investigating agents were "at liberty to secure information by listening devices direct to the conversation of other communications of persons suspected of subversive activities against the United States, including suspected spies." These investigations were to be limited "in so far as possible to aliens."[131]

The Court wrestled with new forms of technological intrusion. Federal agents used a "detectaphone," placed against the wall of a room, to hear conversations on the other side. The Court found no violation of the Fourth Amendment.[132] Law enforcement officers entered the home of a suspect and installed a concealed microphone in the hall. A hole bored in the roof allowed wires to transmit sounds to a nearby garage. Although a trespass and probably a burglary had occurred, the Court found no violation of Section 605.[133] In another case, government agents pushed an electronic listening device through the wall of an adjoining house until it touched the heating duct of a suspect's house. Through the use of this "spike mike," officers with earphones could listen to conversations taking place on both floors of the house. This time the Court found a violation of the Fourth Amendment.[134]

In 1967, the Court finally overturned the "trespass" doctrine announced in *Olmstead* and other holdings. By a vote of 7 to 1, the Court declared unconstitutional the placing of electronic listening and recording devices on

130. 86 Cong. Rec. A1471 (1940).
131. Fisher, American Constitutional Law, at 730.
132. Goldman v. United States, 316 U.S. 129 (1942).
133. Irvine v. California, 347 U.S. 128 (1954).
134. Silverman v. United States, 365 U.S. 505 (1961).

the outside of public telephone booths to obtain incriminating evidence. Although there was no physical entrance into the area occupied by the suspect, individuals had a legitimate expectation of privacy within the phone booth. To the Court, the case involved issues of domestic—not national security—policy: "Whether safeguards other than prior authorization by a magistrate would satisfy the Fourth Amendment in a situation involving the national security is not a question presented by this case."[135] Responding to this decision, Congress passed legislation in 1968 requiring law enforcement officers to obtain a warrant before placing taps on phones or installing concealed microphones. The statute also explained that nothing in it or Section 605 of the Communications Act of 1934

> shall limit the constitutional power of the President to take such measures as he deems necessary to protect the Nation against actual or potential attack or other hostile acts of a foreign power, to obtain foreign intelligence information deemed essential to the security of the United States, or to protect national security information against foreign intelligence activities. Nor shall anything contained in this chapter be deemed to limit the constitutional power of the President to take such measures as he deems necessary to protect the United States against the overthrow of the Government by force or other lawful means, or against any other clear and present danger to the structure or existence of the Government.[136]

Congress did not authorize warrantless national security searches, but did not prohibit them either. However, it placed some limits: "The contents of any wire or oral communication intercepted by authority of the President in the exercise of the foregoing powers may be received in evidence in any trial, hearing, or other proceeding only where such interception was reasonable, and shall not be otherwise used or disclosed except as is necessary to implement that power." For the government to introduce into court evidence it obtained by wiretapping, it had to convince a judge that the interception was reasonable. When Congress enacted FISA, it repealed the passage indented above and made statutory policy the "exclusive means" for authorizing wiretaps and other forms of surveillance in the United States.[137] As noted in a Senate report, the new statutory framework "[put] to rest the notion that

---

135. Katz v. United States, 389 U.S. 347, 358 (Note 23) (1967).
136. 82 Stat. 214 (1968).
137. 18 U.S.C. § 2511(2)(f) (2000).

Congress recognizes an inherent Presidential policy to conduct such surveillances in the United States outside of [statutory] procedures."[138]

The Need for Statutory Action

A unanimous decision by the Supreme Court in 1972 held that the 1968 law merely disclaimed congressional intent to define presidential powers in matters affecting national security and did not authorize warrantless national security surveillance. In the particular dispute before the Court, it ruled that the Fourth Amendment required prior judicial approval for surveillance of domestic organizations. It specifically avoided the question of surveillance over foreign powers, whether within or outside the country.[139] The Court invited Congress to pass legislation to clarify national policy.[140] The decision put pressure on lawmakers to revisit the issue of national security wiretaps and decide what procedures were needed to accompany them.

Congress drafted the FISA legislation at the same time that the country became aware that the Nixon administration had wiretapped 17 government officials and newsmen between May 1969 and February 1971. The first press reports of those activities surfaced in February 1973 and were officially acknowledged in May 1973, when William Ruckelshaus, as FBI Acting Director, discovered that records of the taps had been removed from the FBI and taken to the White House.[141] The Justice Department also admitted that members of Congress and their staffs had been wiretapped by the government.[142] The general premise of FISA was that whenever an electronic surveillance for foreign intelligence purposes involves the Fourth Amendment right of any U.S. person, "approval for such a surveillance should come from a neutral and impartial magistrate."[143] The scope of national security searches was not left to independent and unreviewable decisions by the President and his advisers.

FISA permits the President, through the Attorney General, to authorize electronic surveillance to obtain foreign intelligence information for periods

138. S. Rept. No. 95-604(I), 95th Cong., 2d Sess. 64 (1978).
139. United States v. United States District Court, 407 U.S. 297 (1972).
140. Id. at 322.
141. "Warrantless Wiretapping and Electronic Surveillance," report by the Subcommittee on Surveillance of the Senate Committee on Foreign Relations and the Subcommittee on Administrative Practice and Procedure of the Senate Committee on the Judiciary, 94th Cong., 1st Sess. 5 (Comm. Print, February 1975).
142. Id. at 10.
143. H. Rept. No. 95-1283, Pt. I, 95th Cong., 2d Sess. 24–25 (1978). Also on the legislative history of FISA, see S. Rept. No. 604, 95th Cong., 1st Sess. (1997), S. Rept. No. 95-701, 95th Cong., 2d Sess. (1978), and H. Rept. No. 95-1720, 95th Cong., 2d Sess. (1978).

of up to one year. In such cases the Attorney General must certify in writing, under oath, certain details about the surveillance. He then transmits a copy of that certification under seal to the FISA court, which has jurisdiction to hear applications for and to grant orders approving electronic surveillance anywhere within the United States. The certification remains sealed unless the court, with two exceptions, decides to unseal it.[144] If the Attorney General determines that an emergency situation exists that requires electronic surveillance before a court order can be obtained, he may authorize the emergency use after informing the judge.[145] These emergency actions are for short periods of time, originally 24 hours and now 72 hours as a result of legislation passed in 2001 after the September 11, 2001, terrorist attacks. Without judicial approval they must terminate.[146] If a federal court determines that a surveillance was not lawfully exercised or conducted, it shall suppress the evidence.[147]

The FISA Court in Action

The 1978 statute authorized seven district court judges to serve on the FISA court. Three other judges constitute a court of review. The USA Patriot Act of 2001 increased the court to eleven judges.[148] The only lawyers who argue before the court are from the Justice Department when they submit applications for intelligence surveillance. The court meets in a windowless, highly protected courtroom on the sixth floor of the Justice Department. A rare instance of a published opinion occurred in June 1981, when Presiding Judge George L. Hart Jr. ruled that FISA judges in at least three previous secret orders had overstepped their authority.[149]

The jurisdiction of the FISA court has expanded over the years. Although it was initially limited to approving applications for national security wiretaps (including physical entries to plant eavesdropping devices), in 1994 Congress empowered the court to also authorize physical searches for the purpose of obtaining foreign intelligence.[150] The Justice Department argued that such searches could be defended as part of the President's power to protect national security, but thought it would be safer to have statutory support and

---

144. 92 Stat. 1787, § 102(a)(3) (1978); 50 U.S.C. § 1802 (2000).

145. 50 U.S.C. § 1805(f) (2000).

146. 115 Stat. 1402, §§ 314(a)(1) and 314(a)(2)(B) (2001); 50 U.S.C. § 1801 (Supp. II 2002).

147. 92 Stat. 1794, § 106(g); 50 U.S.C. § 1806(g) (2000).

148. 115 Stat. 272, 283, § 208 (2001).

149. Larry Tell, "The Cloak-and-Dagger Court," National Law Journal, August 10, 1981, at 1, 60.

150. 108 Stat. 3443–53 (1994).

the support of Congress and the judiciary.[151] By the end of 1993, the FISA court had heard 7,554 electronic surveillance cases and had never rejected a government request.[152]

No sitting judge of the FISA court had ever given a public speech about the court until April 4, 1997, when District Judge Royce Lamberth gave a breakfast speech sponsored by the American Bar Association's Standing Committee on Law and National Security. He said the information the court handled was classified either Secret or Top Secret for national security reasons. Speaking at a time when Janet Reno was the Attorney General, he and the other judges of the FISA court found the applications submitted to it "well-scrubbed by the attorney general and her staff before they are presented to us."[153] As to the statistical record showing that no applications had been formally denied by the court, he pointed out that some had been revised and others withdrawn and then resubmitted with additional supporting information.[154] He added that all of the district and circuit courts that had reviewed a FISA court order in a subsequent criminal prosecution had upheld the FISA court's action and that the Supreme Court had never granted certiorari in those cases.[155] In these lower court actions, a district judge would conduct an in camera review of the application submitted to the FISA order to determine whether the surveillance had probable cause.[156]

The uninterrupted pattern of FISA court support for government requests came to an end on May 17, 2002, when the court challenged the government's position that FISA can be used "primarily for a law enforcement purpose, so long as a significant foreign intelligence purpose remains." The court disclosed that the Clinton administration had included errors in 75 FISA applications, and that additional errors appeared in applications submitted by the George W. Bush administration. The court was particularly troubled by an inadequate "wall" between FISA information-gathering and criminal investigations. It charged that procedures adopted by the administration in March 2002 seemed designed to amend the law.[157] The three-judge court of review reversed the FISA court and upheld the authority of criminal prosecutors to be actively involved in foreign intelligence wiretaps.[158] This activity of

151. Benjamin Wittes, "Surveillance Court Gets New Powers," Legal Times, November 7, 1994, at 1.

152. Id. at 22.

153. "Intelligence on the FISA Court," Legal Times, April 14, 1997, at 18.

154. Id.

155. Id.

156. For example, United States v. Isa, 923 F.2d 1300, 1303 (8th Cir. 1991).

157. In re All Matters to Foreign Intelligence Surveil., 218 F.Supp. 2d 611 (Foreign Intel. Surv. Ct. 2002).

158. In re Sealed Case, 310 F.3d 717 (Foreign Intel. Surv. Ct. of Rev. 2002).

the FISA court was remarkable for many reasons, including the publication of both decisions.

The "Graymail" Statute

Over the years, the government's effort to prosecute individuals in national security cases ran into problems. As part of a defense strategy, the accused could threaten to make public certain documents that had been classified. The government could press ahead at the risk of having the classified material disclosed. Prosecution of a defendant for disclosing national security information often threatened to disclose the very information the laws sought to protect. Unwilling to let that happen, the government might decide to drop the case. A Senate report in 1978 explained that the "more sensitive the information compromised, the more difficult it becomes to enforce the laws that guard our national security." The government "must often choose between disclosing classified information in the prosecution or letting the conduct go unpunished." A Justice Department official asked: "To what extent must we harm the national security in order to protect the national security?"[159]

Congress drafted legislation to provide pretrial procedures to enable a trial judge to rule on classified information in camera before the defendant tried to introduce the evidence in open court. The defendant would have to put the government on notice of all motions he might make, including the use of witnesses from the intelligence community, that would require the discovery and disclosure of intelligence information. This pretrial stage allows the government to calculate the damage to national security if the prosecution continued. The judge can allow the government to prepare a substitute statement, containing the relevant facts, provided it does not prejudice the defendant's right to a fair trial.[160]

If the government objects to an order requiring disclosure of the classified information, the judge can consider various sanctions, including dismissing specified counts of the indictment or the entire case. The Attorney General may file with the court an affidavit objecting to disclosure.[161] In the event the judge authorizes the disclose of classified information, or imposes sanctions against the government for failing to disclose the information, the government can take the dispute to a court of appeals. Congress directed circuit courts to act expeditiously on those appeals.[162]

159. S. Rept. No. 96-823, 96th Cong., 2d Sess. 2 (1980).
160. Id. at 4.
161. 94 Stat. 2028, § 6(e) (1980).
162. Id., § 7.

The Classified Information Procedures Act (CIPA) is known as the "Graymail" statute. That label implies unscrupulous and manipulative conduct on the part of a defendant, forcing the government to drop the prosecution and allow criminal activity to go unpunished. However, legitimate defense efforts to obtain or disclose classified information can also present the government "with the same 'disclose or dismiss' dilemma."[163] To iron out disputes at the pretrial stage, the legislation authorizes a judge to meet in camera with both the prosecution and the defense present.[164]

The statute defines classified information as "any information or material that had been determined by the United States Government pursuant to an Executive order, statute, or regulation, to require protection against unauthorized disclosure for reasons of national security."[165] That kind of sensitive information is now entrusted to judicial review. As with FISA, Congress placed in CIPA security procedures that requires the Chief Justice, in consultation with the Attorney General, the CIA Director, and the Secretary of Defense, to prescribe rules to protect against unauthorized disclosure of any classified information.[166]

Lessons Learned in Court

Two Supreme Court decisions in the early 1970s revealed how the executive branch can use "secrecy" to protect not the national interest, or national security, but rather its own internal problems, including efforts to cover up criminal activities. At times concealment is performed by White House aides trying to protect the President. The President may also decide to personally withhold information from Congress and the courts. In these disputes, the Solicitor General can end up misleading Supreme Court Justices about "grave risks" to national security. The political education of Watergate helped dislodge the judiciary from its passive attitude after World War II, when it regularly deferred to presidential claims about military and diplomatic affairs. In 1948, for example, the Court regarded it as "intolerable that courts, without the relevant information, should review and perhaps nullify actions of the Executive taken on information properly held secret. Nor can courts sit *in camera* in order to be taken into executive confidences. But even if courts

---

163. S. Rept. No. 96-823, at 3 (testimony of Assistant Attorney General Philip Heymann).
164. Id. at 7.
165. 94 Stat. 2025, § 1(a) (1980).
166. Id. at 2029, § 9.

could require full disclosure, the very nature of executive decisions as to foreign policy is political, not judicial."[167]

The Court jettisoned that argument four years later with the Steel Seizure Case, striking down President Truman's seizure of steel mills needed to prosecute the war in Korea. The matter was judicial, not political. Gradually the judiciary gained a deeper appreciation of the role it needs to play in matters of foreign policy and national security. Judicial attitudes also changed as a result of statutory grants of power that authorized judges to review classified information in camera and to sit in judgment of executive branch requests for national security wiretaps.

The Pentagon Papers

In 1971, the Supreme Court decided that newspapers were constitutionally entitled to publish a multivolume Defense Department secret study that revealed a pattern of deceptive administration statements about the war in Vietnam. Daniel Ellsberg, one of several analysts who had worked on the study, reproduced 43 of the 47 volumes and gave them to Senator J. William Fulbright. He shared parts of the study with analysts at the Institute for Policy Studies and turned over most of the material to reporter Neil Sheehan of the *New York Times*.[168] The *Washington Post* gained access to some of the documents.[169] More than a dozen other newspapers began publishing parts of what became known as the Pentagon Papers.[170]

The government, moving to prevent publication of the study, initiated separate lawsuits to prosecute Ellsberg and others for leaking the study. Protecting secrets was not the initial reason within the Nixon administration for these legal actions. Nixon and his aides understood that release of the Pentagon study had convenient political value because it damaged the reputations of the Kennedy and Johnson administrations.[171] Moreover, Nixon was prepared to release secret documents to the public concerning the alleged involvement of the Kennedy administration in the assassination of the president of South Vietnam, Ngo Dinh Diem.[172]

A brief prepared by Solicitor General Erwin N. Griswold advised the Court that publication of the Pentagon Papers would pose a "grave and immediate

167. C.&S. Air Lines v. Waterman Corp., 333 U.S. 103, 111 (1948).
168. John Prados and Margaret Pratt Porter, eds., Inside the Pentagon Papers 7–8 (2004).
169. Id. at 57.
170. Id. at 191.
171. Id. at 91, 92, 96, 103, 114.
172. Id. at 59, 85, 88.

danger to the security of the United States."[173] He construed "immediate" to mean "irreparable,"[174] and he reminded the Court that it recognized in *Reynolds* "that the President is uniquely qualified to determine whether the disclosure of 'military and state secrets' would result in danger to the national security."[175]

During oral argument, Griswold identified several items that he said were properly classified as Top Secret.[176] He read language from an executive order that defined Top Secret as information "which requires the highest degree of protection." The Top Secret classification "shall be applied only to that information or material that the defense aspect of which is paramount and the unauthorized disclosure of which could result in exceptionally grave damage to the Nation, such as, leading to the definite break in diplomatic relations affecting the defense of the United States; and an armed attack against the United States or its allies; a war or the compromise of military or defense plans, or intelligence operations; or scientific or technological developments vital to the national defense."[177] Releasing the Pentagon Papers to the public, Griswold warned, "would be of extraordinary seriousness to the security of the United States."[178] Publication of the materials "will affect lives. It will affect the process of the termination of the war. It will affect the process of recovering prisoners of war."[179] Divided 6 to 3, the Court decided that the government had failed to meet the heavy burden needed to place prior restraints on publication.[180]

In a speech in 1984, Griswold described the process he used in trying to identify items in the volumes that, if disclosed, would be a "real threat" to the security of the United States. The study contained seven million words. If one read "them all at a pretty rapid rate of speech, it would take seven weeks— and I had a few hours."[181] He asked three people from the Defense Department, the State Department, and the National Security Agency to tell him "what are the things in this which are really bad." They picked 42 items. He went through those selections, "scanning—I couldn't read everything—and I

173. 71 Landmark Briefs 127 (1975).
174. Id. at 129.
175. Id. at 139.
176. Id. at 221.
177. Id. at 229.
178. Id. at 221.
179. Id. at 228.
180. New York Times Co. v. United States, 403 U.S. 713 (1971).
181. Erwin N. Griswold, "The Pentagon Papers Case: A Personal Footnote," Yearbook 1984, Supreme Court Historical Society, at 115.

picked out eleven of the forty-two and I waived everything else."[182] Years later, in an op-ed piece written in 1989 after the volumes had been made public, Griswold admitted that he had never seen "any trace of a threat to the national security" from their publication.[183] The principal concern of executive officials who classify documents, he said, "is not with national security, but rather with governmental embarrassment of one sort or another."[184]

Nixon aide H. R. Haldeman concluded that publication of the Pentagon Papers was damaging, but not to national security. The Pentagon Papers undercut the credibility of the government and the President. The public would learn "you can't trust the government; you can't believe what they say; and you can't rely on their judgment; and the implicit infallibility of presidents, which has been an accepted thing in America, is badly hurt by this, because it shows that people do things the President wants to do even though it's wrong, and the President can be wrong."[185]

Some have argued that the Pentagon Papers did contain "real secrets" harmful to the nation if published. Whitney North Seymour Jr., lead counsel for the government in the Pentagon Papers case in New York, argued that a "large number of the documents posed immediate threats to United States military operations and diplomatic relations."[186] His observations relied on David Rudenstine's book, *The Day the Presses Stopped,* published in 1996. Rudenstine, however, did not identify particular documents and demonstrate how they harmed the United States. His views were tentative and speculative. A government document "alleged" injury, another "potentially threatened important national security interests," some "would likely" close up diplomatic channels, and others "might" reduce the rate of American troop withdrawals from Vietnam.[187] Rudenstein stated, quite cautiously: "it now appears that the Pentagon Papers did contain some information that could have inflicted some injury—at least to a degree that makes the concerns of national security officials understandable—if disclosed, which it was not."[188] At the end of the book, he appears to find no harm done: "There is no evidence that the newspapers' publication of the Pentagon Papers, followed by the three books

---

182. Id. at 116.

183. Erwin N. Griswold, "Secrets Not Worth Keeping," Washington Post, February 15, 1989, at A25.

184. Id. For the text of this op-ed, see Fisher, American Constitutional Law, at 274–75.

185. H. R. Haldeman to President Nixon, June 14, 1971, 3:09 P.M. meeting; http://www.gwu.edu/~nsarchiv/NSAEBB/NSAEBB48/.

186. Whitney North Seymour Jr., "At Last, the Truth Is Out," 19 Cardozo L. Rev. 1359, 1359 (1998).

187. David Rudenstein, The Day the Presses Stopped: A History of the Pentagon Papers Case 8–9 (1996).

188. Id. at 9. See also at 84–87, 195–201, 218–24, 267–72, 326–29.

during the summer and fall of 1971, harmed the U.S. military, defense, intelligence, or international affairs interests."[189]

The Supreme Court did not prepare a written decision. Instead, it delivered a short per curiam allowing publication, followed by a series of concurrences by individual Justices. In one, Justice Stewart spoke approvingly of independent presidential power: "If the Constitution gives the Executive a large degree of unshared power in the conduct of foreign affairs and the maintenance of our national defense, then under the Constitution the Executive must have the largely unshared duty to determine and preserve the degree of internal security necessary to exercise that power successfully."[190] This passage presents several problems. The first clause begins with a ringing *if*. What if the Constitution does not give the President a large degree of unshared power in the conduct of foreign affairs and the maintenance of our national defense? What if the President must depend on Congress for appropriations to support his conduct of foreign affairs and the maintenance of national defense? Second, there is no necessary connection between the two clauses. The President's largely unshared power *to conduct* foreign affairs does not imply a largely unshared power *to make* national security policy.

The conduct and implementation of foreign policy usually means policy jointly arrived at by Congress and the President. That is especially the case for the "maintenance of our national defense," which requires congressional authorizations and appropriations. In the field of foreign affairs, the Constitution does not give "a large degree of unshared power" to either Congress or the President. Later in his concurrence Justice Stewart acknowledged that the President does not possess a monopoly: "This is not to say that Congress and the courts have no role to play."[191] Congress, through such statutes as FISA and CIPA, can vest important national security powers with the judiciary.

In his dissent, Justice Harlan agreed that the judiciary "must review the initial Executive determination to the point of satisfying itself that the subject matter of the dispute does lie within the proper compass of the President's foreign relations power." Citing language in *Reynolds,* he said that constitutional considerations forbid "a complete abandonment of judicial control."[192] Yet instead of having a federal judge examine the documents, Harlan was satisfied if the head of an executive department determined that disclosure would "irreparably impair the national security." For additional authority, Harlan looked to the British case of *Duncan v. Cammell, Laird & Co.* (1942).[193]

189. Id. at 327.
190. New York Times Co. v. United States, 403 U.S. at 728–29.
191. Id. at 730.
192. Id. at 757 (citing United States v. Reynolds, 345 U.S. at 8).
193. Id.

The Watergate Tapes

To prevent the kind of leaks that occurred with the Pentagon Papers, President Nixon created a "Plumbers Unit," which led, within a few years, to his resignation from office. In June 1972, five people were arrested while trying to burglarize the headquarters of the National Democratic Committee at the Watergate complex. It was quickly established that others were involved and they could be traced to the Republican Committee to Re-elect the President. In August, President Nixon offered advice that would later come back to haunt him: "What really hurts in matters of this sort is not the fact that they occur, because overzealous people in campaigns do things that are wrong. What really hurts is if you try to cover it up."[194]

Special Prosecutor Archibald Cox was appointed to conduct an independent investigation into what became known as the Watergate affair. At the same time, House and Senate committees pursued their own investigations. A Senate hearing disclosed to the public a remarkable fact about White House operations. Alexander Butterfield, administrator of the Federal Aviation Administration, told committee staff about listening and recording devices in the Oval Office. Both Congress and the judiciary sought access to those tapes to determine whether there had been perjury or obstruction of justice by executive officials.

President Nixon insisted on his right to withhold information from a congressional inquiry if he determined that the release of such documents would violate the constitutional doctrine of executive privilege. Faced with subpoenas from the House Judiciary Committee, he argued that the release of presidential conversations to Congress would undermine the independence of the executive branch and jeopardize the operations of the White House. A line had to be drawn somewhere, he told the committee, and he would be the one to do it. The committee would get some documents, but not all, and Nixon would decide whether the documents needed to be edited before their release.[195] The committee denied that a President had any authority to determine what kind of evidence to share with a Congress conducting an impeachment inquiry.[196]

Nixon also asserted his authority to withhold information from the judiciary. On July 23, 1973, he was served with a subpoena directing him to turn over to a federal grand jury the tape recordings of eight specifically identified meetings and one specifically identified telephone conversation that had taken place in his office between June 20, 1972, and April 15, 1973, regarding

194. Public Papers of the Presidents, 1972, at 828.
195. John R. Labovitz, Presidential Impeachment 201–6 (1978).
196. Id. at 205.

the Watergate break-in. The government's brief opposed this subpoena, arguing that any effort to subject the President to the orders of a court "would effectively destroy the status of the Executive Branch as an equal and coordinate element of government," and that in the exercise of his discretion to claim executive privilege the President "is answerable to the nation but not to the courts."[197] The doctrine of separation of powers, said the brief, prevented the judiciary from compelling the President "to produce information that he has determined it is not in the public interest to disclose."[198] No court, according to the brief, "has ever attempted to enforce a subpoena directed at the President of the United States."[199]

These justifications for withholding the tapes were presented in lofty terms of separation of powers and the public interest. Part of the reason was to conceal possible criminal and impeachable conduct. After much legal maneuvering, some of the tapes wound up in the hands of Judge John Sirica. They revealed unmistakable evidence of obstruction of justice, such as Nixon's remarks at a March 22, 1973, meeting: "And, uh, for that reason, I am perfectly willing to—I don't give a shit what happens. I want you to stonewall it, let them plead the Fifth Amendment, cover-up or anything else, if it'll save the plan."[200] The plan, of course, was to save the administration and the President.

President Nixon lost his case in the Supreme Court, which held that in matters of criminal prosecution the decision to release documents is one for the courts, not the President.[201] Chief Justice Warren Burger, writing for the Court, added unfortunate dicta: "Absent a claim of need to protect military, diplomatic, or sensitive national security secrets," the Court found that the confidentiality of presidential communications would not be "significantly diminished" if given to a district court for in camera inspection.[202] This observation was purely extraneous to the decision. The question of military, diplomatic, or national security secrets had not been raised in the litigation. Why mention it at all? If Nixon had claimed that the tapes contained national security secrets, could he have successfully hidden behind unilateral assertions and denied defendants materials they needed in a criminal trial? To allow such presidential power would severely damage such basic constitutional principles as an independent judiciary, the adversary process, and the rights of the accused.

197. "Separation of Powers and Executive Privilege: The Watergate Briefs," 88 Pol. Sci. Q. 582, 586–87 (1973).
198. Id. at 587.
199. Id. at 588.
200. John J. Sirica, To Set the Record Straight 162 (1979).
201. United States v. Nixon, 418 U.S. 683 (1974).
202. Id. at 706.

The tapes that were released as a result of this decision demonstrated that Nixon had agreed to use the CIA to put a halt to the FBI investigation.[203] After release of the tapes, Nixon recognized that a House vote for impeachment "is, as a practical matter, virtually a foregone conclusion."[204] He announced his resignation on August 8, 1974, effective the next day.

Other Court Rulings

Two cases in the late 1980s focused on the authority of Presidents to classify and protect government documents. Language can be pulled from both cases to suggest executive dominance over the process, but the mere fact that they were litigated demonstrates a judicial role, and neither case raised any questions about the capacity of Congress or the courts, under their constitutional powers, to gain access to classified and secret documents.

A memo by the Office of Legal Counsel in 1996 cited the first case, *Department of Navy v. Egan* (1988), to analyze the responsibility of the executive branch to protect classified information.[205] However, the case was fundamentally and solely one of statutory construction. It had nothing to do with the President's constitutional authority. The dispute involved the Navy's denial of a security clearance to Thomas Egan, who worked on the Trident submarine. He was subsequently removed. Egan sought review by the Merit Systems Protection Board (MSPB), but the Supreme Court upheld the Navy's action by ruling that the denial of a security clearance is a sensitive discretionary judgment call committed by law to the executive agency with the necessary expertise for protecting classified information.[206] The conflict in this case was within the executive branch (Navy versus the MSPB), not between Congress and the executive branch or between the judiciary and the executive branch.

The focus on statutory questions was evident throughout the case. As the Justice Department noted in its brief to the Supreme Court: "The issue in this case is one of statutory construction and 'at bottom . . . turns on congressional intent.'"[207] The parties were directed to address this question: "Whether, in the course of reviewing the removal of an employee for failure to maintain a

---

203. H. Rept. No. 93-1305, 93d Cong., 2d Sess. 53 (1974).

204. Public Papers of the Presidents, 1974, at 622.

205. Memorandum from Christopher H. Schroeder, Office of Legal Counsel, Department of Justice, to Michael J. O'Neil, General Counsel to the Central Intelligence Agency, November 26, 1996, at 6–7 (hereafter "OLC Memo").

206. Department of Navy v. Egan, 484 U.S. 518, 529–30 (1988).

207. U.S. Department of Justice, "Brief for the Petitioner," Department of the Navy v. Egan, October Term, 1987, at 22 (citing Clarke v. Securities Industry Ass'n, No. 85–971, January 14, 1987).

required security clearance, the Merit Systems Protection Board is authorized by statute to review the substance of the underlying decision to deny or revoke the security clearance."[208]

The statutory questions centered on four sections of Title 5 of the U.S. Code: sections 7512, 7513, 7532, and 7701. The Justice Department's brief analyzed the relevant statutes and their legislative history and could find no basis for determining that Congress intended the MSPB to review the merits of security clearance determinations.[209] The entire oral argument before the Supreme Court on December 2, 1987, was devoted to the meaning of statutes and what Congress intended by them. At no time did the Justice Department suggest that classified information could be withheld from Congress or that it was an area purely committed to presidential control.

The Court's deference to the Navy did not cast a shadow over the right of Congress or the judiciary to receive sensitive information. The Court decided merely the "narrow question" of whether the MSPB had statutory authority to review the substance of a decision to deny a security clearance.[210] Although the Court referred to independent constitutional powers of the President, including those as Commander in Chief and head of the executive branch,[211] and noted the President's responsibility with regard to foreign policy,[212] the case was decided wholly on statutory grounds. In stating that courts "traditionally have been reluctant to intrude upon the authority of the Executive in military and national security affairs," the Court added this key qualification: "unless Congress specifically has provided otherwise."[213] The Court appears to have borrowed that thought (and language) from the Justice Department's brief: "Absent an unambiguous grant of jurisdiction by Congress, courts have traditionally been reluctant to intrude upon the authority of the executive in military and national security affairs."[214] Nothing in the legislative history of the Civil Service Reform Act of 1978 convinced the Court that the MSPB could review, on the merits, an agency's security clearance determination.[215]

During oral argument before the Supreme Court, the Justice Department and Egan's attorney, William J. Nold, debated the statutory issues. After the

208. Id. at (I).
209. U.S. Department of Justice, "Petition for a Writ of Certiorari to the United States Court of Appeals for the Federal Circuit," Department of the Navy v. Thomas E. Egan, October Term, 1986, at 4–5, 13, 15–16, 18.
210. 484 U.S. at 520.
211. Id. at 527.
212. Id. at 529.
213. Id. at 530.
214. U.S. Department of Justice, "Brief for the Petitioner," Department of the Navy v. Egan, October Term, 1987, at 21.
215. 484 U.S. at 531 (Note 6).

department completed its presentation, Nold told the Justices: "I think that we start out with the same premise. We start out with the premise that this is a case that involves statutory interpretation." Yet Nold remarked on the department's effort to shoehorn in some constitutional dimensions: "What they seem to do in my view is to start building a cloud around the statute. They start building this cloud and they call it national security, and as their argument progresses . . . the cloud gets darker and darker and darker, so that by the time we get to the end, we can't see the statute anymore. What we see is this cloud called national security."[216]

In citing the President's role as Commander in Chief, the Court stated that the President's authority to protect classified information "flows primarily from this constitutional investment of power in the President and exists quite apart from any explicit congressional grant."[217] That gives away too much, even if a number of lower courts would later read it that way. If Congress had never enacted legislation regarding classified or secret information, certainly the President could act in the absence of congressional authority. But once Congress enters the field and supplies statutory direction, it can narrow the President's range of action and the courts then look to congressional policy.

A second case, called *Garfinkel*, started off in district court with the judge acknowledging a large grant of independent constitutional authority for the President over national security information. By the time it reached the Supreme Court, however, the case had pulled back from this executive model to recognize the role of Congress and the value of shared power. The case is of interest because the 1996 Office of Legal Counsel memo cites it for the Justice Department position that Congress cannot "divest the President of his control over national security information in the Executive Branch by vesting lower-ranking personnel in that Branch with a 'right' to furnish such information to a Member of Congress without receiving official authorization [from within the executive branch] to do so."[218] That was indeed the view in district court, but it was quickly vacated by the Supreme Court.

In 1983, President Reagan directed that all federal employees with access to classified information sign nondisclosure agreements or risk the loss of their security clearance.[219] Congress, concerned about the vagueness of some terms in the directive and the loss of access to agency information, passed legislation (§ 630) to prohibit the use of appropriated funds to implement

216. Transcript of Oral Argument, December 2, 1987, at 19.

217. 484 U.S. at 527.

218. OLC Memo, at 3 (quoting from the Justice Department's brief in American Foreign Service Association v. Garfinkel).

219. National Security Decision Directive 84; see Louis Fisher, "Congressional-Executive Struggles over Information Secrecy Pledges," 42 Adm. L. Rev. 89, 90 (1990).

the nondisclosure policy.[220] In 1988, District Judge Oliver Gasch held that Congress lacked constitutional authority to interfere, by statute, with nondisclosure agreements drafted by the executive to protect the secrecy of classified information.[221] From *Egan* he extracted a sentence ("The authority to protect such [national security] information falls on the President as head of the Executive Branch and as Commander in Chief") without acknowledging that *Egan* was decided on statutory, not constitutional, grounds.[222] Judge Gasch concluded that Congress had passed legislation that "impermissibly restricts the President's power to fulfill obligations imposed upon him by his express constitutional powers and the role of the Executive in foreign relations."[223]

On October 31, 1988, the Supreme Court noted probable jurisdiction in the case.[224] Both the House and the Senate submitted briefs protesting Gasch's faulty analysis of the President's powers over foreign affairs. During oral argument, after Edwin Kneedler of the Justice Department spoke repeatedly about the President's constitutional role to control classified information, one of the Justices remarked: "But, Mr Kneedler, I just can't—I can't avoid interrupting you with this thought. The Constitution also gives Congress the power to provide for a navy and for the armed forces, and so forth, and often classified information is highly relevant to that task."[225] The attorney for the association challenging Reagan's nondisclosure policy objected that Gasch's decision, "by declaring that the Executive Branch has such sweeping power, has impeded the kind of accommodation that should take place in this kind of controversy," and hoped that the Court "wipes that decision off the books."[226]

That is what the Court did. It vacated Judge Gasch's order and remanded the case for further consideration.[227] In doing so, the Court warned Gasch to tread with greater caution in expounding on constitutional matters: "Having thus skirted the statutory question whether the Executive Branch's implementation of [Nondisclosure] Forms 189 and 4193 violated § 630, the court proceeded to address appellees' argument that the lawsuit should be dismissed because § 630 was an unconstitutional interference with the President's authority to protect the national security."[228] The Court emphasized that the

---

220. 101 Stat. 1329–432, § 630 (1987); 102 Stat. 1756, § 619 (1988).

221. National Federation of Federal Employees v. United States, 688 F.Supp. 671 (D.D.C. 1988).

222. Id. at 685.

223. Id.

224. 488 U.S. 923 (1988).

225. Transcript of Oral Argument, March 20, 1989, at 57–58.

226. Id. at 60.

227. American Foreign Service Assn. v. Garfinkel, 490 U.S. 153 (1989).

228. Id. at 158.

district court "should not pronounce upon the relative constitutional authority of Congress and the Executive Branch unless it finds it imperative to do
so. Particularly where, as here, a case implicates the fundamental relationship
between the Branches, courts should be extremely careful not to issue unnecessary constitutional rulings."[229]

On remand, Judge Gasch held that the plaintiffs (American Foreign Service Association and members of Congress) failed to state a cause of action
for courts to decide.[230] By dismissing the plaintiff's complaint on that ground,
Judge Gasch did not address any of the constitutional issues.[231] The effect was
to push the dispute back to the two elected branches, to encourage some form
of political accommodation.

The legal landscape shifted fundamentally after the *Reynolds* decision. Congress passed a number of statutes to give the public greater access to agency
information, amended the Housekeeping Statute to strip it of any leverage
for nondisclosure, and brought federal judges into close touch with classified
and national security secrets. The stage was set for a discovery in the year
2000 of evidence that the Justice Department had misled the Supreme Court
in *Reynolds*.

---

229. Id. at 161.
230. American Foreign Service Ass'n v. Garfinkel, 732 F.Supp. 13 (D.D.C. 1990).
231. Id. at 16.

6

DISCOVERING THE ACCIDENT REPORT

Through its ruling in *Reynolds,* the Supreme Court provided a powerful imprimatur to the state secrets doctrine. In subsequent disputes over access to agency documents, the government would regularly cite this decision as legal justification for withholding requested materials. Although much had changed after 1953 to make government more open and to give federal courts greater access to confidential and secret documents, there had been little analysis of the merits of *Reynolds* or the manner in which the Justices decided it. Anyone reading the briefs, the decisions, and the evolution of the case from district court to the Supreme Court would have substantial misgivings about the final ruling. Still, there was little evidence of the government misleading the courts. That picture changed dramatically in 2000 with the discovery of the declassified accident report.

Freedom of Information Act Requests

Before finding the accident report on the Internet, several of the plaintiffs in *Reynolds* attempted to get the report by relying on the Freedom of Information Act (FOIA). Under that statute, Phyllis Brauner sent a letter to the government on July 22, 1991, and another letter on August 23, 1991, requesting release of information. She received a response from the Department of the Air Force on September 10, 1991, stating: "We are not the originating office for the records you requested. We forwarded your request to Air Force Safety Agency/IMA (FOIA), Norton AFB, CA 92409-7001. They will reply directly to you."[1] Other family members asked the government for copies. Phyllis's daughter, Cathy, recalled: "From time to time, one of us would request the accident report from the government. It came, but inevitably much of the information was blacked out. The government claimed it was a matter of national security because the scientists, including my physicist father, had been testing secret electronic equipment."[2] When Cathy Brauner finally had an

1. E-mail to author from Cathy Brauner.
2. Cathy Brauner, "This Is What the Terrorists Really Took," Wellesley Townsman, September 27, 2001, at 4; mailed to author by Cathy Brauner.

opportunity to examine the declassified accident report, she saw that what "had been blacked out all those years ago was not government secrets, but the names of those who had been at fault."[3] Phyllis Brauner, who lived long enough to see the accident report, "felt betrayed by her own government."[4]

Browsing the Internet

As a teenager growing up in southern New Jersey in the 1970s, Michael Stowe began finding small pieces of military airplanes. The local airport had been a World War II fighter training base, and pieces of P-47s "still littered the woods."[5] After an accident, the government would visit the site to recover the plane, but fragments remained scattered over a large territory. Stowe began writing to the U.S. Air Force to obtain aircraft accident reports, but he received only censored versions. In the years that followed, he founded a museum at the airport and began to document all vintage military airplane accidents in New Jersey.

In early 1996, the Air Force decided to release aircraft accident reports covering the period from 1918 to 1955. Stowe was "very anxious to finally see the real story of the New Jersey accidents," but the 1,200 reels of microfilm priced at $30 each put the cost of the collection beyond his reach. After buying some of the reels, the idea of a Web site seemed to him the most logical method of paying for the rest.[6] His Web site (Accident-Report.com; http://www.accident-report.com/) explains: "Whether you're looking for a family member, squadron history, lost warbirds and crash sites," there is available "a wide range of resources to help find the information you need." He organized the Web site around such headings as "Search for Pilots or Crew Members," "Search for Aircraft," "Search for Stations," and "Missing Air Crew Members." Under the heading "USAF & USAAF Pilot and Crew Lists," one can select a particular year. Clicking "1948" takes you to the names of those who died in the Waycross crash. Among those listed: William H. Brauner, Robert Reynolds, and Albert Palya.

Judith Loether was seven weeks old when her father, Albert Palya, died in the accident. As she grew up, she learned that he had been killed in a B-29 plane crash that involved a secret project he had been working on for RCA. The crash "had an aura of mystery about it." One of her uncles (her father's

---

3. Id. at 5.

4. Letter from Susan P. Brauner, Catherine Brauner, and Judith Palya Loether to Mr. Duane Landreth, Latanzi Spaulding & Landreth, PC, 8 Cardinal Lane, Orleans, MA 02653, at 2.

5. This account relies on e-mails sent to the author by Michael Stowe.

6. Id.

brother-in-law) told her that he thought the Russians blew up the plane. She began to read newspaper articles stored in a box in the attic—"big headlines in major papers, with pictures of the wreckage"—but she did not study them in great detail.[7] She knew her mother had been involved in a lawsuit and had received some money. She was not familiar with the specifics of the litigation, the Supreme Court decision, or any controversy about an accident report.

After she had her first son in 1975, she began thinking more about her father. She wrote to Eugene Mechler, the only civilian to survive, and asked questions. When she saw her father's sister, she made further inquiries, but she stopped short of putting questions to her mother. By the time Judy Loether turned 41, in 1989, she had a better appreciation of how young her father was at the time of the crash. She began looking up information about the B-29 and the special equipment that was on the plane.

On February 10, 2000, she stayed overnight with friends and decided to sit down at their computer. For the first time, she entered the combination "B-29" plus "accident" into a search engine. The first hit that came up was Michael Stowe's Web site, Accident-Report.com. Within seconds, she was "staring at the page and comprehending that there was an accident report available that would give me details about the plane crash that killed my father. MOST specifically, I wanted to know WHAT secret project they had been working on, and too, I thought that maybe it would tell if the Russians blew up the plane!"[8]

Within two weeks, she received the accident report and was disappointed that it made no mention of the secret project. There were a few references to "secret equipment," but she already knew that from newspaper stories. She returned to the attic collection and read the newspaper articles and family letters with greater care. She began sending out postcards to find the Brauners. One was addressed to Susan P. Brauner in Harwich Port, Mass. Judy wrote: "Am looking for Susan Brauner, daughter of the late W. H. Brauner and Phyllis Brauner. Our fathers were killed in the same plane crash on 10-06-48." Back came a reply from Susan Brauner on March 4, 2000: "I am the person you are looking for. Needless to say the family is quite curious as to why."[9] By meeting with Susan, her sister Cathy, and their mother Phyllis, she learned about the Supreme Court case. "That very day I looked up the decision on the internet and was stunned to see how it all hinged on the accident report . . . because it was SO secret . . . that the details of the secret equipment and the project had to be withheld from the court. I thought . . . but NO! there isn't

7. Drawn from e-mails sent to the author by Judith Palya Loether.
8. Id.
9. Postcard and letter sent to author by Cathy Brauner.

anything in there about the project . . . or the equipment . . . because that's what I wanted to see!"[10]

Loether gathered up papers her mother had saved about the court case, put them in chronological order, and began to study them. She now understood that her mother had settled for less money than the original court award. During this time, she was "building up steam, getting more and more angry with the government, MY government . . . wondering why they didn't just pay that measly sum and keep their darn accident report." It seemed clear that "the number of mistakes made with the plane and by the crew must have been an embarrassment. But why didn't they pay? THAT was the moral thing to do." She remembered that when she went to college, "every time I had tuition due my mother had to take out a loan." In later years, her mother contracted Alzheimer's disease and started having serious problems by 1992. She died in 2000. Phyllis Brauner also died later that year. Susan Brauner sent a letter to Drinker Biddle & Reath in 2000, asking for old files on the *Reynolds* case. They searched and could not locate anything. Law firms are unlikely to keep records almost 50 years old. Drinker Biddle suggested that Loether and Brauner contact some New York City attorneys who specialized in air crash cases. Loether decided that if they were going to sue, "it's NOT going to be about negligence. It's going to be about lying in court."[11]

After locating Susan Brauner, the next search was for Patricia J. Reynolds, the wife of Robert Reynolds. Susan Brauner found her married name, Herring, and sent out blind postcards to a number of Herrings in Indiana. There she discovered Patricia J. Herring.[12] Loether, Brauner, and Herring could now coordinate their plans and resources to decide the best strategy for challenging the government.

Judy Loether drove to Florida with a friend in 2002 and on the way home stopped in Waycross to see the scene of the crash. It was during that visit that she decided to sue the government. She thought of the "enormous tragedy of those men dying, while on a project to develop highly technical equipment for their country, and how that country did not step in to take care of those that were left behind." Suing the government "seemed like a farfetched idea. But I thought I ought to try." She remembers watching the television show *Superman* when she was a child, with its spine-tingling message: "Truth, Justice, and the American Way." After reading the accident report and the Supreme Court decision, she kept thinking "this was NOT the Truth, this was

10. E-mail to author from Judith Palya Loether.
11. Id.
12. E-mail to author from Patricia J. Herring.

NOT Justice and this surely was NOT the American Way."[13] She talked to the Brauners when she returned home, and they spent several weeks jointly drafting a letter and sending it to local attorneys.

The first batch of letters to attorneys was not promising. Loether and the Brauners were about to send out more when Fred Thys, a Boston reporter for National Public Radio, took an interest in their story. His research uncovered more about Charles Biddle and his role in representing the three widows. Loether searched the Internet for more information about him and checked the Drinker Biddle Web site to see what it had on Charles Biddle. It now occurred to Loether that if she couldn't give the accident report to Charles Biddle, it should go to someone in his law firm. She felt that if the law firm said it was a lost cause, "then my mind would be at peace, because I knew that they would have more interest in it than how much money they would make."[14]

On July 18, 2002, Judy Loether sent an e-mail to Gregg Melinson, the firm's government attorney. She wrote: "We have contacted your firm and you have kindly given us some names of other attorneys. But I can't help but think that if Mr. Biddle were still alive HE would want to right this injustice himself." She urged the firm to "finish the case he started and so passionately tried. The firm with the name of Charles Biddle on it should be the firm that sees that justice is finally done in this case."[15] Within days she heard that Drinker Biddle was very interested. The firm decided to file a motion for a writ of *coram nobis,* charging that the government had misled the Supreme Court and committed fraud against it.

A Writ of *Coram Nobis*

The writ of *coram nobis,* originating in England, is a motion to a court to review and correct its judgment because it was based on an error of fact. The writ identifies an error of fact—not an error of law—that remained unknown at the time of the trial by the court and the party seeking relief. Without the error, the court would not have entered the judgment.[16] In 1827, Justice Joseph Story of the U.S. Supreme Court recognized the fundamental principle at play: "Every Court must be presumed to exercise those powers belonging to it, which

13. E-mail to author from Judy Loether.
14. Id.
15. Id. (forwarding the e-mail that she had sent to the firm).
16. Abraham L. Freedman, "The Writ of Error Coram Nobis," 3 Temple L. Q. 365, 370–71 (1929). For a *coram nobis* during this period, see New England Furniture & Carpet Co. v. Willcuts, 55 F.2d 983 (D. Minn. 1931).

are necessary for the promotion of public justice; and we do not doubt that this Court possesses the power to reinstate any cause, dismissed by mistake."[17]

Two principles of law compete. One is the general rule of judicial finality. As expressed by the Supreme Court in 1944, society is well served "by putting an end to litigation after a case has been tried and judgment entered."[18] Bringing finality to a legal dispute offers important benefits. Closure is needed. Disputes need to be settled and put behind. But a second principle demands respect. A court must have the capacity and willingness to revisit a judgment after it has discovered that a fraud has cast a shadow over the original ruling. Courts must be able to correct injustices deemed to be "sufficiently gross."[19] Tolerating fraud in a particular case reduces respect for judges and lowers confidence in the courts. The Supreme Court explained the serious consequences of allowing fraud to infect a ruling:

Tampering with the administration of justice in the manner indisputably shown here involves far more than an injury to a single litigant. It is wrong against the institutions set up to protect and safeguard the public, institutions in which fraud cannot complacently be tolerated consistently with the good order of society. Surely it cannot be that preservation of the integrity of the judicial process must always wait upon the diligence of litigants. The public welfare demands that the agencies of public justice be not so impotent that they must always be mute and helpless victims of deception and fraud.[20]

As originally placed in Rule 60(b) of the Rules of Civil Procedure, a writ of *coram nobis* was accompanied by other arcane motions for relief, including *coram vobis* and *audita querela*. Federal and state judges bridled at those terms and the laborious, tiresome efforts of counsel to distinguish one from another. An Arizona judge in 1898 said he did not "encourage the digging into the moldering dust heaps of the past for worn-out and discarded remedies."[21] An advisory committee in 1946 acknowledged that the use of *coram nobis, coram vobis,* and *audita querela* "is shrouded in ancient lore and mystery."[22]

17. The Palmyra, 12 Wheat 1, 10 (1827).
18. Hazel-Atlas Co. v. Hartford Co., 322 U.S. 238, 244 (1944).
19. Id.
20. Id. at 246.
21. Billups v. Freeman, 5 Ariz. 268, 52 Pac. 367 (1898), cited in Lester B. Orfield, "The Writ of Error Coram Nobis in Civil Practice," 20 Va. L. Rev. 423 (Note 1) (1934). Orfield had earlier written two notes on the use of *coram nobis* in Nebraska: 10 Neb. L. Bull. 314 (1932) and 11 Neb. L. Bull. 421 (1933). See also his article, still focusing on Nebraska: "Writ of Error Coram Nobis," 8 Ind. L. J. 247 (1933).
22. 28 U.S.C. Rule 60(b) (1946) (notes by Advisory Committee on Rules, at page 3320).

Those three terms were stripped from Rule 60(b) when it was revised in 1946. The new rule, effective in 1948, closed with this sentence: "Writs of coram nobis, coram vobis, audita querela, and bills of review and bills in the nature of a bill of review, are abolished, and the procedure for obtaining any relief from a judgment shall be by motion as prescribed in these rules or by an independent action."[23] The revision of Rule 60(b) responded to the "plaintive cries of parties who have for centuries floundered, and often succumbed, among the snares and pitfalls of the ancillary common law and equitable remedies."[24]

Even though the Latin terms disappeared, litigants continued to need a procedure to challenge judgments based on false and possibly corrupt information. The Seventh Circuit in 1968 explained that judicial bodies have an inherent power "to undo that which has been obtained from it by fraud."[25] A decision produced by fraud on the court "is not in essence a decision at all, and never becomes final."[26] When judges interpret Rule 60(b), they must preserve a balance between the "sanctity of final judgments" and the "incessant command of the court's conscience that justice be done in light of all the facts."[27] Upon discovering corruption, a district court said in 1960 that it "is under a duty to take whatever action may be appropriate to sustain its integrity and to undo any harm or injustice which has resulted."[28] However, the burden falls on litigants to produce specific facts and documentary evidence. Mere allegations of fraud or corruption are not enough.[29]

Several high-profile *coram nobis* cases illustrate how the process works and where it falls short. In 1943 and 1944, the Supreme Court handed down two decisions against Japanese Americans, most of them natural-born U.S. citizens. The first case, *Hirabayashi v. United States,* upheld a nighttime curfew.[30] The second, *Korematsu v. United States,* provided judicial support for the placement of Japanese Americans in detention camps.[31] The executive branch prevailed in those lawsuits because it was willing to deceive the judiciary and withhold vital evidence from the courts. At the time of the second case, Justice Department attorneys learned that a 618-page document called *Final Report,*

---

23. 28 U.S.C. Rule 60(b) (2000).

24. Bankers Mortgage Company v. United States, 423 F.2d 73, 77 (5th Cir. 1970).

25. Kenner v. C.I.R., 387 F.2d 689, 690 (7th Cir. 1968).

26. Id. at 691.

27. Id. See also Universal Oil Co. v. Root Rfg. Co., 328 U.S. 575, 580 (1946).

28. Chicago Title & Trust Co. v. Fox Theatres Corporation, 182 F.Supp. 18, 28 (S.D. N.Y. 1960).

29. Id. at 31.

30. 320 U.S. 81 (1943).

31. 323 U.S. 214 (1944).

prepared by the War Department, contained erroneous claims about alleged espionage efforts by Japanese Americans. Analyses by the FBI and the Federal Communications Commission disproved War Department conclusions that Japanese Americans had sent signals from shore to assist Japanese submarine attacks along the Pacific coast.

Justice Department attorneys knew they had an obligation to alert the Court to the false information. They drafted a footnote, to be included in their brief for *Korematsu,* that identified errors and misconceptions in the *Final Report.* As originally drafted, the footnote specifically repudiated the claim of shore-to-ship signaling by persons of Japanese ancestry. After much maneuvering within the administration, the footnote was progressively reworked and so watered down that the Court could not possibly have understood how it had been misled.[32]

In subsequent years, scholarship and archival discoveries uncovered this fraud on the Court and a series of *coram nobis* cases reached the judiciary in the 1980s. The first was brought by Fred Korematsu, who petitioned for *coram nobis* relief to vacate his 1942 conviction involving the detention camps. A district judge explained that although the revised Rule 60(b) abolished *coram nobis* in civil cases, "the writ still obtains in criminal proceedings where other relief is wanting."[33] The government, although not prepared to confess error, was willing to have the court set aside the conviction.[34] On the basis of documents submitted to it, the court concluded that the government during World War II "knowingly withheld information from the courts when they were considering the critical question of military necessity in this case."[35] The court compared the first version of the footnote, which alerted the judiciary to conflicts within the Roosevelt administration, to the final version that made no mention of contradictory reports.[36]

The district court concluded that "there is substantial support in the record that the government deliberately omitted relevant information and provided misleading information in papers before the court." It added that the judicial process "is seriously impaired when the government's law enforcement officers violate their ethical obligations to the court."[37] In granting the petition for a writ of *coram nobis* and vacating Korematsu's conviction, the court underscored the point that it was responding only to errors of fact, not to errors

32. Peter Irons, Justice at War 278–92 (1983).
33. Korematsu v. United States, 584 F.Supp. 1406 (D. Cal. 1984).
34. Id. at 1413.
35. Id. at 1417.
36. Id. at 1417–18.
37. Id. at 1420.

of law, and that the Supreme Court's decision in 1943 "stands as the law of this case and for whatever precedential value it may still have."[38]

A second *coram nobis* suit came from Gordon Hirabayashi, who was convicted of violating the curfew order. The Justice Department argued to the Supreme Court in 1943 that the exclusion of everyone of Japanese ancestry from the West Coast was due to military necessity and the lack of time to separate loyal Japanese from those who might be disloyal. It did not claim that it was impossible to separate loyal Japanese from the disloyal.[39] However, General John L. DeWitt, the commanding general of the Western Defense Command, had taken the position that because of racial ties, filial piety, and strong bonds of common tradition, culture, and customs, it was impossible to make such a distinction.[40] To him, there wasn't "such a thing as a loyal Japanese."[41] The initial draft report contained DeWitt's sentiments. The final report, after changes made by the War Department, did not. The Justice Department received the final report but not the original one.

A district court held in 1986 that although the department "did not knowingly conceal from petitioner's counsel and from the Supreme Court the reason stated by General DeWitt for the exclusion of the Japanese, the government must be charged with the concealment because it was information known to the War Department, an arm of the government."[42] The court found that the government's failure to disclose to Hirabayashi, his counsel, and the Supreme Court the reason stated by DeWitt for excluding all those of Japanese ancestry "was an error of the most fundamental character" and that Hirabayashi "was in fact seriously prejudiced by that non-disclosure in his appeal from his conviction of failing to report."[43] Consequently, the court vacated his conviction for failing to report to civilian control stations. At the same time, the court declined to vacate his conviction for violating the curfew order.

On appeal, the Ninth Circuit vacated both convictions.[44] Although Hirabayashi had served his sentence for misdemeanor offenses, the court noted that a U.S. citizen "convicted of a crime on account of race is lastingly aggrieved."[45] As to the distinction drawn by the district court between the two convictions, the Ninth Circuit pointed out that the Justice Department's brief

38. Id.
39. Hirabayashi v. United States, 627 F.Supp. 1445, 1453, 1454 (W.D. Wash. 1986).
40. Id. at 1149.
41. Id. at 1452.
42. Id. at 1454.
43. Id. at 1457.
44. Hirabayashi v. United States, 828 F.2d 591 (9th Cir. 1987).
45. Id. at 607.

to the Supreme Court in 1943 had argued "a single theory of military necessity to support both the exclusion and curfew orders."[46]

A third example of *coram nobis* comes from a series of nuclear tests conducted by the government during the spring of 1953 at the Nevada Proving Ground, northwest of Las Vegas. Ranchers in surrounding areas reported abnormal losses of sheep and lambs, but the government denied that radioactive fallout from the tests caused the deaths or contributed to them. When sheep owners brought an action under the Federal Tort Claims Act, the government attributed the losses to unprecedented cold weather during the lambing and shearing of sheep, inadequate feeding, infectious diseases of various types, and other factors unrelated to the tests.[47]

Congressional hearings, conducted more than two decades later in 1979, revealed a "cover-up" by the government.[48] Government records had been changed to remove evidence of a causal relationship between radiation exposure of the sheep and their deaths, and the final report of the Atomic Energy Commission had falsely claimed a unanimous view of experts who participated in the investigation and signed the report.[49] The sheep owners returned to court and charged that fraud had been practiced upon the courts by U.S. officials. District Judge Christenson (who had handled the original trial in the 1950s) concluded that evidence wrongfully withheld by the government would have benefitted the plaintiffs' claims for damages.[50] He found that one or more of the government attorneys "knowingly participated" in the concealment from the district court of facts that the court was entitled to have.[51] He now reflected on his earlier belief that government officials would tell the truth:

> And it is quite true that judged by modern insights I took a somewhat pristine view at the original trial of the general integrity of government officials in the absence of evidence impugning it in specific instances.

---

46. Id. at 608. For a third *coram nobis* action stemming from the treatment of Japanese Americans during World War II, see Yasui v. United States, 772 F.2d 1496 (9th Cir. 1985). Another Japanese American case, although not raising *coram nobis,* also focused on the government's fraudulent concealment of information from the courts. Hohri v. United States, 586 F.Supp. 769 (D.D.C. 1984); Hohri v. United States, 782 F.2d 227 (D.C. Cir. 1986); United States v. Hohri, 482 U.S. 64 (1987); Hohri v. United States, 847 F.2d 779 (Fed. Cir. 1988).

47. Bulloch v. United States, 145 F.Supp. 824, 826 (D. Utah 1956). See also Bulloch v. United States, 133 F.Supp. 885 (D. Utah 1955).

48. Bulloch v. United States, 95 F.R.D.123, 126 (D. Utah 1982).

49. Id. at 131.

50. Id. at 133.

51. Id. at 142.

I suppose that I shall continue to do so, despite the buffetings of Watergate, these proceedings and other current disclosures. Nonetheless, I have concluded that by whatever standard or as of whatever period the circumstances found here are to be judged, they clearly and convincingly demonstrate a species of fraud upon the court for which a remedy must be granted even at this late date.[52]

Concluding that the government had perpetrated a fraud upon the court, Judge Christenson vacated the 1956 judgment and ordered a new trial.[53] The Tenth Circuit reversed, concluding that the sheep owners had failed to establish proof of fraud on the district court or any other kind of fraud sufficient to set aside the original judgment.[54] To the appellate court, the plaintiffs had access to government information, data, and witnesses when they brought their case in the 1950s, and if they failed to make a sufficient showing of fraud at that stage, they could not attempt to make it 25 years later. The plaintiffs "have a heavy burden to demonstrate why they waited these many years to make the assertions they have made in this action."[55] To prevail on the charge of fraud on the court, the plaintiffs need to produce "clear and convincing evidence."[56]

Subsequent efforts by the plaintiffs to show that the government had withheld information from them in the 1950s and had committed fraud were turned aside by the Tenth Circuit.[57] Separate litigation, brought by individuals ("downwinders") who linked cases of leukemia and cancer to the Nevada tests, was successful in district court but reversed by the Tenth Circuit.[58] With judicial relief unavailable, Congress passed legislation in 1990 to establish procedures for claims due to exposure to radiation from nuclear tests and uranium mines. The statute authorized a $100 million special Radiation Exposure Trust Fund.[59]

---

52. Id. at 143.
53. Id. at 145.
54. Bulloch v. United States, 721 F.2d 713 (10th Cir. 1983).
55. Id. at 718.
56. Id.
57. Bulloch v. United States, 763 F.2d 1115 (10th Cir. 1985) (en banc), cert. denied, 474 U.S. 1086 (1986). See also Bulloch v. Pearson, 768 F.2d 1191 (10th Cir. 1985), cert. denied, 474 U.S. 1086 (1986).
58. Allen v. United States, 588 F.Supp. 247 (D. Utah 1984); Allen v. United States, 527 F.Supp. 476 (D. Utah 1981), rev'd, 816 F.2d 1417 (10th Cir. 1987), cert. denied, 484 U.S. 1004 (1988).
59. 104 Stat. 920 (1990), amended by 104 Stat. 1835, § 3139 (1990). For an excellent analysis of the litigation that challenged the Nevada tests, see Howard Ball, Justice Downwind: America's Atomic Testing Program in the 1950s (1986).

The experience with these *coram nobis* actions suggests a significant difference between criminal and civil cases. Hirabayashi and Korematsu prevailed in part because they had been found guilty of a criminal offense and those convictions, wrongly decided, needed to be wiped clean from their records. The ranchers brought a civil case and were expected to discover fraud by the government at the discovery stage. A heavier burden may fall on plaintiffs in a civil case, which is what the *Reynolds* case presented.

First Stop: Supreme Court

On March 4, 2003, Wilson M. Brown III, of Drinker Biddle & Reath, petitioned the Supreme Court for a "writ of error *coram nobis* to remedy fraud upon this Court." Plaintiffs in the case included Patricia J. Herring (formerly Patricia J. Reynolds), the widow of Robert Reynolds; Susan and Catherine Brauner, the daughters of William H. Brauner; and Judith Palya Loether, William Palya, and Robert Palya, the children of Albert H. Palya. By the time of the filing, the wives of William H. Brauner and Albert H. Palya had died: Phyllis Brauner on December 23, 2000, and Elizabeth Palya on October 3, 2000.

Plaintiffs' Brief

The petition presented by the plaintiffs began by listing three questions, identifying where fraud had been perpetrated against the Court and the kinds of relief that might be appropriate:

1. Where recently declassified documents show that the United States defrauded this Court in securing the Court's decision in *United States* v. *Reynolds,* 345 U.S. 1 (1953), should the Court issue a writ of error *coram nobis* pursuant to 28 U.S.C. § 1651, or exercise its inherent equitable powers, to vacate its decision and now affirm and reinstate the original judgments?

2. Where the government defrauded the Court and thereby deprived petitioners of the benefit of their judgments, should the Court award petitioners damages to compensate them for their loss pursuant to 28 U.S.C. § 1912 or pursuant to the Court's equitable powers as a sanction for the government's misconduct?

3. Where the government defrauded the Court and thereby deprived petitioners of the benefit of their judgments, should the Court award petitioners their attorneys fees and single or double costs pursuant to

28 U.S.C. § 1912, pursuant to 28 U.S.C. § 2412(b), or pursuant to the Court's equitable powers as a sanction for the government's misconduct?[60]

The three sections cited from Title 28 authorize judicial procedures. Section 1651 provides that the Supreme Court and all courts established by Congress "may issue all writs necessary or appropriate in aid of their respective jurisdictions and agreeable to the usages and principles of law." Section 1912 covers damages and costs: "Where a judgment is affirmed by the Supreme Court or a court of appeals, the court in its discretion may adjudge to the prevailing party just damages for his delay, and single or double costs." Section 2412 contains other details on costs and fees. Unless expressly prohibited by statute, a court "may award reasonable fees and expenses of attorneys," in addition to the costs for the prevailing party in any civil action brought by or against the United States. Similar to the principle included in the Federal Tort Claims Act, which treats the United States on a par as with any other private litigant, Section 2412(b) states that the United States "shall be liable for such fees and expenses to the same extent that any other party would be liable under the common law or under the terms of any statute which specifically provides for such an award."

The preliminary statement of the petition reviewed the judgments that had been awarded to the three widows by Judge Kirkpatrick. Afterward, the United States "was bent on overturning their judgments, and—to accomplish this—it committed a fraud not only upon the widows but upon this court." Patricia Herring and the children of Brauner and Palya "now ask the court to right this wrong."[61] By refusing to produce the accident report and survivors' statements, even to the district court in camera, the United States "advanced a sweeping claim of executive privilege, contending that the reports contained 'military secrets' so sensitive not even the district court should see them." Yet the recently declassified reports "include nothing approaching a 'military secret.' Indeed, they are no more than accounts of a flight that, due to the Air Force's negligence, went tragically awry." In "telling the Court otherwise, the Air Force lied." By relying on that lie, the Supreme Court "deprived the widows of their judgments." The petition urged the court to issue a writ of error *coram nobis,* in the exercise of its inherent power to remedy fraud, "to put things right."[62]

---

60. Petition for a Writ of Error *Coram Nobis* to Remedy Fraud upon This Court, In re Patricia J. Herring, No. O2M76, at i (hereafter "Petition").

61. Id. at 1.

62. Id.

The petition explains the government's nondisclosure of the documents in this manner: "The Air Force presumably sought to protect these materials to avoid the embarrassment and public scrutiny their production would have generated."[63] The Air Force became a separate branch of the armed services in September 1947 "and was still seeking to establish itself." The B-29, one of the most effective weapons during World War II, "had long been plagued with technical and mechanical problems," especially the tendency of its engines to catch fire.[64] The declassified documents on the B-29 crash over Waycross identify the main cause of the accident as the Air Force's failure to comply with two technical orders that mandated changes to the exhaust manifold assemblies to eliminate a fire hazard. The orders required the installation of heat shields to avoid overheating. Without that installation, the aircraft was not considered "to have been safe for flight." The declassified reports show that the shields were not installed on the B-29 that crashed on October 6, 1948.[65]

The petition points out the contradiction between the declassified reports and the Air Force's response to interrogatories. Question 31 asked: "(a) Have any modifications been prescribed by defendant for the engines in its B-29 type aircraft to prevent overheating of the engines and/or to reduce the fire hazard in the engines? (b) If so, when were such modifications prescribed? (c) If so, had any such modifications been carried out on the engines of the particular B-29 type aircraft involved in the instant case? Give details." Response by the Air Force: "No."[66] That was false. Question 27 asked whether the pilot bailed out with his parachute. The government answered: "Pilot did not appear to have bailed out. Body was found near wreckage, with no parachute attached." The accident report stated this about Captain Erwin: "Apparently tried to use parachute which became fouled on the aircraft upon exit, preventing him from falling free."[67]

The declassified reports and survivor statements reveal other negligent acts by the Air Force. The civilian engineers were not given preflight briefings on the use of parachutes and emergency aircraft evacuation, as required by Air Force regulations.[68] Various factors contributed to risk. The aircraft commander, copilot, and engineer had never flown together as a crew before the flight. As noted in an Air Force report, this lack of experience meant that

63. Id. at 8.
64. Id. at 8 (Note 5).
65. Id. at 9.
66. Id.
67. Army Air Forces [sic], Report of Major Accident, AAF Form No. 14, Aircraft No. 45-21866, accident two miles South of Waycross, Ga., Attachment # 4.
68. Petition, at 9.

"their coordination was not as good as could have been expected had they been accustomed to acting as a fixed crew."[69] The fact that the pilot feathered the wrong propeller and the copilot "got up from his seat to aid in depressurization indicates that confusion did exist among the pilot, copilot and engineer."[70]

When the fire broke out in engine No. 1, the pilot (according to the copilot's testimony) inadvertently "feathered" the propeller for the No. 4 engine, and the copilot tried to correct that mistake. Feathering changes the blade's angle to make it parallel to the line of flight. At the crash site, however, the propellers of both the No. 1 and No. 4 engines were found in feathered positions.[71] Feathering is typically done when an engine fails, to avoid drag. Feathering an operating engine creates torque, or twist, that does damage to an engine and puts stress on the mounts holding the engine to the wing. As the plane went into a spin, the load on the engine increased, eventually tearing it from the plane. In its answer to interrogatory question 8, the government stated that the pilot eventually feathered the No. 1 engine.

The declassified documents reveal other areas of negligence by the government. The B-29 that exploded over Waycross was on a "red diagonal," meaning that it was not in compliance with a technical order. The plane was released for flight only "by signing of the exceptional release." Because the technical orders required "changes in the exhaust systems to eliminate a definite fire hazard" and they were not complied with, "the aircraft is not considered to have been safe for flight."[72]

The plaintiffs' petition reviewed the purpose of *coram nobis*. Courts have an inherent right to set aside fraudulently obtained judgments: "to hold the public trust and confidence that are the bedrock of its authority, this Court must have the power to root out and remedy abuses of its jurisdiction by those appearing before it."[73] The petition quotes from a 1944 decision by the Supreme Court: "Tampering with the administration of justice . . . involves far more than an injury to a single litigant. It is a wrong against the institutions set up to protect and safeguard the public, institutions in which fraud

69. Department of the Air Force, Headquarters United States Air Force, Washington, "Information Concerning Comments Contained in Letter from Mr. Frank Folsom, RCA," January 10, 1949, at 2 (section g(1)) (hereafter "Folsom").

70. Id. at 3 (section i(1)).

71. Petition, at 10.

72. Folsom, at 2 (section f(1)). The special investigation report of the accident over Waycross also concluded that the aircraft "is not considered to have been safe for flight because of non-compliance with Technical Orders 01-20EJ-177 and 01-20EJ-178." Report of Special Investigation of Aircraft Accident Involving TB-29-100BW No. 45-21866, September 14, 1950, at 8.

73. Petition, at 10.

cannot complacently be tolerated consistently with the good order of society.
. . . The public welfare demands that the agencies of public justice be not so
impotent that they must always be mute and helpless victims of deception
and fraud."[74]

Although revisions to Rule 60(b) had abolished the writ of *coram nobis* in
1948, the petition argued that the All Writs Act (Section 1651) offered the
Court "a 'residual source of authority' to issue any of the historic common law
suits not otherwise covered by statute."[75] The writ "is tailor-made for this case,
where an error in a matter of fact—this Court's crediting as true government
affidavits that were false—has undermined the validity and regularity of the
Court's decision-making."[76] To the petition, it "seems clear . . . that only this
Court can undo what it has done and reinstate the judgments it reversed."[77]
As an alternative to *coram nobis*, "the Court may treat this petition as simply a
petition or motion in equity to vacate the Court's decision in *Reynolds*."[78]

The petition speculates on the government's strategy in lower court. The
Air Force "must have calculated that its scheme entailed little risk. If the false
affidavits convinced the district court to back down, the Air Force could continue its cover-up. If the district court did not back down and the Air Force
persisted in its noncompliance, the Air Force would suffer nothing beyond a
compensatory damage award under the Tort Claims Act (an award it almost
certainly would have to pay anyway if the documents were produced)." If
the Air Force lost in district court it would have a right of appeal "and an
opportunity to test the reach of a privilege for 'military secrets' and 'national
security' at a favorable time, in a sympathetic context, with the full backing
of the Justice Department."[79] This analysis could be correct. It could also be
the case that the driving force behind the litigation strategy was not the Air
Force but rather the Justice Department, in search of a case to lock in the state
secrets privilege, and it saw *Reynolds* as the ideal vehicle for achieving a victory
not merely for the Air Force but for executive power.

As to the timeliness of the petition, the plaintiffs' brief pointed out that *coram nobis* relief is available "without limitation of time."[80] It further remarked:
"The government, moreover, has no cause to complain of delay. The govern-

74. Id. at 10–11 (quoting from Hazel-Atlas Glass Co. v. Hartford-Empire Co., 322 U.S.
238, 246 (1944)).

75. Id. at 11 (citing Carlisle v. United States, 517 U.S. 416, 429 (1996), which quotes
from Pennsylvania Bureau of Correction v. United States Marshals Service, 474 U.S. 34, 43
(1985)).

76. Id. at 12.

77. Id. at 13 (Note 7).

78. Id.

79. Id. at 18.

80. Id. at 20 (citing United States v. Morgan, 346 U.S. 502, 507 (1954)).

ment concealed its fraud for decades, holding the accident reports and witness statements as 'classified materials' until the 1990s, even though they contained no secrets and had no conceivable further utility."[81] The government's purpose in classifying them was "to bury them so deep and so long that no one would find them."[82] Although the government "practiced fraud in three courts, it succeeded only here [the Supreme Court]."[83] Only the Court "can correct its error and undo what it [the government] has done."[84]

The petition asked the Court to vacate its 1953 decision and to affirm and reinstate the district court's original judgment entered in the widows' favor. Starting with the amount the widows were denied as a result of the settlement on June 22, 1953 ($55,000), and calculating what that amount would bring if invested (an average rate of return of 6% per annum for corporate bonds and other investments), the petition determined that the families were entitled to $1.14 million.[85] The petition also asked for attorneys' fees and costs, in line with earlier rulings regarding the Court's inherent powers to redress fraud on the Court or to sanction misconduct.[86]

Attached to the petition was an appendix containing such documents as the June 22, 1953, compromise settlement and the declassified accident report and survivor statements. The accident report signed by Colonel John W. Persons explains that the B-29 took off on October 6, 1948, "on a research and development mission" for the purpose of "completing an electronics project."[87] There was nothing privileged or sensitive about that information. It was disclosed in newspaper coverage a day after the accident. More significantly, the report notes that "Technical Orders 01-20EJ-177 and 01-20EJ-178, dated May 1947, were not complied with." The orders provided for changes "in the exhaust manifold assemblies for the purpose of eliminating a definite fire hazard."[88] Moreover, the "passengers and crew including the civilian passengers were not briefed prior to take-off on emergency procedures in accordance with AF Regulation 60-5."[89] The report concluded that the "aircraft is not considered to have been safe for flight because of non-compliance" with the two technical orders, and that the fire that developed in the No. 1 engine was the result "of the failure of the right exhaust collector ring."[90]

81. Id.
82. Id.
83. Id.
84. Id.
85. Id. at 23–24.
86. Id. at 26–27.
87. Appendix, at 14a.
88. Id. at 16a.
89. Id. at 19a.
90. Id. at 22a.

A summary of the B-29 accident by Lieutenant Colonel Murl Estes stated that the access door on the No. 1 engine "was turning brown from excessive heat." Fire extinguishers were used, without effect, "and then a severe engine fire was observed."[91] He concluded that the fire was "probably caused" by breaks found in the right exhaust collector ring. The fire "may have been aggravated" by noncompliance with Technical Order 177 "in that heat shields were not installed at the rear lower cowl assembly to prevent excessive heat from entering the accessary section."[92] He pointed out that the Accident Investigation Board singled out, as "the most probable cause factor" for the accident, "the failure to comply with" Technical Order 177.[93]

A supplemental aircraft accident report, dated December 14, 1948, also noted that Technical Order 177 was only "partially complied with in that the exhaust manifold has been installed but the heat shields were not installed at the rear lower cowl assembly."[94] A clamp assembly, part of the exhaust rear manifold assembly, was cracked.[95] The fire in the No. 1 engine "appears to have started" in the area surrounding the flexible joint assembly and "progressed into the accessory section because of the absence of the heat shields."[96] The failure to comply with Technical Order 177 "results in a very serious fire hazard prevailing in all engines."[97]

Government's Brief

The government responded to plaintiffs' petition in May 2003, stating that they had not provided grounds for the Supreme Court to issue an extraordinary writ. To the government, the Court was divested of its jurisdiction over the case when it decided *Reynolds* in 1953 and the district court subsequently entered the final settlement judgment.[98] The government's brief called attention to the original offer that the plaintiffs depose the surviving crew members, enabling them, as the Court put it, "to adduce the essential facts as to causation without resort to material touching upon military secrets."[99] The Court regarded that procedure as sound: "We think that offer should have

91. Id. at 33a.
92. Id. at 34a.
93. Id.
94. Id. at 64a.
95. Id.
96. Id. at 65a.
97. Id.
98. Response of the United States to Motion for Leave to File a Petition for a Writ of Error Coram Nobis, In re Patricia J. Herring, No. 02-M76 (hereafter "Response").
99. Id. at 9 (quoting from United States v. Reynolds, 345 U.S. at 11).

been accepted."[100] The government's brief states that when the case was remanded to the district court, the plaintiffs "did not avail themselves of the government's offer to interview the surviving crew members" and chose to settle their claims.[101] Plaintiffs maintain that Charles J. Biddle took the depositions before settling, although copies of the transcripts of the depositions are not available and may never have been transcribed.[102] The Supreme Court decided *Reynolds* on March 9, 1953. A little over two weeks later, on March 27, Biddle filed with the district court a notice of depositions, requesting the government to produce for depositions at his office, on "April 10, 1952 [1953]," the three surviving crew members, Moore, Peny, and Murrhee.[103] Biddle wrote to Phyllis Brauner on April 29, 1953, that the depositions had been taken.[104]

The government reviewed the essential elements of Rule 20 of the Supreme Court, governing procedures on a petition for an extraordinary writ. Issuance of a writ "is not a matter of right, but of discretion sparingly exercised." To justify the granting of this writ, "the petition must show that the writ will be in aid of the Court's appellate jurisdiction, that exceptional circumstances warrant the exercise of the Court's discretionary powers, and that adequate relief cannot be obtained in any other form or from any other court."[105] Clearly the Court had discretion to issue the writ, particularly because the fraud had been committed primarily against it. Or it had the option of denying the writ with the understanding that the plaintiffs could seek relief in a lower court. The government urged the latter course, insisting that the petitioners had not shown that adequate relief was unavailable "in any other form or from any other court."[106]

The government argued that the fraud alleged by the petitioners was committed, "if at all, in the trial court, court of appeal, as well as the Supreme Court in *Reynolds,* because the claim of privilege was asserted on the same foundation in each of those courts."[107] It is true that the statements by Finletter and Harmon surfaced in trial court, but the reasons given by the

---

100. United States v. Reynolds, 345 U.S. at 11.

101. Response, at 9.

102. Plaintiffs' Memorandum in Opposition to Defendant's Motion to Dismiss, Herring v. United States, Civil Action No. 03-5500 (LDD) (E.D. Pa. 2004), at 24 (Note 9).

103. Notice of Depositions, Brauner and Palya v. United States, Civil Action No. 9793, and Reynolds v. United States, Civil Action No. 10,142 (E.D. Pa. March 27, 1953).

104. Letter from Charles J. Biddle to Mrs. William Brauner, April 29, 1953; http://www.wbur.org/photogallery/news%5Fbrauner/default.asp?counter=5.

105. Response, at 10.

106. Id. at 11.

107. Id. at 12–13.

government for nondisclosure in district court centered on the Housekeeping Statute and the privileged nature of aircraft accident reports. Those reasons reappeared in the Third Circuit. The foundation for the claim of privilege changed fundamentally at the Supreme Court, after the government had lost two times in a row. Only at the Supreme Court did the state secrets privilege fully emerge as the government's dominant rationale.

The remainder of the government's brief dismissed the allegations of fraud, finding them to be "without merit."[108] It claimed that the Supreme Court "did not decide that the documents at issue were protected by the Air Force's claim of privilege, but rather remanded the case for further proceedings."[109] The Court did indeed remand the case, but it is false to say it did not decide that the documents were protected by the claim of privilege. The remand was merely to encourage the plaintiffs to depose the surviving crew members. There would be little opportunity for the plaintiffs (or the district judge in chambers) to see the disputed documents. Repeatedly the Court accepted the state secrets privilege: "Certainly there was a reasonable danger that the accident investigation report would contain references to the secret electronic equipment which was the primary concern of the mission."[110] The district judge was not allowed to examine the documents in camera, for there was a "reasonable danger that compulsion of the evidence will expose military matters which, in the interest of national security, should not be divulged."[111] These "electronic devices must be kept secret if their full military advantage is to be exploited in the national interests."[112] In view of the Finletter and Harmon statements, there was "a reasonable possibility that military secrets were involved," and there was "certainly a sufficient showing of privilege to cut off further demand for the documents."[113] Even when there is "the most compelling necessity" for access to documents it "cannot overcome the claim of privilege if the court is ultimately satisfied that military secrets are at stake."[114] The plaintiffs should have interviewed the surviving members of the crew to avoid "material touching upon military secrets."[115]

The government's brief objected that the petition for *coram nobis* "would create needless friction between the branches of government, and under such a rule, there would never be finality in cases involving classified information."

---

108. Id. at 13.
109. Id. at 14.
110. United States v. Reynolds, 345 U.S. at 10.
111. Id.
112. Id.
113. Id. at 11.
114. Id.
115. Id.

The government found "nothing exceptional about the declassification of the documents at issue in this case that would warrant reopening this long-settled case."[116] The case was "long-settled" because it was based on fraud, and there is no justification for finality when the judiciary is deceived by the facts, especially when the deception comes from the government. The "needless friction" here is part of the system of checks and balances, where an abuse by one branch is subject to review and reversal by another branch. The process has a purpose. The system of separation of powers was adopted to protect the rights of citizens by limiting the abuse that occurs when power is concentrated in a single branch.

Curiously, the government argued that the "fraud alleged by petitioners in this case was not a basis for this Court's decision in *Reynolds.*"[117] The Court's opinion in 1953 turned not only on the privileges asserted by the government in the lower court (such as the Housekeeping Statute), but also on the heightened claims of state secrets pressed upon the Supreme Court. Had the Justices taken the time to read the accident report and the statements of survivors, they would have learned that the documents contained no state secrets, and thus there was no justification for withholding them from the plaintiffs or the trial judge.

The government reasoned that the allegation of fraud lacks merit because "there was a well-recognized privilege in 1950, as there is today, for accident investigation reports like the one that was at issue in the underlying case."[118] That privilege, limited and checked by the courts, was acknowledged by the district court and the Third Circuit, but held to be less weighty than the needs of plaintiffs for documentary evidence under the Federal Tort Claims Act. Only at the Supreme Court level did the government jettison the privilege for investigation reports in favor of the emotionally laden state secrets privilege. The government cited the Civil Aeronautics Act of 1938 for its provision that "no part of any report or reports of the [Air Safety] Board or the [Civil Aeronautics] Authority relating to any accident, or the investigation thereof, shall be admitted as evidence or used in any suit or action for damages growing out of any matter mentioned in such report or reports."[119] Significantly, no such statutory provision applies to the military or to the Federal Tort Claims Act. The government's brief adds that Finletter's claim of privilege "relied on regulations that embodied the same public policy of encouraging full and frank cooperation with accident investigations in order to promote flying safety."[120]

116. Response, at 16.
117. Id. at 17.
118. Id. at 19.
119. Id. at 20 (52 Stat. 1013, § 701(e) (1938)).
120. Id.

Probably so—but there is a wide gap between the legal authority that Congress puts in a statute and what an agency puts in a regulation.

The fact that the documents withheld from the plaintiffs and the district judge did not contain secrets of national security is addressed by the government this way: "The claim of privilege did not state that the particular accident reports or witness statements in this case in fact contained military or state secrets." Rather, Finletter's claim of privilege "expressed concern that because the particular aircraft was engaged on a secret mission to test highly secret equipment, production of the report might lead to disclosure of information touching on the classified equipment."[121] It is disingenuous to argue that the affidavits did not state that the documents contained military or state secrets. They were written for that purpose, and so understood by the courts, even if they can be parsed for some degree of ambiguity. Second, the government is presenting a slippery-slope defense. Under its theory, all documents, no matter how innocuous, must be withheld for fear that somewhere down the line, a state secret might be jeopardized. This analysis makes everything a state secret to be withheld from plaintiffs and courts.

As an example of what could have happened had the plaintiffs, or the district judge, been given access to documents they requested, the government points to a letter in the file that refers to RCA's role in Project Banshee, a classified project to develop a pilotless aircraft guided missile system.[122] The ability of plaintiffs to read the accident report and the survivor statements would have been more than enough to establish negligence on the part of the government. There was no need for them to go further.

If the government's argument were to prevail, no discovery could proceed because every document surrendered might lead to the disclosure of others, without end. The discovery process is not boundless. Yet the government insisted: "The Secretary's claim of privilege over the accident and ancillary reports responsibly and accurately sought to protect highly classified information about the Banshee project."[123] How would one know if that was the motive, or whether it was to keep from plaintiffs evidence of government negligence?

Plaintiffs' Reply

The plaintiffs, in their reply to the government, stated that it was never the object of discovery or court orders to gain access to the "accident investigative

121. Id. at 21.
122. Id. at 22.
123. Id. at 23.

file" or to "ancillary" materials in that file.[124] The only documents sought in discovery were the official accident report and the survivor statements. The district court's September 21, 1950, order directing in camera review was confined to "the report and findings of the official investigation of the defendant's B-29 type aircraft near Waycross, Georgia on October 6, 1948," and statements by the crew survivors Moore, Peny, and Murrhee.[125] The plaintiffs also disputed the government's claim that the statements by Finletter and Harmon were truthful. Harmon, for example, told the district court that the "information and findings of the Accident Investigation Board and statements which have been demanded by the plaintiffs cannot be furnished without seriously hampering national security, flying safety and the development of highly technical and secret military equipment."[126] Reading the accident report and the survivor statements would not have revealed anything about the development of highly technical and secret military equipment.

To the plaintiffs, Finletter and Harmon did not tell the truth: "they lied."[127] It was because of the government's claim that the disputed documents contained classified or sensitive information that Judge Kirkpatrick proposed that he read the materials in camera. The Third Circuit understood the government to assert that the documents "sought to be produced contain state secrets of a military character."[128] The Finletter and Harmon statements led the Supreme Court to believe that "there was a reasonable danger that the accident investigation report would contain references to the secret electronic equipment which was the primary concern of the mission."[129] The focus was on the accident report, not "ancillary" materials. Even if the RCA letter about Project Banshee had been released to the plaintiffs, no sensitive national security information would have been disclosed. In January 1947, almost two years before the B-29 crash, the *Washington Star* had published several articles on Project Banshee, describing Air Force efforts to create a pilotless remote-controlled drone.[130]

To the government's claim that "there is nothing unique about the particular allegations of fraud in this case that excuse petitioners from presenting their allegations to a lower court first by way of an independent action," the plaintiffs replied: "There is one extraordinarily unique thing about this

---

124. Petitioners' Reply in Support of Their Motion to File Petition for a Writ of Error *Coram Nobis,* In re Patricia J. Herring, No. 02-M76, at 2 (hereafter "Reply").
125. Id. at 3.
126. Id. at 4.
127. Id. at 3.
128. Id. at 5 (quoting from Reynolds v. United States, 192 F.2d at 996).
129. Id. (quoting from United States v. Reynolds, 345 U.S. at 10).
130. Id. at 6–7 (Note 4).

particular fraud: It did not succeed in the courts below. *It only succeeded in this Court.*[131] In response to the government's remark that the three widows after the Supreme Court's decision "made a strategic decision to settle their cases,"[132] the petitioners disagreed. The settlement "could hardly be called 'informed' much less 'strategic.' The widows were entirely ignorant that their judgments had been vitiated through fraud."[133]

As a further point, the plaintiffs focused on the futility of the three widows following the advice of the Supreme Court to return to district court and interview the surviving crew members. The record indicates that they took that step. But as the declassified statements reveal, "not a single one of those crewmen knew that the main cause of the accident was the Air Force's failure to comply with Technical Orders mandating changes to the aircraft's exhaust manifold assemblies."[134]

Finally, with regard to the government's position that the issue of *coram nobis* relief should be sent back to district court to be decided there, rather than by the Supreme Court, the plaintiffs offered this objection: "it would deny this Court any power to correct its *own* mistakes, whether through *coram nobis* or otherwise. . . . This Court is not powerless in the face of fraud. It should now act in this case to set things right."[135] Without explanation, the Court on June 23, 2003, issued this decision: "Motion for leave to file a petition for writ of error *coram nobis* denied."[136]

In District Court Again

On October 1, 2003, the plaintiffs filed an action in district court for relief from judgment in order to remedy fraud on the court. It argued that the government's action "was intended to and did subvert the processes of this Court, the Court of Appeals, and the United States Supreme Court."[137] The government's brief, filed January 23, 2004, moved to dismiss the case. The opening paragraph of the brief highlights the importance of *Reynolds,* where the Supreme Court recognized "for the first time in its modern jurisprudence

---

131. Id. at 9 (emphasis in original).
132. Response, at 15.
133. Reply, at 10.
134. Id.
135. Id. at 12 (emphasis in original).
136. In re Herring, 539 U.S. 940 (2003).
137. Independent Action for Relief from Judgment to Remedy Fraud on the Court, Herring v. United States (E.D. Pa. 2003), at 14.

the state secrets privilege—the government's privilege against disclosures of information that could be harmful to national security."[138]

Opposing Briefs

The protection of privileged information, argued the government, should not be compromised by plaintiffs unskilled in understanding the needs of national security: "plaintiffs lack the informed expertise of Executive Branch officials who are responsible for determining what information should or should not be withheld in the interests of national security."[139] Plaintiffs could not be expected to understand "how seemingly trivial information contained in these documents may have provided valuable intelligence to the nation's enemies—all the more so considering that the events in question took place over 50 years ago."[140] If plaintiffs lacked expertise, what of courts? Did the government's argument also exclude in camera inspection by federal judges? Did expertise reside solely in the executive branch?

The logic of the government's argument would put plaintiffs in a federal tort claims case at a permanent disadvantage in any dispute concerning the military or other areas of governmental activity deemed sensitive to national security. The government would be the sole judge of what information "should or should not be withheld in the interests of national security." What safeguards would prevent the government from withholding information not in the interests of national security but to conceal corruption, hide embarrassments, or promote other agendas unrelated to national security? There is no reason to assume that in the struggle over "national security" information the executive branch is guided solely or even primarily by the national interest.

The government's brief describes the type of fraud that should concern the courts. Fraud on the court involves "only the most egregious misconduct, such as the subornation of perjury by an officer of the court, the bribery of judges, or other unconscionable schemes to subvert a court's impartiality."[141] Who gets to define egregious and unconscionable? How would one know that an action satisfying those standards occurs if the government alone decides what information shall be disclosed? The brief adds: "It is well-

---

138. Brief in Support of Defendant's Motion to Dismiss, *Herring v. United States*, Civil Action No. 03-5500 (LDD) (E.D. Pa. 2004), at 1 (hereafter "Defendant's Motion").
139. Id. at 2.
140. Id.
141. Id. at 3.

established that perjury, standing alone, does not rise to that level."[142] Although perjury "must be and is condemned by the courts," the remedies for perjury do not include "a right of action to set aside judgments so long ago taken as the judgment assailed here."[143] The government cited a number of cases to demonstrate that perjury, withholding documents during discovery, and false or misleading interrogatory answers do not constitute fraud upon the court.[144] Those cases, however, involved misconduct by private litigants and witnesses.[145] They did not concern perjury by officers of the court and government attorneys. Far more damaging to the integrity of the judiciary, and far more dangerous to the abuse that comes from concentrated political power, is when perjury, withholding documents, and false or misleading interrogatory answers are done by the government.

Later in its brief, the government explains why it believes courts should not be entrusted to review confidential documents in camera. The government refused to give Judge Kirkpatrick the accident report and the statements of survivors "on the ground that doing so would vitiate the privilege it had asserted."[146] Its position at the Supreme Court was that executive branch agencies have inherent authority "to withhold any documents . . . from judicial view if they deem it to be in the public interest."[147] The brief conceded that the Supreme Court in *Reynolds* chose "a narrower ground for decision."[148]

The fact that plaintiffs would later find in the accident report and the survivor statements no information about military secrets does not, according to the government, represent fraud against the courts. Determinations of what information "is and is not appropriately protected in the interests of national security involve predictive judgments about the potential future harm of premature [*sic*] disclosure, where informed expertise and even intuition 'must often control in the absence of hard evidence.'"[149] In short: Leave it to the executive branch.

The government denied that the statements signed by Finletter and Harmon constituted lies: "neither Secretary Finletter's claim of privilege, nor

142. Id.
143. Id.
144. Id. at 16.
145. E.g., Simon v. Navon, 116 F.3d 1, 6 (1st Cir. 1997) ("perjury alone, absent allegation of involvement by an officer of the court . . . has never been sufficient," citing Geo. P. Reintjes Co. v. Riley Stoker Corp., 71 F.3d 44, 49 (1st Cir. 1995); Great Coastal Exp. v. International Broth., Etc., 675 F.2d 1349, 1355–57 (4th Cir. 1982); Petry v. General Motors Corporation, Chevrolet Division, 62 F.R.D. 357 (E.D. Pa. 1974).
146. Defendant's Motion, at 7.
147. Id. at 8.
148. Id. (citing United States v. Reynolds, 345 U.S. at 6).
149. Id. at 18.

General Harmon's affidavit, makes any specific representation concerning the contents of those documents [the accident report and the witness statements]."[150] This point has already been examined. It was because of the Finletter-Harmon statements that both the district court and the Third Circuit supported in camera review and the Supreme Court was convinced that the accident report contained secret information. The government further asserted: "The Executive Branch's familiarity with matters of national security means that it has unmatched expertise and insight when it comes to 'what adverse [e]ffects might occur as a result of public disclosure' of information in the government's hands."[151] As shown by the experience of Solicitor General Griswold and the Pentagon Papers (Chapter 5), the executive branch also has unmatched ability to call something national security when it is not.

From a number of cases, the government concluded that not only is it appropriate for courts to give "utmost deference" to governmental judgments about the dangers of disclosing national security information, but also "little weight, if any, is given to the opinions of litigants," such as those in the relitigation of the *Reynolds* case.[152] The government cites a 1989 opinion by the Fifth Circuit for the proposition that "even the most apparently innocuous [information] can yield valuable intelligence."[153] And "even if plaintiffs had a sound basis for leveling charges of fraud, plaintiffs have not alleged a fraud on the court—a subversion of the courts' impartiality—that justifies relief from a judgment entered more than 50 years ago."[154]

Returning to the plaintiffs' allegation that Finletter and Harmon committed perjury, the government cites a 1993 district court case for this observation: "it is well settled that a witness' perjured testimony does not constitute fraud upon the court."[155] The alleged perjured testimony in this case was by the General Electric Company, not by the government. What if the government presented perjured testimony to a federal judge? Would that constitute fraud upon the court, especially when it is submitted in the form of an affidavit signed by a government official who is an attorney? Should the government be allowed to lie and deceive in court without penalty?

To the government, the plaintiffs would have to allege or show that the government's counsel in *Reynolds,* "as officers of this Court, the Third Circuit, or the Supreme Court, either suborned or otherwise knowingly participated in the submission of perjured testimony, as might give rise to a fraud on the

150. Id., Note 6.
151. Id. at 19.
152. Id.
153. Id. (citing Knight v. CIA, 872 F.2d 660, 663 (5th Cir. 1989)).
154. Id. at 21.
155. Id. (citing Lacy v. Gen. Elec. Co., No. 81-2958, 1993 WL 53570 (E.D. Pa. 1993)).

court."[156] That is, the plaintiffs would have to produce documentary evidence that attorneys for the federal government directed Finletter and Harmon to sign false statements. It is improbable that a government attorney would ever put that legal advice on paper, and even more unlikely that the government would ever surrender such a document, if it existed, to plaintiffs during the discovery process.

The government's brief faults the plaintiffs in *Reynolds* for failing to interrogate the surviving crew members. Apparently they did. Had they done so, argued the government, "they may well have adduced the facts essential to their case, as the Supreme Court anticipated."[157] Interrogating the surviving crew members would have shed no light on the truth or falsity of the Finletter and Harmon statements. Had the plaintiffs' attorney even edged in that direction, the government—present at the deposition—would have objected that the area under inquiry constituted confidential and privileged information.

Finally, the government denied that the plaintiffs should have any opportunity to contest matters they could have pursued in 1953 "but did not." Consequently, "the evidence and recollection of the facts, and judgments, giving rise to the government's assertion of privilege now lie beneath the sands of 50 years' time."[158] That was not true. The evidence existed in the form of declassified documents released to the public in 1996.

Several other briefs were prepared by the plaintiffs and the government for the district court. The plaintiffs' memorandum in opposition to the government motion to dismiss, dated February 24, 2004, rejected the idea that the plaintiffs in 1953 could have better established fraud by the government had they taken discovery of the surviving crew members: "the notion that the widows, through depositions of the crash survivors, would have been able to divine that Air Force officials had defrauded the courts is absurd; those survivors did not even know the chief cause of the accident, much less the contents of the Air Force's classified reports."[159]

As to the government's effort to withhold the accident report from the plaintiffs and the courts, the plaintiffs' brief remarks: "The Air Force presumably sought to protect these materials to avoid the embarrassment and public scrutiny their production would have generated."[160] The accident report revealed negligence on the part of the Air Force for failing to install the heat shields and for failing to brief the civilian engineers before the flight on the

156. Id. at 22.
157. Id. at 23.
158. Id. at 24.
159. Plaintiffs' Memorandum in Opposition to Defendant's Motion to Dismiss, Herring v. United States, Civil Action No. 03-5500 (LDD) (E.D. Pa. 2004), at 4.
160. Id. at 10.

use of parachutes and emergency aircraft evacuation. Having become a separate branch of the armed services in September 1947, the Air Force may have wanted to withhold any information that could have damaged its reputation and competence. Still, had the accident report been shown to Judge Kirkpatrick in his chambers, and had he awarded the widows the original amount, the government could have accepted that judgment and not appealed. End of story. There was no risk that what Judge Kirkpatrick saw would have become public knowledge. He would have known he was looking at classified information, and he would have been aware that he had a duty to protect it from public disclosure.

The dilemma for the government, however, went beyond negligence. Had Judge Kirkpatrick looked at the accident report, it would have been clear that the government had lied on its response to Question 31, which asked whether any modifications had been prescribed for the B-29 engines to prevent overheating and reduce the risk of fire hazard. The government's answer: "No."[161] Reading the declassified accident report today, it is obvious that other answers by the government were either inaccurate or false.

Thus, the government, through its own doing, had a number of problems to deal with. First: negligence by the Air Force. To keep that information from being disclosed, the government chose to lie when it responded to the interrogatories. It was a classic tale of one lie requiring another. Finletter and Harmon would have to imply, without ever saying so explicitly, that the accident report and the survivor statements contained military secrets. After the dispute was relitigated in 2003, the government decided to continue with falsehoods, including representations that the Finletter and Harmon statements were true and that the plaintiffs in 1953 might have uncovered fraud by the government had they deposed the surviving crew members. Once false statements are made, the next step is to cover it up and obstruct justice. To the plaintiffs, the Finletter and Harmon statements were offered "in order to cover-up and suppress conclusive evidence that the Air Force's negligence had caused the deaths of Reynolds, Palya, and Brauner."[162] Moreover, the statements were submitted "with a view toward fabricating a 'test case' for a favorable judicial ruling on claims of an executive or 'state secrets' privilege—a case built on the fraudulent premise that the documents in question contained 'secret' military or national security information."[163]

The plaintiffs' brief reviewed the meaning of "fraud upon the court." From Moore's *Federal Practice* comes the guidance that fraud on the court "is

161. Id. at 11.
162. Id. at 11–12.
163. Id. at 12.

limited to fraud that does, or at least attempts to, 'defile the court itself,' or that is perpetrated by officers of the court 'so that the judicial machinery cannot perform in the usual manner its impartial task of adjudicating cases.'"[164] The brief continues: "Thus, a 'fraud on the court' is a fraud designed not simply to cheat an opposing litigant, but to 'corrupt the judicial process' or 'subvert the integrity of the court.'"[165] To prevent the executive branch from committing fraud on the courts, the federal judiciary must place a higher value on preserving its independence, integrity, and credibility than in swallowing at face value the government's assertions about national security and state secrets. A lack of judicial resolve and probity invites executive branch manipulation and lies. If there is no price to be paid for deceiving the judiciary, executive officials—including attorneys in the Justice Department—will continue to misrepresent the facts and withhold documents that plaintiffs, the courts, and the public are entitled to receive.

In a reply brief dated March 19, 2004, the government stated that "perjury alone, absent involvement by an officer of the court, has never been accepted as a fraud on the court."[166] It concluded that Finletter and Harmon "were not acting in a capacity as 'officers of the court,' however, when they asserted the military secrets privilege on the government's behalf."[167] As to the plaintiffs' claim that Finletter and Harmon were officers of the court "on the ground that they assumed the role of fiduciaries to this Court when they asserted the state secrets privilege on the government's behalf," the government insisted that the plaintiffs offered no authority for this proposition "except their own say-so."[168]

Oral Argument

Judge Legrome D. Davis issued an order setting May 11, 2004, as the day for oral argument.[169] James J. Gilligan of the Justice Department presented the government's position, summarizing some of the points made in earlier briefs. First: "it is undisputed that on remand from the Supreme Court the plaintiffs neither attempted to make a showing of need for the [accident] report nor

---

164. Id. at 14.
165. Id.
166. Reply Brief in Support of Defendant's Motion to Dismiss, Herring v. United States, Civil Action No. 03-5500 (LDD) (E.D. Pa. 2004), at 3.
167. Id. at 5.
168. Id.
169. Order, Herring v. United States, Civil Action No. 2:03-CV-05500-LDD (E.D. Pa. 2004).

did they press their claims through discovery to trial."[170] Of course that was disputed. Second: "as the Courts have long recognized, lay persons lack the experience, the expertise and the knowledge that the executive branch possesses, and in particular the military departments possess, when it comes to making judgments as to what disclosures of information might be harmful to national security."[171] Third: "the Government is not aware of any case where a Court has permitted litigants to reopen judgments that have lain undisturbed for any period approaching 50 years."[172]

Gilligan then reviewed the standards for setting aside a judgment on grounds of fraud on the court, "requiring narrowly defined conduct of only the most egregious sort." Examples would include "bribery of a Judge or jurors, or a fraud which involves officers in the Court and its perpetuation, such as the subornation of perjury by a parties counsel." He said that the plaintiffs made no allegation that the government bribed Judge Kirkpatrick "or otherwise corrupted the ability of the Courts to decide the *Reynolds* case impartially."[173] (If a court is denied evidence from one side needed to understand the merits, its decision will be partial and uninformed.) Gilligan claimed that it was established as a matter of law that perjured testimony, "while not to be condoned, does not constitute a fraud on the Court, at least absent the involvement of an officer of the Court."[174] This became a key issue. Were Finletter and Harmon, when they signed their statements, operating as officers of the court? To the government, no. To the plaintiffs, yes. Gilligan said that the plaintiffs "cite no precedence for the proposition that a party or witness assumes the mantel of an officer of the Court simply by asserting a privilege."[175] Again: "it cannot be said that Secretary Finletter or General Harmon acted as trustees or officers of the Court when they asserted the military secrets privilege on behalf of the Government."[176]

Gilligan next argued that even assuming that the Air Force "was, in fact, misrepresenting the case when it asserted the military secrets privilege," the plaintiffs were not denied a recovery.[177] After the Supreme Court's decision they were allowed to use tools of discovery, including depositions of the surviving crew. They could return to the district court and, upon a showing of

170. Transcript of Hearing Before the Honorable Legrome D. Davis, Herring v. United States, CV-03-5500 LDD (E.D. Pa. May 11, 2004), at 5.
171. Id. at 6.
172. Id. at 8.
173. Id.
174. Id. at 9.
175. Id. at 11.
176. Id.
177. Id. at 12.

necessity, ask the court to reconsider the government's assertion of privilege. Curiously, Gilligan said that the plaintiffs, on remand, "were no worse off than if the crash investigation report had never existed."[178] Of course it was the accident report that revealed a number of negligent acts on the part of the Air Force.

In response to Gilligan's opening statement, Wilson Brown insisted that the Finletter statement "could not have been clearer" in saying that the Air Force objected to releasing the documents to the plaintiffs because the documents were "concerned with this confidential missions and equipment of the Air Force," and that there was an intent on the part of government to suggest to the courts that these documents "contained references to confidential missions and descriptions of confidential equipment that were secret."[179] Moreover, the Finletter and Harmon statements "were directed to the Federal Courts, not the widows," and both Finletter and Harmon were lawyers.[180] The statements themselves "were fraudulent" because they contained "false statements" that were either knowingly false or were made in reckless disregard of whether they were true or false. They were "intended to and did mislead the Courts and ultimately the Courts, in the person of the United States Supreme Court, relied on them for precisely the purpose they were intended and vacated judgments that the widows had won."[181]

Brown reviewed earlier cases that defined fraud on the court as "an unconscionable plan or scheme which is designed to influence the Court in its decisions," which would be "something short of bribery." He suggested that such actions include "a mocked up test case based on a phony proposition of fact that the Air Force deliberately us[ed] our widows to take up to the United States Supreme Court." The result, to Brown, was "to subvert the integrity of the judicial process in a rather conscious shocking way."[182] In rebuttal, Gilligan read the case law on fraud on the court in more limited fashion as "a corruption of the Court's ability to decide the matter impartially."[183] The question was whether the Finletter and Harmon statements, however interpreted, prevented the courts from deciding the matter impartially.

A striking part of oral argument focused on whether the Finletter and Harmon statements provide evidence of fraud. Gilligan characterized Brown's position in this manner: "it's obvious because the affidavit submitted by General Harmon and Secretary Finletter say that these crash investigation reports and

178. Id. at 13.
179. Id. at 18.
180. Id. at 19.
181. Id. at 22.
182. Id. at 23.
183. Id. at 35.

witness statements talk about the secret mission and the secret equipment. And, then you look at the reports and there's nothing in there about the mission or the equipment." Gilligan disputed that understanding: "But Your Honor, when you read these affidavits, it's quite clear there are no representations made by either the Secretary or the Judge Advocate General regarding the contents of the report or that the reports—or that the report actually contains any specific description of the equipment or the nature of the mission, although there actually is an allusion to the nature of the mission."[184]

It is true that the Finletter and Harmon statements are written with great ambiguity, whether by design or otherwise, and allow different readers to walk away with different impressions. Yet it is also a fact that the Third Circuit and the Supreme Court read the affidavits to mean that the accident report and the survivor statements contained state secrets. Apparently none of the judges on the Third Circuit and none of the Justices on the Supreme Court ever said to the government: "We're not sure what these statements mean. Do they say that the accident report and the survivor statements contain military secrets or state secrets?" Would the government, in 1952 and 1953, have replied, as Gilligan did in oral argument: "Why, no, Your Honor. Those documents, requested by the plaintiffs, do not contain any military secrets or state secrets." It was to the government's advantage to allow the statements to cloud the facts. It was the responsibility of the plaintiffs and the judiciary to remove the cloud. Instead, they left it there.

The Decision

Judge Davis released his decision on September 10, 2004, granting the government's motion to dismiss and instructing the Clerk of Court to "statistically close this matter."[185] He first looked at the legal standard for motion to dismiss. The government in this case would prevail with its motion to dismiss if the plaintiff "can prove no set of facts in support of the claim which would entitle him to relief."[186] Thus, the court found that the conflict between the Finletter-Harmon statements and the contents of the accident report did not represent a sufficient "set of facts," nor did the clear conflict between the government's answers to interrogatories and the conclusions of the accident report.

The court reviewed the legal standard for finding "fraud upon the court." A number of the provisions of Rule 60(b) appear to fit the government's

184. Id. at 41.
185. Memorandum and Order, Herring v. United States, Civil Action No. 03-CV-5500-LDD (E.D. Pa. Sept. 10, 2004), at 21.
186. Id. at 4.

conduct in *Reynolds,* including "(2) newly discovered evidence which by due diligence could not have been discovered in time to move for a new trial under Rule 59(b)" and "(3) fraud (whether heretofore denominated intrinsic or extrinsic), misrepresentation, or other misconduct of an adverse party."[187] However, the court's review of the complaint and the attached exhibits (including the declassified documents) "does not suggest that the Air Force intended to deliberately misrepresent the truth or commit a fraud on the court."[188] How did Judge Davis know that? Some of the government's answers to the interrogatories and the statements signed by Finletter and Harmon misrepresented the truth, but apparently to the court, it was not "deliberate." It would be difficult for Judge Davis, the plaintiffs, or anyone else to speak with confidence about what was deliberate or not 50 years ago, unless memos surfaced (unlikely) showing criminal intent on the part of government to defraud.

Relying on a judgment of a lower court decision, Judge Davis said: "In all likelihood, fifty years ago the government had a more accurate understanding 'on the prospect of danger to [national security] from the disclosure of secret or sensitive information' than lay persons could appreciate or than hindsight now allows."[189] That is pure assumption on the part of the court and represents judicial deference to military judgments without any supporting evidence. The court also accepted the theory that a single piece of evidence, no matter how innocuous, may open the door to the discovery of a national security secret: "because 'each individual piece of intelligence information, like a piece of [a] jigsaw puzzle, may aid in piecing together bits of information even when the individual piece is not of obvious importance itself.'" It therefore becomes "proper to defer on some level" to governmental claims of privilege even for "information that standing alone may seem harmless, but that together with other information poses a reasonable danger of divulging too much to a 'sophisticated intelligence analyst.'"[190] That is a different way of expressing judicial deference, or judicial abdication, and places a minimal standard on the government to justify nondisclosure. The government frequently advances this "mosaic theory" to withhold documents.

In examining the Finletter statement, Judge Davis summarized the position of the plaintiffs as saying that "only the mission and electronic equipment were confidential." To the court, "a broader reading of the affidavit suggests that beyond the mission itself, disclosure of technical details of the

187. Id. at 5.
188. Id. at 7.
189. Id. at 8 (citing Halperin v. NSC, 452 F.Supp. 47 (D.D.C. 1978)).
190. Id. (citing Fitzgerald v. CIA, 911 F.2d 755, 763 (D.C. Cir. 1990) and In re United States, 872 F.2d 472, 475 (D.C. Cir. 1989), quoting Halkin v. Helms, 598 F.2d 1, 9 (D.C. Cir. 1978)).

B-29 bomber, its operation, or performance would also compromise national security."[191] After reviewing the accident report, the court acknowledged that "it offers no thorough exploration of the secret mission, [but] it does describe the mission as an 'electronics project' and an 'authorized research and development mission.'"[192] That is quite true, but it is equally true that newspapers around the country, in reporting the accident, talked openly about the secret electronics mission.

Judge Davis then drew from the accident report information that was not common knowledge to newspaper readers, such as the technical orders and the installation of heat shields to reduce the danger of engine fire.[193] That information is somewhat sensitive, but sharing it with the district court for in camera review would not have made it public. Davis warned: "Details of flight mechanics, B-29 glitches, and technical remedies in the hands of the wrong party could surely compromise national security."[194] Yes, but examination of the accident report by Judge Kirkpatrick would not have put the document in the hands of the wrong party, nor would it have compromised national security.

Of interest to Judge Davis were published reports that three B-29s were forced to land in Vladivostok, Russia, in 1944, during bombing missions against Japanese targets, and that Russia confiscated the planes and used them as the model for its Tu-4. The replicas "copied the B-29 almost exactly, including the fire-prone engines."[195] Russia used the Tu-4 to detonate its first atomic bomb in 1949.[196] Given this context, Davis found it reasonable that the Air Force, in 1948, would be "eager to protect from public view the accident investigation report that mentions modifications needed for the B-29, and by extension the Tu-4."[197] It may have been reasonable to protect the report from public view, but it was not reasonable to withhold the report from Judge Kirkpatrick's review, unless one regards in camera inspection as tantamount to making the report public.

There are no grounds for that conclusion. Making that assumption is an unwarranted attack on the integrity of a federal judge, yet Judge Davis reasoned: "It is at least conceivable that were the accident investigation report released, it might have alerted the otherwise unaware Soviets to a technical problem in the Tu-4 that the May 1, 1947 technical order sought to remedy in

---

191. Id. at 9.
192. Id. at 10.
193. Id.
194. Id. at 11.
195. Id. at 15.
196. Id. at 16.
197. Id.

the B-29."[198] First, the technical orders were not classified and were available to anyone. Second, if the Russian Tu-4 "copied the B-29 almost exactly, including the fire-prone engines," the Soviets were hardly unaware of technical problems. Third, as explained in the next section, the Tu-4 did not copy the B-29 engine. Fourth, such details were safe in Judge Kirkpatrick's chambers. Fifth, why assume that in camera inspection would lead to the report being "released"?

Judge Davis agreed with the government's argument that the plaintiffs "cannot undo the careful and prudent decision to settle their claims and relitigate issues they voluntarily put to rest more than fifty years ago."[199] That they settled their claims on the basis of misleading statements and false answers to interrogatories did not, to him, disturb his analysis or conclusions. Judge Davis found no evidence of "egregious conduct by any Air Force representatives" and could not, "in good conscience, find a gross miscarriage of justice or grant Plaintiffs the relief from judgment they seek."[200]

The Third Circuit

The plaintiffs appealed to the Third Circuit, challenging Judge Davis on a number of points of law, especially for going outside the information contained in the briefs and constructing his own "public record" on what happened to the B-29s in Russia. The government responded with a brief, the plaintiffs countered with a reply brief, and the case was heard for oral argument on July 15, 2005.

Plaintiffs' Brief

Wilson Brown faulted the district court's decision on a number of grounds, including its failure to view the plaintiffs' allegations in the most favorable light, its "broader reading" of the Finletter statement, and for going beyond the plaintiffs' complaint to assemble a "public record" that the plaintiffs had no opportunity to see and respond to. The plaintiffs had taken the position that only the mission and electronic equipment were confidential, but Judge Davis decided that "a broader reading" of the Finletter statement "suggests that beyond the mission itself, disclosure of technical details of the B-29 bomber, its operations, or performance would also compromise national

198. Id. at 16–17.
199. Id. at 19.
200. Id. at 20.

security."[201] Judge Davis concluded that he was entitled to develop this "public record" because the plaintiffs in their brief had cited certain books on the B-29.[202]

To Brown, the plaintiffs "never cited in their complaint to a 'public record' or gave the district court any license to engage in 'fact-finding' on a motion to dismiss." Nor did the plaintiffs "have any opportunity to respond to the court's judicially-noticed findings, in violation of basic rules of procedure and evidence."[203] He also objected to the district court's standard of review for granting the government's motion to dismiss. Under Rule 12(b)(6) of the Federal Rules of Civil Procedure, a court is bound "to accept all well-pleaded allegations in the complaint as true and to draw all reasonable inferences in favor of the non-moving party. The inquiry is not whether plaintiffs will ultimately prevail in a trial on the merits, but whether they should be afforded an opportunity to offer evidence in support of their claims. Dismissal under Rule 12(b)(6) is not appropriate unless it appears *beyond doubt* that plaintiffs can prove no set of facts in support of his claim which would entitle him to relief."[204]

By concluding that the plaintiffs had failed adequately to allege that the Air Force "intended to deliberately" misrepresent the truth or commit a fraud on the court, Judge Davis had, Brown argued, tilted toward the government. Davis undertook to give the Finletter statement a "broad" construction, "with a view toward drawing all inferences in favor of the government."[205] Brown charged that Davis's reasoning "turns the standards governing Rule 12(b)(6) motions on their head."[206] Although Brown agreed that courts "undoubtedly should afford some deference to executive branch determinations with respect to 'state secrets,'" deference by the judiciary "does not give the government a license to lie."[207] However one reads the Finletter statement, Brown said that the Harmon affidavit "claims no protection broader than Secretary Finletter does."[208]

Brown also disputed the conclusion by Judge Davis that the accident report contained secret or confidential information, such as an electronics project that required "aircraft capable of dropping bombs [and operating] at

---

201. Brief for Appellants, Herring v. United States, No. 04-4270 (3d Cir. 2005), at 14 (citing Judge Davis's decision, at 9).

202. Id. at 15.

203. Id. at 18.

204. Id. at 20 (citing In re Rockefeller Center Properties, Inc. v. Securities Litigation, 311 F.3d 198, 215 (3d Cir. 2002) [emphasis added]).

205. Id. at 25.

206. Id.

207. Id. at 26.

208. Id. at 30.

altitudes of 20,000 feet and above."[209] Brown pointed out that a front page story in the *Waycross Journal-Herald* on October 7, 1948, the day after the accident, reported that the plane "was flying at an altitude of 20,000 feet" when the No. 1 engine caught fire. Earlier newspaper stories, from 1944, described the B-29 as capable of operating at 40,000 feet and higher.[210] With regard to matters of "public record," Brown said that the Third Circuit permitted access to documents "filed of record by public authorities, and not popular histories or internet articles," as Judge Davis had relied on.[211]

Continuing to analyze the court's creation of a "public record," Brown cited Federal Rule of Evidence 201(b) as establishing the standards for judicial notice: "A judicially noticed fact must be one not subject to reasonable dispute in that it is either (1) generally known with the territorial jurisdiction of the trial court or (2) capable of accurate and ready determination by resort to sources whose accuracy cannot reasonably be questioned."[212] In addition, in the context of a motion to dismiss, "if the court takes judicial notice of matters on its own initiative, it must notify the parties that it is doing so, and afford them an opportunity to be heard."[213] Furthermore, the findings by Judge Davis are not "generally known," are not "capable of accurate and ready determination" through unquestioned sources, and the statement that the Soviets "copied the B-29 almost exactly, including the fire-prone engines," is false. The "public record" that Judge Davis relied on—an article in the *Air & Space/Smithsonian* magazine—explains that the Soviets did not use the B-29 engine. Instead, it used a different U.S. engine that Russia had acquired in earlier years under license from the United States.[214] Brown could find no evidence that the Russian plane, the Tu-4, "ever figured into the Air Force's calculations about the accident report and witness statements."[215]

Government's Brief

In a brief filed March 8, 2005, the government responded to the plaintiffs' arguments. After reviewing familiar ground, the brief offered new information

209. Id. at 34 (citing Judge Davis, at 10).
210. Id. at 35 (Note 15).
211. Id. at 40–41.
212. Id. at 42.
213. Id. (quoting from Kurtis A. Kemper, "What Matters Not Contained in the Pleadings May Be Considered in Ruling on a Motion to Dismiss Under Rule 12(b)(6) of the Federal Rules of Civil Procedure or Motion for Judgment on the Pleadings Under Rule 12(c) Without Conversion to Motion for Summary Judgment," 138 A.L.R. Fed. 393, § 2 (1997)).
214. Id. at 43 (citing Von Hardesty, "Made in the USSR," Air & Space/Smithsonian, February–March 2001, at 76, available at http://www.airspacemag.com/ASM/Mag/Index/2001/FM/TU-4.html).
215. Id. at 46.

by rejecting the plaintiffs' position that the accident report did not contain state secrets. The report "actually does contain details about the secret military equipment aboard the B-29 when it crashed, as the district court concluded. Most notably, the report identified the altitude at which the secret equipment needed to be tested and the fact that in order to test it, an airplane with bomb bay doors was required."[216] Later: "The information as to bomb bay doors and required testing altitude plainly constitute puzzle pieces that help in putting together a picture of the United States' program to develop a guided missile."[217] Here is an attempt to use the mosaic theory, but anyone reading a newspaper in 1948 knew that the B-29 was involved in secret testing, and obviously a B-29 bomber has bomb bay doors. Where is the secret?

On the issue of officers of the court, the government insisted that "the submissions [Finletter and Harmon statements] in the *Reynolds* litigation were not made by officers of the court, and there is no allegation here that officers of the court [attorneys from the Justice Department] participated in any way in their creation."[218] Finletter "did not submit an affidavit to the district court, but a formal claim of privilege, more akin to a pleading, that did not purport to be made under oath or under penalty of perjury."[219] The government cautioned the Third Circuit against trying to apply the standards for fraud on the court "to unsworn pleadings filed in court by non-lawyer government officials."[220] Finletter, in fact, was a lawyer.

Even assuming that the Finletter statement and the Harmon affidavit were not truthful, the government regarded both men as "witnesses, not officers of the court."[221] The cases the government cited on this issue are contradictory. One decision held that "an attorney is an 'officer of the court,'"[222] which would fit Finletter and Harmon. Other cases referred to officers of the court as "attorneys authorized to practice before that court."[223] That might exclude Finletter and Harmon. The government's bottom line: "Persons who appear in court as government witnesses . . . are not serving as officers of the court."[224]

The government defended Judge Davis's citation of history books and articles and described his use of that material as "not erroneous."[225] Cases were

216. Brief for Appellee, Herring v. United States, No. 04-4270 (3d Cir. 2005), at 24–25.
217. Id. at 40.
218. Id. at 25–26.
219. Id. at 33 (Note 11).
220. Id.
221. Id. at 53.
222. Id. (citing Traveler's Indemnity Co. v. Gore, 761 F.2d 1549, 1551 (11th Cir. 1985)).
223. Id. at 54 (citing Ex parte Garland, 71 U.S. 333, 378 (1866)).
224. Id.
225. Id. at 47.

cited to show that judges may take judicial notice of facts outside the pleadings, including the contents of newspaper articles and history books.[226] Yet
Judge Davis was in error when he said that the Russians "copied the B-29 almost exactly, including the fire-prone engines." To the government, that error
was of "no moment" because the Air Force "could easily have been concerned
that the engines might be copied by the Soviets in the future and want[ed] to
withhold information on the engine's problems and solutions to those problems for that reason."[227]

Plaintiffs' Reply Brief

The reply brief by Wilson Brown focused on the elements needed to show
fraud on the court, which "encompasses all misleading statements or omissions that are directed to the court for the purpose of influencing the court in
its decision." Those who commit fraud on the court "need not be 'officers of
the court,' although Secretary Finletter and Major General Harmon unquestionably were." To Brown, it was not "essential that the court's 'impartiality'
be corrupted." It was essential "only that the lie be directed to the court to
influence the court's decision-making and be relied upon by the court in making its ruling."[228]

Brown charged that the government "ignores the fact" that the Finletter
and Harmon statements specifically represented the accident report and the
witness statements as "concerned with confidential missions and equipment
of the Air Force," when, "in fact, they were not." To that extent the statements
"were deceitful—and it was this deceit that proved dispositive in the Supreme
Court." Whether the statements would support a perjury prosecution was
not, to Brown, the question. "The misleading affidavits were designed to and
did work a fraud on the court."[229] The principal issue before the court was
whether the allegations put forth by the plaintiffs, "viewed in the light most
favorable" to them, "state a claim for relief." If they did, as Brown concluded,
all the other issues (whether the statements were knowingly or recklessly deceitful, whether anything "secret" was in the accident report and the witness
statements, and the question of Judge Davis going outside the record in the
search for facts) should be dealt with in later motions or at trial.[230]

---

226. Id. at 50.
227. Id. at 52 (Note 17).
228. Reply Brief for Appellants, Herring v. United States, No. 04-4270 (3d Cir. 2005),
at 2.
229. Id. at 3.
230. Id.

An essential issue for Brown was the need to select and follow a proper standard of review. He insisted that the case be governed by Rule 12(b)(6), requiring plenary or de novo review by the court. The government regarded the plaintiffs' action as a Rule 60(b) motion, leading to a standard more favorable to the government. Also, the government wanted the issue to be perjury, defined by criminal perjury standards. Under that procedure, the plaintiffs could prevail only if the Finletter and Harmon statements "are not susceptible to any truthful interpretation." To Brown, the issue was fraud, requiring the plaintiffs only "to allege facts that give rise to an inference that the government engaged in *deceit.*"[231] Brown was certain that the plaintiffs had met that test.

The government argued that fraud on the court could be based only on the knowing participation of an "officer of the court." Brown rejected that position, insisting that a claim of fraud on the court "may be based on an unlawful scheme or plan undertaken entirely without the involvement of counsel."[232] He rejected also the government's contention that Finletter and Harmon were "witnesses" and not "officers of the court." Brown defined the latter term broadly to cover "all persons who stand in a fiduciary or other special relationship to the court given the nature of the proceedings."[233] Both Finletter and Harmon were attorneys and both "had a special duty and responsibility to the federal courts in asserting a 'state secrets' privilege."[234] Brown cited this passage from Judge Davis's ruling, where he rejected the government's contention that Finletter and Harmon were "mere affiants":

Adopting the Government's position would directly contravene the role contemplated in *United States* v. *Reynolds* for military officers; the military secrets privilege standard demands that only the head of the department with control over the matter lodge the formal claim of privilege following her/his personal consideration. *Reynolds,* 345 U.S. at 8. The Court depends on the experience, expertise, and truthfulness of the official lodging the military secrets privilege claim, such that the official must speak truthfully.[235]

Brown maintained that the Finletter and Harmon statements "falsely represented" that the documents requested by the three widows were "concerned with confidential missions and equipment of the Air Force." The documents

231. Id. at 12 (emphasis in original).
232. Id.
233. Id. at 13.
234. Id.
235. Id. (quoting from Judge Davis's memorandum opinion, at 11 [Note 3]).

206 CHAPTER SIX

did not contain that information, "*and this falsehood was dispositive in the Supreme Court.*"[236] In *Reynolds,* the Court concluded that the statements established "there was a reasonable danger that the accident investigation report would contain references to the secret electronic equipment which was the primary concern of the mission."[237]

Oral Argument

On July 15, 2005, the Third Circuit heard oral argument. Sitting on the panel were Judges Samuel A. Alito Jr., Franklin S. Van Antwerpen, and Ruggero J. Aldisert. Wilson Brown began by saying that Judge Davis had turned Rule 12 standards "upside down" and reached outside the record to find facts "and use those facts to bolster his conclusions." Plaintiffs "had no opportunity to test those facts," a procedure that was "clear error" on the part of the district court.[238] Brown said that the standard for fraud on the court was egregious misconduct and a grave miscarriage of justice. When asked whether he was accusing the government of perjury and whether that was fraud on the court, he replied that perjury is a criminal offense and "it is not the standard here." The government knew what it was doing, he said, and it didn't tell the truth. Executive officials signed statements that were not true. "If it was intended to mislead the court and did mislead the court, and the court relied on the representations to decide this case, I think that makes out a claim" for fraud on the court.

The court asked whether there was some ambiguity in the statements signed by Finletter and Harmon. Brown said there might have been, but ambiguity would not help the government's case. If the statements were intended to mislead the court as to state secrets, and it had that effect, "I think you've got a fraud on the court even if the ambiguity exists on the interpretation." Brown kept fraud on the court front and center. One of the judges asked: "You're seeking more money here, basically." Brown agreed that the plaintiffs sought more money. Next question: "Is that really a miscarriage of justice that you didn't get all the money you could?" Brown clarified the issue: "I think the miscarriage of justice is that the Supreme Court was asked a question of first impression on a bogus record. I think that's the miscarriage of justice. I don't think it has to do with how much money we're entitled to, if any. I think it really has to do with the truth."

236. Id. at 27 (emphasis in original).
237. Id. (quoting from United States v. Reynolds, 345 U.S. at 10).
238. Herring v. United States, oral argument before the Third Circuit, July 15, 2005 (tape).

For the government, August E. Flentje from the Justice Department insisted that the bar for alleging fraud on the court had to be set very high to protect the important principle of judicial finality. He said he would probably disagree with Brown that reckless disregard for the truth would be enough. There has to be intentional deception, and it must involve government counsel taking part in perjured testimony. The plaintiffs would have to show bribery, collusion, witness tampering, or fabrication of evidence.

Flentje told the court that the accident report did contain some secrets: the confidential equipment required testing at 20,000 feet and it required testing in a plane with bomb bay doors. He denied there was a miscarriage of justice. In 1953, the Supreme Court sent the case back to district court to enable the plaintiffs to show why it was necessary to further probe the government's claim of privilege. It was almost impossible, he said, to determine today whether the details in the accident report had any intelligence significance at the time. No one should attempt to second-guess 50 years later the government's decision in 1948. Finally, Flentje said that it was acceptable for Judge Davis to go outside the record to understand what happened a half century ago. Other courts had done that.

Court's Decision

On September 22, 2005, the Third Circuit decided in favor of the government. Judge Aldisert, writing for the three-judge panel, explained at the outset that the case was "whether the Government's assertion of military secrets privilege for an accident report discussing the October 6, 1948 crash of a B-29 bomber which killed three civilian engineers along with six military personnel, at Waycross, Georgia, was fraud upon the court." The next two sentences signaled how the court would likely rule: "Actions for fraud upon the court are so rare that this Court has not previously had the occasion to articulate a legal definition of the concept. The concept of fraud upon the court challenges the very principle upon which our judicial system is based: the finality of a judgment."[239] What counted most for the Third Circuit was not having to revisit and redo an earlier decision, even if the evidence was substantial that the judiciary had been misled by the government.

For the Third Circuit, a *coram nobis* case places a heavy burden on plaintiffs: "The presumption against the reopening of a case that has gone through the appellate process all the way to the United States Supreme Court and reached final judgment must be not just a high hurdle to climb but a steep cliff-face to scale."[240] Why? What was significant about the fact that a case

239. Herring v. United States, 424 F.3d 384, 386 (3d Cir. 2005).
240. Id.

had gone through the appellate process and reached final judgment by the Supreme Court? Layers of appeal should not matter if the government had, at every step, misled the judiciary. In fact, if the deception occurred at each level, the burden on the plaintiffs should be less, not more.

In order to meet the standard for proof of fraud upon the court, the Third Circuit identified four ingredients: "there must be: (1) an intentional fraud; (2) by an officer of the court; (3) which is directed at the court itself; and (4) in fact deceives the court."[241] The history of the *Reynolds* litigation indicated that all four standards had been satisfied. However, the Third Circuit decided to use "a demanding standard" for finding intentional fraud. It agreed with the Eighth Circuit that fraud on the court must constitute "egregious misconduct . . . such as bribery of a judge or jury or fabrication of evidence by counsel."[242] That was also the government's position in this case. To determine whether that standard had been met, the Third Circuit examined the Finletter and Harmon statements. Given the court's standards, it appeared that false or misleading content in the documents would be insufficient proof of fraud. How could the plaintiffs show that the documents had been fabricated? How would plaintiffs ever obtain such evidence during discovery?

The Third Circuit agreed with other rulings that "perjury by a witness is not enough to constitute fraud upon the court."[243] This position is sound when private parties are in court. Litigants are expected through the adversary process to catch false statements "through discovery and cross-examination, and, where warranted, motion for relief from judgment to the presiding court."[244] However, the standard should be different when perjury is committed by the government and when the government, at the discovery stage, refused to release an accident report that would have shown the Finletter and Harmon statements were false or misleading. The Japanese American cases in the 1980s explained the damage done to the judicial process when officers of the court (government attorneys) present misleading documents and testimony.

The government denied that Finletter and Harmon were "officers of the court," even though both men were lawyers and had signed their statements as truthful documents. The court acknowledged that the two men did not represent the United States in the litigation, but "they did represent the United States Air Force's claim of privilege over a document central to that litigation."[245] It agreed with the district court's conclusion on September 10,

241. Id.
242. Id. at 390.
243. Id.
244. Id.
245. Id.

2004, that the Supreme Court in 1953 had depended upon the "experience, expertise and truthfulness" of Finletter and Harmon when it decided to reverse and remand.[246]

The Third Circuit focused on the stature of the documents in which allegedly fraudulent representations were made. The representations were made in Harmon's affidavit and Finletter's formal claim of privilege, with both statements made under oath. "To allege that false statements were made in these documents is to allege perjury; a particularly serious type of perjury because of the high degree of faith the Court placed in the truth of Finletter and Harmon's representations." This part of the court's decision is confusing and seemingly irrelevant. The court had already ruled out perjury as evidence of fraud: "proof of perjury is not enough to establish fraud upon the court. . . . In this case, however, an accusation of perjury forms the basis of the fraud upon the court claim."[247]

To rule out perjury, the court found it necessary to determine whether the two documents "are susceptible to a truthful interpretation."[248] In a footnote, it indicated that any effort by the court to analyze the statements in light of the contents of the accident report "would require a certain amount of deference to the Government's position because of the near impossibility of determining with any level of certainty what seemingly insignificant pieces of information would have been of keen interest to a Soviet spy fifty years ago."[249] That type of analysis was not necessary because the court decided that the Finletter statement was so ambiguous that it could not be classified as either perjurious or misleading. Here is the part of the statement the court focused on:

> The defendant [the government] further objects to the production of this report, together with the statements of witnesses, for the reason that the aircraft in question, together with the personnel on board, were engaged in a confidential mission of the Air Force. The airplane likewise carried confidential equipment on board and any disclosure of **its** mission or information concerning **its** operation or performance would be prejudicial to this department and would not be in the public interest.[250]

The two "its" are in bold, for reasons to be discussed. The first 48 words of the above passage are of no consequence. Newspaper readers across the country

246. Id.
247. Id. at 391.
248. Id.
249. Id. (Note 3).
250. Id. at 392 (emphasis added).

knew that the aircraft was engaged in a confidential mission and carried confidential equipment on board. The dispute comes with the next 27 words. Specifically, what does the pronoun "its" refer to? The first use would refer to the airplane ("its mission"). What of the second use? Is it to the electronic equipment on board (the plaintiffs' position) or to the airplane (the government's choice)? The court decided that both readings "are conceivable, [but] the Government's is more logical." The court regarded it as "more natural to refer to an airplane's mission than to refer to the confidential equipment's mission. At the very least, the statement is readily susceptible to the reading preferred by the Government."[251] The court pointed to an earlier brief by the plaintiffs that seemed to point to the aircraft rather than to the equipment.[252]

Never made clear in this discussion was what difference it made if the second "its" referred to the airplane or to the equipment. Resorting to this kind of labored, ponderous, and cryptic analysis gave an easy out to the court, but it ignored the larger issue. The government convinced the judiciary that the accident report contained state secrets, and it is extremely difficult to locate such material. Obviously the Third Circuit did not want to go through that exercise, and if it did, it would have deferred heavily to the government. By deciding that the Finletter statement had "an obviously reasonable truthful interpretation," the court found that the plaintiffs were unable to make out a claim for the perjury, which, "as explained above, forms the basis for their fraud upon the court claim. We, therefore, conclude that [they] failed to state a claim upon which relief can be granted."[253]

The *coram nobis* litigation in district court and the Third Circuit recalls T. S. Eliot's observation about how the world ends: not with a bang but a whimper. The case turned on the meaning of "its." When the government invokes the state secrets privilege, one expects information that is so crucial to national security that it cannot be shared even with the court in chambers. Nothing in the accident report or the survivor statements rises to that level. The alleged state secrets were thin in substance and of marginal quality. The Third Circuit pointed to three possible candidates: "The accident report revealed, for example, that the project was being carried out by 'the 3150th Electronics Squadron,' that the mission required an 'aircraft capable of dropping bombs' and that the mission required an airplane capable of 'operating at altitudes of 20,000 feet and above.'"[254] The second element cannot be a state secret. It was

251. Id. at 392.
252. Id.
253. Id.
254. Id. at 391 (Note 3).

public knowledge that the confidential equipment was on board a B-29 and that the aircraft was capable of dropping bombs. That's what bombers do. It is implausible to regard the other two elements as so sensitive in nature that they could not have been submitted for in camera review.

On December 21, 2005, the plaintiffs filed a cert petition with the Supreme Court. The government filed a brief in opposition on March 31, 2006. The case went to conference on April 28 and on May 1 the Court denied cert.

7

THE SCOPE OF STATE SECRETS

The *Reynolds* decision in 1953 marked a triumph for the Justice Department, but in the decades that followed, only on occasion did the executive branch claim "state secrets" to prevent disclosure of documents to courts or private parties. Instead, the government typically invoked "national security" or "foreign affairs" to withhold documents. In this past decade, however, matters have changed dramatically, with the government now routinely citing "state secrets" as the ground for denying private litigants access to agency information. That trend, well in place before the terrorist attacks of September 11, 2001, has been on an upward climb.[1]

This chapter begins by looking at two early court cases frequently cited as the origin of the state secrets privilege: the Aaron Burr trial, and a government contract entered into during the Civil War with a spy. Neither precedent provides solid support for the privilege. The chapter then identifies two types of secrets: those recognized in statute and those executive-made. Subsequent sections explore the types of decisions that the government faces in criminal and civil cases when it wants to invoke the state secrets privilege, and the damage done to the rights of plaintiffs and an independent judiciary when courts defer to executive assertions.

Aaron Burr Trial

Federal courts often point to the trial of Aaron Burr in 1807 as the source of the state secrets privilege. A district court in 1977 claimed that the state secrets privilege "can be traced as far back as Aaron Burr's trial in 1807."[2] In 1989, the D.C. Circuit said that although "the exact origins" of the state secrets privilege "are not certain," the privilege in the United States "has its initial roots in Aaron Burr's trial for treason . . . and has its modern roots in *United States* v. *Reynolds*."[3] In the government's brief to the Supreme Court

---

1. William G. Weaver and Robert M. Pallitto, "State Secrets and Executive Power," 120 Pol. Sci. Q. 85 (2005).
2. Jabara v. Kelley, 75 F.R.D. 475, 483 (D. Mich. 1977).
3. In re U.S., 872 F.2d 472, 474–75 (D.C. Cir. 1989).

in *Reynolds,* the Justice Department cited early examples, "more directly apposite to the power of department heads to withhold production, [which] include . . . Burr's trials, where counsel for the Government refused to divulge, in response to subpoenas, confidential portions of documents in the possession of the executive."[4] Later in the brief, the department produced a list of examples "of successful assertions of the [evidentiary] privilege, comprising partly assertions by the President and partly assertions by department heads." The second example: "Confidential information and letters relating to Burr's conspiracy."[5] The brief relies on an article written by Herman Wolkinson, an attorney with the Justice Department. These descriptions of the Burr trial are misleading and superficial.

A decision in 2004 by District Judge Reggie B. Walton remarked: "The origins of the state secrets privilege can be traced back to the treason trial of Aaron Burr in *United States* v. *Burr.*"[6] He cited two contemporary federal appellate cases to support that position. One case involved the person who leaked the Pentagon Papers, Daniel Ellsberg: *Ellsberg v. Mitchell* (1983). The other is called *In re United States* (1989). As explained later, neither case offers convincing support for the state secrets privilege.

Judge Walton noted that Aaron Burr had sought access to a letter that General Wilkinson—the primary government witness against him—had sent to President Jefferson "that purportedly contained information" about Burr, "of whose guilt," Wilkinson said, "there can be no doubt." According to Judge Walton, the government objected to producing the letter, asserting that it was "improper to call upon the president to produce the letter of Gen. Wilkinson, because it was a private letter, and probably contained confidential communications, which the president ought not and could not be compelled to disclose. It might contain state secrets, which could not be divulged without endangering the national safety."[7]

As Judge Walton pointed out, Chief Justice John Marshall wrote for the circuit court and "noted that 'such circumstances present a delicate question' because this was a capital case in which the defendant claimed that the letter was material to his defense." Marshall did not have to decide whether the letter "should be disclosed because there was 'nothing before the court which show[ed] that the letter in question contain[ed] any matter the disclosure of which would endanger the public safety.'" Marshall reasoned that "if it does

4. Brief for the United States, United States v. Reynolds, No. 21, U.S. Supreme Court, October Term, 1952, at 10–11.
5. Id. at 24.
6. Edmonds v. U.S. Dept. of Justice, 323 F.Supp.2d 65, 70 (D.D.C. 2004).
7. Id., citing United States v. Burr, 25 Fed. Cas. 30, 31 (C.C.D. Va. 1807) (No. 14,692d).

contain any matter which it would be imprudent to disclose, which it is not the wish of the executive to disclose, such matter, if it be not immediately and essentially applicable to the point, will, of course, be suppressed."[8]

Judge Walton failed to flesh out what Marshall said. Although it is accurate to say that the Burr trial involved what might have been "confidential communications" and "state secrets," it is not true that the Jefferson administration told the Court it could not see the letter. Marshall concluded that the letter did not contain "any matter the disclosure of which would endanger the public safety." He did not take at face value the word of the administration, as the Supreme Court did in *Reynolds* when it deferred to the judgment of the Finletter and Harmon statements. Marshall made an independent assessment. He stated his willingness to suppress the letter upon learning "it is not the wish of the executive to disclose," but immediately said: "if it be not immediately and essentially applicable to the point." In a criminal trial, where the death penalty loomed as a possibility, Marshall stood ready to give Burr access to the documents he needed to defend himself.

Jefferson's Indictment

With extraordinary carelessness, President Jefferson publicly condemned Burr as guilty before he ever had a trial. In his Sixth Annual Message, delivered December 2, 1806, Jefferson alerted Congress to the plans of several private individuals who had armed themselves to carry out a military expedition "against the territories of Spain."[9] In response to a House resolution adopted on January 16, 1807, requesting additional information on the situation,[10] Jefferson submitted a message on January 22. He cautioned that much of the information was in the form of letters "containing such a mixture of rumors, conjectures, and suspicions" that it would be inappropriate and unjust to identify particular individuals involved in the conspiracy "except that of the principal actor, whose guilt is placed beyond question."[11] He then singled out Aaron Burr as "the prime mover." Jefferson referred to several letters he had received from General Wilkinson concerning Burr's activities: letters of October 21, December 14, and December 18, 1806. Having watched Jefferson function as both executive and supreme judge, if not executioner, Burr had every right to see the letters.

8. Id. at 71, citing United States v. Burr, 25 Fed. Cas. at 37.
9. 1 A Compilation of the Messages and Papers of the Presidents 394 (Richardson ed. 1925) (hereafter "Richardson").
10. Annals of Cong., 9th Cong., 2d Sess. 334–59 (1807).
11. 1 Richardson 400.

Chief Justice Marshall recognized that if he issued a subpoena to Jefferson for the letters, it might be interpreted as a sign of disrespect to the office of the presidency. However, Marshall was more concerned that his own branch would lose respect if it failed to give an accused access to information needed for his defense. He declined to say whether that result would "tarnish the reputation of the government; but I will say, that it would justly tarnish the reputation of the court which had given its sanction to its being withheld." If Marshall were a party to the withholding of documents needed by a defendant, "it would be to deplore, most earnestly, the occasion which should compel me to look back on any part of my official conduct with so much self-reproach as I should feel, could I declare, on the information now possessed, that the accused is not entitled to the letter in question, if it should be really important to him."[12]

Jefferson's letter of June 12, 1807, to George Hay, one of the government attorneys handling the prosecution, contained some caveats about the President's right to independently decide "what papers coming to him as president the public interest permits to be communicated, and to whom." He then assured the court of his "readiness under that restriction voluntarily to furnish on all occasions whatever the purposes of justice may require." As to the October 21 letter from General Wilkinson, Jefferson said he had given it to Attorney General Caeser Rodney to be taken to Richmond for the trial. He closed by expressing "a perfect willingness to do what is right."[13] Nothing in this record indicated a determination by Jefferson to prevent Burr from gaining access to documents needed for his defense.

Writing again on June 17, Jefferson was satisfied that the correspondence he had released to Attorney General Rodney "will have substantially fulfilled the object of a subpoena from the district court of Richmond."[14] He added that if Burr believed "there are any facts within the knowledge of the heads of department or of myself, which can be useful for his defense, from a desire of doing anything our situation will permit in furtherance of justice," those officials would be available for deposition in Washington, D.C.[15] He drew the line only at having to personally attend the trial at Richmond, pointing to the impracticality of the President being drawn from one court to another throughout the country.[16]

Jefferson returned to this theme in a letter of June 20 to Hay, stating that the "leading principle of our Constitution is the independence of the

12. United States v. Burr, 25 Fed. Cas. 30, 37 (C.C.D. Va. 1807) (No. 14,692d).
13. Id. at 65.
14. Id. at 69.
15. Id.
16. Id.

legislature, executive and judiciary of each other." The President could not be independent of the judiciary "if he were subject to the *commands* of the latter, and to imprisonment for disobedience; if the several courts could bandy him from pillar to post, keep him constantly trudging from north to south and east to west, and withdraw him entirely from his constitutional duties."[17] Here the threat to executive independence was the need to appear in person, not in releasing documents required by Burr in criminal court.

When Jefferson wrote to Hay three days later, his willingness to give Burr access to requested documents is evident. Jefferson reminded Hay that he had written to Rodney "to send on the letter of General Wilkinson of October 21st, referred to in my message of January 22d." When Jefferson received the letter he "immediately saw that it was not the one desired, because it had no relation to the facts stated under that reference." Rodney searched through the papers and could not locate the one that Jefferson (and Burr) wanted. Jefferson told Hay that "no researches shall be spared to recover this letter, and if recovered, it shall immediately be sent on to you." Jefferson offered an option to Hay: "General Wilkinson probably has copies of all the letters he wrote me, and having expressed a willingness to furnish the one desired by the Court, the defendant can still have the benefit of it."[18] Writing to Hay on August 7, Jefferson stated: "With respect to the paper in question it was delivered to the Attorney Genl with all the other papers relating to Burr."[19]

Burr at Trial

Aaron Burr faced two charges: one of treason, and the second a misdemeanor for "setting on foot" a military expedition against the territory of Spain. On September 1, 1807, the jury found him not guilty of treason.[20] The court then moved to consider seven counts of the misdemeanor charge. Two days later, Burr referred to the letter he had demanded from President Jefferson, "which had often been promised but not yet produced." He asked whether that letter was in court. Hay said he had searched for the letter but could not find it. He had a copy, "which was ready to be produced." Burr replied that he "was not disposed to admit a copy." Chief Justice Marshall announced that "unless the loss of the original be proved, a copy cannot be admitted."[21] Burr insisted

17. 11 The Writings of Thomas Jefferson 241 (Bergh ed. 1904) (emphasis in original).
18. Id. at 253–54.
19. 9 The Writings of Thomas Jefferson 61n (Ford ed. 1898). This volume, edited by Paul Leicester Ford, reproduces many of the letters from Jefferson to Hay regarding the Burr trial. See Notes 52 to 64.
20. United States v. Burr, 25 Fed. Cas. 180–81 (C.C.D. Va. 1807) (No. 14,693).
21. Id. at 189.

that the letter written by Wilkinson on November 12, 1806, to Jefferson "was material to his defense." Hay responded that he "had that letter, and would produce it."[22] Indicating that there were some matters in the Wilkinson letters "which ought not to be made public," he was willing to put them "in the hands of the clerk confidentially, and he could copy all those parts which had relation to the cause." There then followed this discussion:

> The counsel for Colonel Burr were not satisfied with this proposal. They demanded the whole letters.
>
> Mr. Hay said he was willing that Mr. Botts, Mr. Wickham, and Mr. Randolph [Burr's attorneys] should examine them. He would depend on their candor and integrity to make no improper disclosures; and if there should be any difference of opinion as to what were confidential passages, the court should decide.
>
> Mr. Martin [representing Burr] objected to this as a secret tribunal. The counsel had a right to hear the letters publicly, without their consent.
>
> Mr. Burr's counsel united in refusing to inspect anything that was not submitted to the inspection of their client.
>
> The CHIEF JUSTICE saw no real difficulty in the case. If there were any parts of the letters confidential, then a public examination would be very wrong; otherwise they ought to be read.
>
> Mr. Hay said the president wrote to him when he understood the process had been awarded, that he had reserved to himself the province of deciding what parts of the letters ought to be published and what parts required to be kept secret; that they wished everything to be as public as possible except those parts which were really confidential. The discussion continued till the court adjourned.[23]

The next day, Burr requested two letters that Wilkinson sent to Jefferson, one of which had been subpoenaed. Regarding Jefferson as in contempt of court, Burr said he had a right to demand process of contempt, but the procedure would be "unpleasant" and would "produce delay." Of the October 21 letter, he now said a copy would be sufficient "if duly authenticated." As to the November 12 letter, Burr said he had reason to believe that the whole letter had been shown to others to cause him injury, and that the whole letter ought therefore be produced. When Hay inquired on what ground Burr had such a suspicion, Burr asked whether the November 12 letter had been shown

22. Id. at 190.
23. Id.

to the grand jury. Hay said he was not as familiar with the grand jury "as some other gentlemen were."[24]

Turning Over Documents

What now transpired demonstrates that the Burr trial is not a precedent for the state secrets privilege, under which a President or department head may withhold certain documents and bar their release to a litigant or federal judge. Hay told the court he would produce the November 12 letter, except for two passages "which he could not submit to public inspection." The key word here is *public*, because Hay was willing to show the entire letter to the court. He agreed to turn over the letter, with certain parts removed because they were "not material for the purposes of justice, for the defense of the accused, or pertinent to the issue now about to be joined." As a check on the accuracy of the proposed substitute, he was "willing to refer to the judgment of the court, by submitting the original letter to its inspection."[25] This admission, by itself, distinguishes the Burr trial from executive claims that it has an absolute right to withhold documents.

Chief Justice Marshall ruled on access to the letter. As usual, his reasoning is highly cautious and circumspect in trying to weave a result that is fair to Burr without being needlessly offensive to Jefferson. In criminal cases, courts "will always apply the rules of evidence to criminal prosecutions so as to treat the defence with as much liberality and tenderness as the case will admit."[26] Marshall recognized that the President "might receive a letter which it would be improper to exhibit in public, because of the manifest inconvenience of its exposure." Notice again the word *public*. Withholding a document from the public does not mean withholding it from a court or a litigant. Marshall advised Burr: "The occasion for demanding it ought, in such a case, to be very strong, and to be fully shown to the court before its production could be insisted on." He admitted that "much reliance must be placed on the declaration of the president."

Having given some ground here, Marshall proceeds to reject the conventional distinction between a President's private and public (or official) papers. He explains: "Letters to the president in his private character, are often written to him in consequence of his public character, and may relate to public concerns. Such a letter, though it be a private one, seems to partake of the character of an official paper, and to be such as ought not on light ground

24. Id.
25. Id.
26. Id. at 191.

to be forced into public view."[27] Forcing a letter into "public view" is not the same as sharing it with a judge.

Marshall summed up his dilemma. Jefferson had not personally objected "to the production of any part of this letter." He had left it in the hands of Hay. Marshall assumed that Jefferson "has no objections to the production of the whole, if the attorney has not." If Jefferson had transmitted the letter and stated that "in his judgment the public interest required certain parts of it to be kept secret," Marshall would have paid "all proper respect."[28] All proper respect is not the same as blind acquiescence to executive assertions, which is what the Supreme Court did in *Reynolds*. Marshall said he was inclined to let Burr see the letter. After he looked at it, "it will yet be a question whether it shall go to the jury or not." On September 5, Hay asked the court for time to seek guidance from Jefferson.

Verdict: Not Guilty

On September 9, Hay presented a certificate from Jefferson, indicating the parts of Wilkinson's letter that should not be made public. Jefferson, describing certain passages as "entirely confidential," provided a "correct copy of all those parts which I ought to permit to be made public." The parts "not communicated are in nowise material for the purposes of justice on the charges of treason or misdemeanor depending against Aaron Burr; they are on subjects irrelevant to any issues which can arise out of those charges, & could contribute nothing towards his acquittal or conviction."[29]

Marshall's decision on September 9 explored a number of legal issues. Could hearsay or the declarations of third persons be received in evidence? What are the elements of a conspiracy? What is the statutory meaning of "setting on foot" a military expedition? Can a military expedition be set on foot when a single soldier has been enlisted for that purpose? What is an expedition? An enterprise? Must mental crimes of an accused be translated into open deed? What use could be made in court of charges about Burr from a different district? Suppose that Burr originated the enterprise (which Marshall said "is very probably the case")? Others might have provided the means. Marshall pointed out that Burr was not indicted for being "connected with the enterprize, but for providing certain specific means."[30] As questions from Marshall multiplied and he revealed his answers, the government's case grew bleak. Much of the evidence it had hoped to introduce was progressively ruled out.

27. Id. at 192.
28. Id.
29. 9 The Writings of Thomas Jefferson 64n (Ford ed. 1898).
30. United States v. Burr, 25 Fed. Cas. 193–98 (C.C.D. Va. 1807) (No. 14,694).

At one point Marshall observed that the testimony produced by the government's attorney "disproves his own charge."[31] He inquired of the government: "gentlemen will consider whether they are not wasting the time and money of the United States, and of all those persons who are forced to attend here, whilst they are producing such a mass of testimony which does not bear upon the cause."[32] When the government moved to discharge the jury, Burr objected and insisted on a verdict. The jury retired and returned a verdict of "Not guilty."[33] With this result, no further discussion was necessary on access to documents held by the government. The record shows that Jefferson had not prevented Burr from gaining access to documents needed for his defense.

The Watergate Tapes Case

In *United States v. Nixon* (1974), the Supreme Court replayed the issue posed by the Burr trial: the need of a defendant in criminal court to evidence held by the executive branch. President Nixon insisted that he had exclusive and final authority to decide which documents he would allow to be shared with Special Prosecutor Archibald Cox and the courts. The Supreme Court ruled against Nixon. In a criminal case, where defendants need information to protect their rights in court, the President's general authority over executive privilege could not override the specific need for evidence in a criminal proceeding.[34]

Having established that important principle, Chief Justice Burger proceeded to drop in some unfortunate dicta, talking about confidentiality "of nonmilitary and nondiplomatic discussions" and saying that Nixon did not "place his claim of privilege on the ground they are military or diplomatic secrets. As to these areas of Art. II duties the courts have traditionally shown the utmost deference to Presidential responsibilities."[35] Suppose Nixon *had* claimed military or diplomatic secrets. Would individuals in criminal court be denied evidence they needed to prove their innocence? Or would the government be faced with a choice: either release the documents or drop the charges? The Burger Court left that fundamental issue confused. Marshall did not make that mistake.

Neither of the two contemporary cases cited by District Judge Walton justify using the Burr trial as a credible precedent for the state secrets privilege. In the 1983 Ellsberg case, the D.C. Circuit remarked, "Prior to World War Two, the government rarely had occasion to exercise this prerogative [the state se-

31. Id. at 200.
32. Id. at 201.
33. Id.
34. United States v. Nixon, 418 U.S. 683 (1974).
35. Id. at 710.

crets privilege], and, consequently, the scope of the privilege remained some-what in doubt."[36] In a footnote, the D.C. Circuit observes: "Various early decisions alluded to some such evidentiary privilege, see *e.g.*, *United States v. Burr,* 25 F.Cas. 30, 37 (C.C.D.Va. 1807) (No. 14692d) (Marshall, C.J.), but none attempted to prescribe any comprehensive doctrine regarding the circumstances in which it might legitimately be invoked."[37] Those comments caution against using the Burr trial as a legitimate precedent for the state se-crets privilege. In the other case, *In re United States* (1989), the reference to Burr is so brief as to have no analytical value: "Although the exact origins of the privilege are not certain, . . . the privilege in this country has its initial roots in Aaron Burr's trial for treason."[38]

Government Spies

In *Reynolds,* the Supreme Court described Secretary Finletter's attempt to in-voke "the privilege against revealing military secrets" as a privilege "which is well established in the law of evidence." Among the cases the Court cited for that proposition—and standing first in line—is the Civil War government spy case, *Totten v. United States* (1875).[39] Judge Walton also cited this case as a precedent for the state secrets privilege. President Lincoln had entered into a contract with William A. Lloyd to proceed south and collect data on the number of Confederate troops stationed at different points, plans of forts and fortifications, and other information that might be useful to the federal government. For his services, Lloyd was to be paid $200 a month, but he re-ceived funds only to cover his expenses. After he died, his family sought to re-cover compensation for his services. According to Judge Walton, the Supreme Court "had the occasion to address the state secrets privilege" in *Totten.*[40] However, here are the reasons the Court rejected the lawsuit:

It may be stated as a general principle, that public policy forbids the maintenance of any suit in a court of justice, the trial of which would inevitably lead to the disclosure of matters which the law itself regards as confidential, and respecting which it will not allow the confidence to be violated. On this principle, suits cannot be maintained which would

36. Ellsberg v. Mitchell, 709 F.2d 51, 56 (D.C. Cir. 1983).
37. Id. (Note 21).
38. In re U.S., 872 F.2d 472, 474–75 (D.C. Cir. 1989). See also Irwin S. Rhodes, "What Really Happened to the Jefferson Subpoenas," 60 A.B.A.J. 52 (1974).
39. United States v. Reynolds, 345 U.S. at 6–7 (Note 11).
40. Edmonds v. U.S. Dept. of Justice, 323 F.Supp.2d at 71.

require a disclosure of the confidences of the confessional, or those between husband and wife, or of communications by a client to his counsel
for professional advice, or of a patient to his physician for a similar purpose. Much greater reason exists for the application of the principle to
cases of contract for secret services with the government, as the existence
of a contract of that kind is itself a fact not to be disclosed.[41]

Obviously, this decision is far afield from the state secrets privilege. The
Court was merely addressing the confidentiality that exists in certain types of
communications: between confessor and priest, husband and wife, client and
attorney, patient and doctor. To those privileged communications the Court
added the confidentiality that exists between a President and someone he hires
as a spy. Lincoln paid Lloyd from a contingent fund that Congress had placed
under presidential control.[42] By its very nature, a secret contract could not be
taken into court at some later date to be enforced. At issue was not a secret
that the government had a right to keep privileged. Rather, it was a matter of
ordinary contracts (enforceable in court) and secret contracts (which are not).
Whoever enters into a secret agreement with the government cannot expect
relief in the courts. If there is a dispute, the only part of government that can
provide a remedy is the executive agency that entered into the agreement.
That is the basic difference between *Totten* and the state secrets privilege. The
case in *Totten* was not justiciable. A state secrets case is justiciable, but the private litigant may not be able to gain access to certain agency documents.

The Supreme Court in *Totten* described the service stipulated in Lloyd's
contract as "a secret service; the information sought was to be obtained clan-
destinely, and was to be communicated privately; the employment and the
service were to be equally concealed." Both Lincoln and Lloyd, said the Court,
"must have understood that the lips of the other were to be for ever sealed respecting the relation of either to the matter."[43] Any effort in court to publicize
the agreement "would itself be a breach of a contract of that kind."[44] Nothing
can be drawn from this unique and narrow case to justify withholding state
secrets over the broad domains of national security and foreign affairs. The
doctrine of state secrets covers evidentiary questions and claims of privilege,
and those issues were not at stake in *Totten*.[45]

41. Totten v. United States, 92 U.S. 105, 107 (1875).
42. Id. at 106.
43. Id.
44. Id. at 107.
45. Theodore Francis Riordan, "*Totten* Doctrine—Judicial Sabotage of Government Contracts for Sabotage Services, *Guong* v. *United States,* 860 F.2d 1063 (Fed. Cir. 1988), cert. denied, 109 S. Ct. 1751 (1989)," 13 Suffolk Transnat'l L. J. 807, 808 (Note 2) (1990).

Subsequent Reliance on Totten

The *Totten* principle has been applied to a number of cases—appropriately for spy cases and inappropriately for other legal disputes. Charles de Arnaud served as a spy for General John Fremont during the Civil War and was paid for his services. Twenty-four years later he tried to obtain additional compensation from the government. Relying on *Totten,* the Supreme Court in 1894 rejected his request. Aside from being barred by the statute of limitations (requiring claims to be presented within six years), the Court found unpersuasive Arnaud's argument that he was not really a spy, and thus covered by *Totten,* but rather a "military expert."[46] Two years earlier, the Court of Claims had rejected a petition by another spy for General Fremont who sought compensation for his services.[47]

In 1954, the Court of Claims dismissed a petition seeking expenses and compensation for secret services allegedly performed for the psychological warfare branch of the Military Intelligence Department and other federal agencies, partly behind enemy lines. The necessity for secrecy prevented any effort to recover funds in court.[48] In disallowing recovery, the court said it was governed by the Supreme Court's decision in *Totten.*[49] In two rulings in 1980 and 1981, the Court of Claims rejected efforts by two individuals to be compensated for work they did for the CIA, one in performing undercover intelligence activities and the other for espionage.[50] A Vietnamese man, claiming that he did covert work for the CIA from 1962 to 1964, later tried in federal court to receive back pay for his services and additional compensation. The Federal Circuit, in 1988, relied on *Totten* to deny him relief.[51] In 2001, a district court applied *Totten* against an individual who tried to recover damages for breach of an alleged contract with the CIA.[52]

Totten has become a popular citation for the government and for courts. An article in 2001 reported that although the *Totten* doctrine had been invoked only six times between 1875 and 1951, since 1951, it had been cited more than 65 times. Many of those cases had nothing to do with contracts for secret services.[53] A good example is a 1981 decision by the Supreme Court.

46. De Arnaud v. United States, 151 U.S. 483, 493 (1894).
47. Allen v. United States, 27 Ct. Cl. 89 (1892).
48. Tucker v. United States, 118 F.Supp. 371 (Ct. Cl. 1954).
49. Id. at 372–73.
50. Simrick v. United States, 224 Ct. Cl. 724 (1980); Mackowski v. United States, 228 Ct. Cl. 717 (1981), cert. denied, 454 U.S. 1123 (1981).
51. Guong v. United States, 860 F.2d 1063 (Fed. Cir. 1988).
52. Kielczynski v. U.S. C.I.A., 128 F.Supp.2d 151 (E.D.N.Y. 2001).
53. Sean C. Flynn, "The *Totten* Doctrine and Its Poisoned Progeny," 25 Vt. L. Rev. 793, 793–94 (2001). See also Daniel L. Pines, "The Continuing Viability of the 1875 Supreme Court Case of *Totten v. United States,*" 53 Adm. L. Rev. 1273 (2001); and Major Kelly D. Wheaton, "Spycraft and Government Contracts: A Defense of *Totten* v. *United States,*" Army Lawyer, August 1997, at 9–17.

The issue was whether the Navy had to prepare and release to the public an environmental impact statement for the construction in Hawaii of a facility for storing nuclear weapons. The Court held that the statement was not required. It closed with this passage from *Totten:* "we have held that 'public policy forbids the maintenance of any suit in a court of justice, the trial of which would inevitably lead to the disclosure of matters which the law itself regards as confidential, and respecting which it will not allow the confidence to be violated.'"[54] The issues in the Hawaiian case were unrelated to a narrowly confined secret contract.

"Mr. and Mrs. Doe"

Totten was tested most recently in a case decided by the Supreme Court in 2005. A husband-and-wife team ("John and Jane Doe") sued the United States and the CIA director, alleging that the agency failed to provide them with financial assistance it had promised for their espionage services during the Cold War. As citizens of a foreign country, they wanted to defect to the United States. It was their understanding that if they agreed to conduct espionage for a certain period of time, the CIA would arrange for their travel to and resettlement in the United States and would provide financial security for the remainder of their lives. After conducting espionage, they were brought to the United States, given false identities, and provided with education, medical benefits, and a living stipend. When Mr. Doe's salary from professional employment reached a certain level, the stipend was discontinued with the understanding that if he lost his job, the CIA would resume making payments. After he was laid off, he and his wife contacted the CIA and learned that the stipend would not be restored because of agency budget constraints. Yet they were told that the agency had various types of appeal processes. They tried them, without success.[55]

A district court found that their claims were not barred by *Totten.*[56] The record indicated that the CIA had told the couple that a process existed through which they could appeal their request. Thus, even if *Totten* foreclosed any court from judging their contractual benefits, it appeared that the agency had offered certain procedural safeguards that could be litigated.[57] The court concluded that having the judiciary look at CIA's procedures for reviewing complaints would not jeopardize a national security secret.[58]

54. Weinberger v. Catholic Action of Hawaii, 454 U.S. 139, 146–47 (1981).
55. Doe v. Tenet, 99 F.Supp.2d 1284, 1285–88 (W.D. Wash. 2000).
56. Id. at 1293–94.
57. Id. at 1289–90.
58. Id. at 1290.

The Ninth Circuit, affirming in part, agreed that issues of fact existed as to whether the couple had been deprived of due process under CIA regulations.[59] The essence of the case was not about breaching a secret agreement. The Does went to court "not to reveal secret information: They filed suit under fictitious names and revealed only minimal, nonidentifying details in their complaint."[60] The Ninth Circuit pointed out that the government "has not thus far asserted the state secrets privilege in this case and has therefore not complied with the required procedures."[61] The next year, the Ninth Circuit denied a petition for rehearing and another petition for rehearing en banc.[62]

The Justice Department, in a brief requesting the Supreme Court to take the case, argued that the Ninth Circuit's decision was "inconsistent with this Court's decision in *Totten*."[63] The Civil War case barred the suit "because respondents' claims cannot proceed without disclosing facts that would damage national security: whether respondents actually had an espionage relationship with the CIA and, if so, the details of that relationship."[64] For that reason such suits were "non-justiciable."[65] The "extent of any remedy for an alleged spy is a matter uniquely for the Executive Branch."[66] The government disagreed that *Totten* was somehow "subsumed" under the state secrets privilege announced in *Reynolds*. Indeed, *Reynolds* confirmed that *Totten* posed a jurisdictional bar "where the very subject matter of the action [is] a contract to perform espionage."[67] *Totten*'s rule of dismissing contractual spy cases "does not require formal invocation of the state secrets privilege."[68]

The lawyers representing the Does treated *Totten* as part of the state secrets privilege and not a jurisdictional bar. They viewed *Totten* "as an early kernel of the state secrets privilege (or of its broader family, Executive privilege)."[69] By including *Totten* within the broad principle of *Reynolds,* the plaintiffs' attorneys insisted that a formal claim of privilege must be lodged by the head of the department with control over the matter, and that the officer must give personal consideration of the evidence withheld.[70] The government's reply

59. Doe v. Tenet, 329 F.3d 1135 (9th Cir. 2003).
60. Id. at 1148.
61. Id. at 1151.
62. Doe v. Tenet, 353 F.3d 1141 (9th Cir. 2004).
63. Petition for a Writ of Certiorari, Tenet v. Doe (U.S. Supreme Court 2004), at 7.
64. Id. at 9.
65. Id. at 11.
66. Id.
67. United States v. Reynolds, 345 U.S. 1, 11 (Note 26) (1953).
68. Petition for a Writ of Certiorari, at 17.
69. Response to Petition for Writ of Certiorari, Tenet v. Doe, No. 03-1395 (U.S. Supreme Court 2004), at 12.
70. Id. at 19.

brief denied that *Reynolds* overruled *Totten.*[71] The Civil War case retained an "independent force after *Reynolds,*" it represented a "jurisdictional bar" that prohibits any contractual dispute, and "agreements for espionage services are inherently secret, and are not justiciable."[72] Those positions were elaborated in other briefs submitted by the government and plaintiffs.[73]

In a unanimous opinion, the Supreme Court held that the suit was barred by *Totten.* It denied that *Reynolds* replaced or altered *Totten*'s categorical bar to lawsuits that involve espionage agreements. It also rejected the plaintiffs' argument that conditions had changed since *Totten,* with federal courts given greater access to classified documents. Said the Court: "The state secrets privilege and the more frequent use of *in camera* judicial proceedings simply cannot provide the absolute protection we found necessary in enunciating the *Totten* rule."[74] The decision underscores the point that *Totten* applies to a unique category of government spy cases that are unenforceable in court. In contrast, state secrets cases can be litigated and require certain procedural steps by the government to withhold documents from plaintiffs. Courts have a range of options, including in camera review. Depending on the type of case—criminal or civil—the government faces a number of hurdles and may find that invoking the state secrets privilege can cause it to lose the case.

Con Man or CIA Agent?

In 1990, John Patrick Savage presented himself as a CIA agent to a British company, asking that he borrow $8 million with the promise to pay $35 million within a matter of weeks. The only person named on the promissory note was Savage. The note made no mention of the CIA, the United States, or any other third party. When the company received nothing on the due date, it sued Savage's agent in the English courts and won a $35 million judgment. After collecting nothing on the judgment, the company filed suit against the United States in federal court. The government cited *Totten* and the state secrets privilege as a defense, but the case turned on two questions. Was Savage actually a CIA agent? If he was, did the agency authorize him to enter into the contract? The evidence was mixed on the first, nonexistent on the second. As noted by the Court of Federal Claims, Savage's promise to pay back the

71. Reply Brief for the Petitioners, Tenet v. Doe, No. 03-1395 (U.S. Supreme Court 2004), at 3.

72. Id. at 4–5.

73. Brief for the Petitioners, Tenet v. Doe, No. 03-1395 (U.S. Supreme Court 2004); Brief for the Respondents, Tenet v. Doe, No. 03-1395 (U.S. Supreme Court 2004); Reply Brief for the Petitioners, Tenet v. Doe, No. 03-1395 (U.S. Supreme Court 2004).

74. Tenet v. Doe, 544 U.S. 1, 11 (2005).

money in such a short time, with a profit to the company of $27 million on an $8 million note, amounted to 330% interest, a rate "that would make a loan shark blush."[75] Individuals are ill-advised to enter into a "contract" with someone who purports to be a CIA agent but lacks proper credentials. Any party entering into an agreement with the government "accepts the risk of correctly ascertaining the authority of the agents who purport to act for the Government."[76]

Statutory Secrets

No one questions the need of the government to protect certain types of secrets. In a series of statutes, Congress has identified the kinds of information that must be protected from disclosure and has specified the penalties to be applied to those who violate the law. Individuals who release information to a foreign government, with reason to believe it will be used to injure the United States or advantage the foreign nation, can be punished by death or imprisonment up to a life term. Prohibited actions include efforts to communicate any "document, writing, code book, signal book, sketch, photograph, photographic negative, blueprint, plan, map, model, note, instrument, appliance, or information relating to the national defense." This statute covers efforts to reveal information about nuclear weaponry, military spacecraft or satellites, early warning systems, "or other means of defense or retaliation against large-scale attack," and also includes war plans, communications intelligence or cryptographic information, and any other major weapons system or major element of defense strategy.[77]

Criminal penalties apply to whoever, in time of war, intends to communicate to the enemy any information with respect to the movement of U.S. armed forces or plans for the conduct or military operations. Individuals may be prosecuted for releasing information to the enemy regarding any measures undertaken for fortifications or other information related to public defense. These offenses may be punished by death or by imprisonment for any term of years or for life.[78]

Statutes cover other military activities. Whenever the President, in the interest of national defense, defines certain vital military and naval installations

---

75. Monarch Assur. P.L.C. v. United States, 42 Fed.Cl. 258, 264 (1998). See also Monarch Assur. P.L.C. v. United States, 36 Fed.Cl. 324 (1996).

76. Monarch Assur. P.L.C. v. United States, 244 F.3d 1356 (Fed. Cir. 2001).

77. 18 U.S.C. § 794(a) (2000).

78. Id. at § 794(b).

or equipment as requiring protection against general dissemination of information, it is unlawful to make any photograph, sketch, or graphical representation of the installations or equipment without first obtaining permission from the commanding officer. Persons who violate this law are subject to fines and to imprisonment for not more than one year, or both.[79] Whoever uses or permits the use of an aircraft or "any contrivance" to make a photograph, sketch, or graphical representation of "vital" military installations shall be fined or imprisoned not more than one year, or both.[80] Once the President defines a military or naval installation or equipment as vital, whoever reproduces, publishes, sells, or gives away any photograph, sketch, or graphical representation of those installations and equipment, without first obtaining permission of the commanding officer of the station or higher authority, may be fined and imprisoned for not more than one year, or both.[81]

Disclosure of classified information is subject to fines, imprisonment, and loss of personal property. Classified information is defined as information that, at the time of violation of this section of the criminal code, is—for reasons of national security—specifically designated by a U.S. government agency for limited or restricted dissemination or distribution. The crime applies to whoever knowingly and willingly communicates, furnishes, transmits, or otherwise makes available classified information to an unauthorized person. It applies to anyone who publishes or uses classified information in any manner prejudicial to the safety or interest of the United States, or for the benefit of any foreign government to the detriment of the United States. The categories of classified information include the nature, preparation, or use of any code, cipher, or cryptographic system of the United States or any foreign government. Second: the design, construction, use, maintenance, or repair of any device, apparatus, or appliance used or prepared or planned for use by the United States or any foreign government for cryptographic or communication intelligence purposes. Third: communication intelligence activities of the United States or any foreign government. Fourth: classified information obtained by the process of communication intelligence from any foreign government. Imprisonment shall not be more than ten years. Persons convicted of violating this section of the law shall forfeit to the United States property derived from the illegal transaction.[82]

A number of federal laws provide fines and imprisonment for those entrusted with atomic energy information (such as documents, sketches, and

79. Id. at § 795.
80. Id. at § 796.
81. Id. at § 797.
82. Id. at § 798.

photographs). Penalties apply to whoever communicates, transmits, or discloses the information to any individual with intent to injure the United States or with intent to secure an advantage to any foreign nation.[83] Fines and imprisonment await those who, without permission, make sketches, pictures, or graphical representations of atomic energy installations owned by the government, after the President has designated the installations or equipment as requiring protection against the dissemination of information.[84]

The Intelligence Identities Protection Act of 1982, made popular by the Bush II White House leak of the name of Valerie Plame in late 2003, makes it a criminal offense for those authorized to have access to classified information to intentionally identify a covert agent to an individual not authorized to receive that information. Those convicted of that offense shall be fined or imprisoned not more than ten years, or both.[85] An employee with the federal government who has custody of or access to any official diplomatic code is subject to fines and not more than ten years of imprisonment for willfully publishing or furnishing to another the information without authorization.[86]

The protection of grand jury secrets is well known. Not less than 16 nor more than 23 citizens meet in closed sessions to decide whether to indict someone of a federal crime. In the room are attorneys for the government, the witness under examination, interpreters when needed, a stenographer or operator of a recording device, and the jurors. A grand juror, an interpreter, a stenographer, an operator of a recording device, a typist who transcribes recorded testimony, an attorney for the government, or any person to whom disclosure is made "shall not disclose matters occurring before the grand jury," except as provided by the rules. No obligation of secrecy may be imposed on any person except in accordance with this rule. A knowing violation of Rule 6 may be punished as a contempt of court.[87] The rule on grand jury secrecy does not apply to witnesses. Part of the purpose of grand jury secrecy is to protect the names of innocent individuals discussed during the proceedings.

Executive Secrets

Other than these statutory provisions, "state secrets" are wholly executive made and rest on a common law foundation. During the Aaron Burr trial, the

83. 42 U.S.C. § 2274 (2000).
84. Id. at § 2278b.
85. 96 Stat. 122, § 601(a) (1982); 50 U.S.C. §§ 421–26 (2000).
86. 18 U.S.C. § 952 (2000).
87. 18 U.S.C. app. Rule 6(e) (2000).

Jefferson administration suggested that a letter sent to Jefferson by Wilkinson "might contain state secrets, which could not be divulged without endangering the national safety."[88] However, the state secrets privilege was not used as a reason for withholding documents either from Burr or the court in a criminal trial. In 1865, Attorney General James Speed was asked whether the Secretary of the Navy, or any of his subordinates, was bound by law from furnishing copies of court-martial records to a state court. Speed said that under "principles of public policy there are some kinds of evidence which the law excludes or dispenses with. Secrets of state, for instance, cannot be given in evidence, and those who are possessed of such secrets are not required to make disclosure of them."[89] Yet it was his opinion that when the proceedings of a court-martial "are at an end through the action of the competent revisory power, the contents of the records of such proceedings are not state secrets" and may be given to a state court.[90]

Federal agencies and departments are always at liberty to invoke the state secrets privilege. The extent to which that discretion is honored and successful, however, depends on the type of case and the determination of judges to exercise their authority to decide what evidence is admitted or excluded. Do they run the trial or allow executive officials, through affidavits and declarations, to dictate questions of evidence? In some cases, the government's decision to invoke state secrets may mean that it loses and the private citizen wins.

The leverage of the executive branch in withholding documents depends on which of four categories of cases the privilege is asserted. First, if the government is prosecuting someone in a criminal case, it is constitutionally repugnant to claim that the privilege allows the government to conceal evidence needed for an individual's defense. This is especially so when a defendant faces the death penalty. Raising the state secrets privilege in a civil case opens up the second and third categories: Did the government bring the case? Is it the defendant? A fourth category exists when the government is not a party but intervenes because state secrets might be disclosed in litigation between private parties.

Criminal Prosecution

The Aaron Burr case highlights a fundamental constitutional principle. If the government chooses to prosecute an individual and decides at the same time

---

88. United States v. Burr, 25 Fed. Cas. 30, 31 (C.C.D. Va. 1807) (No. 14,692d).
89. 11 Ops. Att'y Gen. 137, 142 (1865).
90. Id. at 143–44.

to withhold documents needed by the defendant on the ground that they are confidential or "state secrets," due process requires the government to drop the charges. Otherwise, the accused may be denied evidence needed to mount a successful defense. As the Supreme Court explained in *United States v. Nixon* (1974):

> The ends of criminal justice would be defeated if judgments were to be founded on a partial or speculative presentation of the facts. The very integrity of the judicial system and public confidence in the system depend on full disclosure of all the facts, within the framework of the rules of evidence. To ensure that justice is done, it is imperative to the function of courts that compulsory process be available for the production of evidence needed either by the prosecution or by the defense.[91]

This constitutional value arises frequently in American trials. In 1944, Judge Learned Hand of the Second Circuit decided a case involving someone convicted for violating a section of the tax code. Certain official reports were excluded from the trial because the district judge thought their disclosure was forbidden under Treasury Department regulations, based on the Housekeeping Statute. The regulation provided: "Whenever a subpœna shall have been served on [agency employees], they will, unless otherwise expressly directed, appear in Court and answer thereto and respectfully decline to produce the records or give testimony called for on the ground of being prohibited therefrom, from the regulations of the Treasury Department. Officers disobeying these instructions will be dismissed from the service and may incur criminal liability."[92]

Judge Hand reviewed the cases, including *Boske v. Comingore,* that the district judge had relied on, but concluded that "none of these cases involved the prosecution of a crime consisting of the very matters recorded in the suppressed document, or of matters nearly enough akin to make relevant the matters recorded."[93] He then announced this guiding principle:

> While we must accept it as lawful for a department of the government to suppress documents, even when they will help determine controversies between third persons, we cannot agree that this should include their suppression in a criminal prosecution, founded upon those very dealings to which the documents relate, and whose criminality they will, or may,

---

91. United States v. Nixon, 418 U.S. at 709.
92. United States v. Andolschek, 142 F.2d 503, 505 n. (2d Cir. 1944).
93. Id. at 506.

tend to exculpate. So far as they directly touch the criminal dealings, the prosecution necessarily ends any confidential character the documents may possess; it must be conducted in the open, and will lay bare their subject matter. The government must choose; either it must leave the transactions in the obscurity from which a trial will draw them, or it must expose them fully."[94]

Hand ruled that the district judge should not have read the Treasury regulation to exclude the reports in question. The conviction of the accused was reversed and the case remanded for a new trial. A similar case arose two years later, when the Second Circuit again reversed a conviction because the accused was denied access to documents needed in his defense. The defendant had subpoenaed the chief clerk of the Office of Price Administration to produce all agency records related to the pending suit. The clerk appeared in court and stated under oath that he had not brought the records with him because an OPA regulation prohibited the release of agency records unless the OPA administrator determined that withholding "would be contrary to the interests of national defense and security."[95] Citing its 1944 ruling, the Second Circuit stated: "We have recently held that when the government institutes criminal proceedings in which evidence, otherwise privileged under a statute or regulation, becomes importantly relevant, it abandons the privilege."[96]

When the Second Circuit revisited this issue in 1948, it acknowledged that there might be situations where a privilege over documents created by a departmental regulation would prevail, but at a cost. The Justice Department and federal agencies are put "collectively to a choice, either not to suppress all evidence within their control which bore upon the charges, or to let the offences go unpunished."[97] In 1950, the Second Circuit reversed a conviction because a district judge, after reading suppressed documents in his chambers, withheld the materials from the defendant.[98] The Second Circuit agreed that "there may be evidence—'state secrets'—to divulge which will imperil 'national security'; and which the Government cannot, and should not, be required to divulge." For criminal prosecutions, however, "the refusal to allow the defence to see [documents] was, as we have said, a denial of their constitutional rights, and we can see no significant distinction between introducing evidence against an accused which he is not allowed to see, and denying him the right to put in evidence on his own behalf."[99]

94. Id.
95. United States v. Beekman, 155 F.2d 580, 582 (2d Cir. 1946).
96. Id. at 584.
97. United States v. Grayson, 166 F.2d 863, 870 (2d Cir. 1948).
98. United States v. Coplon, 185 F.2d 629, 637 (2d Cir. 1950).
99. Id. at 638.

These issues, thrashed out in the lower courts, reached the Supreme Court in 1957. In the first case, Albert Roviaro was convicted of buying and attempting to transport heroin. Before trial, he requested the name, address, and occupation of "John Doe," an informer for the government who assisted in his arrest. The government regarded Doe's identity as privileged. The Court described "the informer's privilege" as the government's privilege "to withhold from disclosure the identity of persons who furnish information of violations of law to officers charged with enforcement of that law."[100] By preserving their anonymity, the privilege encourages informers to tell the government about the commission of crimes. The scope of the privilege is limited by several factors, one of which is the requirement of fairness: "Where the disclosure of an informer's identity, or of the contents of his communication, is relevant and helpful to the defense of an accused, or is essential to a fair determination of a cause, the privilege must give way."[101] In such situations, the trial court may require disclosure. If the government refuses to identify the informant, the next step is for the court to dismiss the action.[102] The Court said that Roviaro had a need to know the identity of the informer and to call him as a witness. His testimony might reveal entrapment by the government or Roviaro's lack of knowledge about the contents of a package that was later analyzed to contain heroin.[103] Other than Roviaro, the informer was the sole participant in the transaction charged. Moreover, a witness for the government testified that the informer denied knowing Roviaro or ever having seen him before.[104]

Justice Clark, dissenting, agreed that in cases where the government's refusal to disclose the identity of an informer deprives the accused of a fair trial, the nondisclosure policy "must either be relaxed or the prosecution must be foregone."[105] In this case, however, Clark said that "undisputed evidence" indicated that Roviaro knew the informer and that when the informer denied knowing him, or having seen him before, he was "carrying out a pretense that he too was arrested, was involved, and was not 'squealing.'"[106] Accepting the rule that under certain conditions the government must either name the informer or drop the prosecution, Clark insisted that the principle did not apply to Roviaro's case.

Also in 1947, the Court released a second and much more controversial decision. Clifford Jencks had been convicted of filing an affidavit stating falsely that he was not a member of the Communist Party or affiliated with it. To

100. Roviaro v. United States, 353 U.S. 53, 59 (1957).
101. Id. at 60–61.
102. Id. at 61.
103. Id. at 64.
104. Id. at 64–65.
105. Id. at 67.
106. Id. at 68.

prosecute and convict Jencks, the government relied on statements of two paid undercover agents for the FBI. Jencks asked that the FBI reports on the two informers be turned over to the trial court for examination to determine whether they had value in impeaching their testimony. If the judge found that the reports had value for impeachment purposes, the court would turn them over to him to be used in cross-examination. The district judge denied his motion.

In reversing the lower court, the Supreme Court went beyond Jenck's request to have the reports submitted to the judge. The Court ordered the government to produce for *his* inspection the FBI reports "touching the events and activities" at issue in the trial.[107] The Court explained: "Because only the defense is adequately equipped to determine the effective use for purpose of discrediting the Government's witness and thereby furthering the accused's defense, the defense must initially be entitled to see them to determine what use may be made of them. Justice requires no less."[108] The Court specifically rejected the option of giving documents solely to the trial judge to determine questions of relevancy and materiality, "without hearing the accused."[109]

The Court noted that in the lower courts, the government did not assert that the reports were privileged against disclosure on grounds of "national security, confidential character of the reports, public interest, or otherwise."[110] Here the Court offered the unnecessarily broad generality that it is "unquestionably true that the protection of vital national interests may militate against public disclosure of documents in the Government's possession."[111] What does that observation have to do with the right of an accused in a criminal case to obtain documents needed for a defense? The Court recognized that in previous decisions, "in civil causes," it considered statutory authority conferred upon agencies to adopt regulations regarding its records and papers.[112] It cited the Housekeeping Statute and also *Reynolds* and *Totten,* but for what purpose?

Having ceded some ground to the government in civil cases, the Court concluded that in criminal cases the government can invoke its evidentiary privilege only by letting the defendant go free.[113] The Court's position is straightforward: "The burden is the Government's, not to be shifted to the

---

107. Jencks v. United States, 353 U.S. 657, 668 (1957).
108. Id. at 668–69.
109. Id. at 669.
110. Id. at 670.
111. Id.
112. Id.
113. Id. at 670–71.

trial judge, to decide whether the public prejudice of allowing the crime to go unpunished is greater than that attendant upon the possible disclosure of state secrets and other confidential information in the Government's possession."[114] There was no reason for the Court to suggest that the government's choice was any different if the documents involved national security or "vital national interests." The defendant's right to evidence to establish innocence is the same.

Justice Clark issued the only dissent. He admitted that in this case, where a witness had recanted his testimony, "the trial judge should have examined the specific documents called for, as the defense requested, and if he thought justice required their delivery to the defense, [to] order such delivery to be made. I would have no objection to this being done."[115] But he disagreed sharply with the Court fashioning "a new rule of evidence which is foreign to our federal jurisprudence."[116]

In a criminal case, is it constitutionally sufficient for the government to submit national security documents to a court, to be read in camera, and not shared with the defendants? In *Alderman* (1969), the Supreme Court said no. The government, after engaging in illegal electronic eavesdropping, urged that the surveillance records should be first inspected in camera by the trial judge, who would then turn over to the defendants and their counsel only those materials relevant for their prosecution.[117] The Court decided that the procedure gave inadequate protections to the defendants. The hazards were too great in allowing a trial judge to winnow through surveillance records to decide what is relevant:

> An apparently innocent phrase, a chance remark, a reference to what appears to be a neutral person or event, the identity of a caller or the individual on the other end of a telephone, or even the manner of speaking or using words may have special significance to one who knows the more intimate facts of an accused's life. And yet that information may be wholly colorless and devoid of meaning to one less acquainted with all relevant circumstances. Unavoidably, this is a matter of judgment, but in our view the task is too complex, and the margin for error too great, to rely wholly on the *in camera* judgment of the trial court to identify those records which might have contributed to the Government's case.[118]

---

114. Id. at 672.
115. Id. at 681.
116. Id. at 680.
117. Alderman v. United States, 394 U.S. 165, 168, 176 (1969).
118. Id. at 182.

Emphasizing that adversary proceedings "are a major aspect of our system of criminal justice," the Court regarded in camera inspection and ex parte procedures as wholly inadequate for protecting the defendants' rights.[119] If the government objected to disclosing national security materials to the defendants, it could dismiss the prosecution.[120] Otherwise, the materials should go to the defendants and their attorneys. The trial court "can and should, where appropriate, place a defendant and his counsel under enforceable orders against unwarranted disclosure of the materials which they may be entitled to inspect."[121] In a dissent, Harlan and Fortas agreed that the government was obligated to surrender the surveillance documents to the court, but wanted in camera inspection in cases where an unauthorized disclosure would present a substantial risk to the national security.[122]

When Government Brings a Civil Case

When the government initiates a civil case, it is obliged, as it is in a criminal case, to make needed evidence available to a defendant. If it chooses not to, because the documents are privileged or covered by the state secrets doctrine, courts can tell the government to drop the suit or they can rule in favor of the defendant. The exact line between criminal and civil cases with regard to evidence is unclear. Although the Supreme Court in *Nixon* insisted that government documents be turned over in a criminal proceeding, it added: "We are not here concerned with the balance between the President's generalized interest in confidentiality and the need for relevant evidence in civil litigation."[123] Still, lower courts in several cases have told the government that when it brings a civil case against a private party, it must be prepared to either surrender documents needed by the defendant or drop the charges.

A district court decision in 1941 concerned an order by the Labor Department to enjoin a private citizen from violating the provisions of the Fair Labor Standards Act. In an interrogatory, the defendant asked for the names of the employees the government claimed were paid wages less than that prescribed by law. The government objected that to answer the interrogatory would disclose confidential and privileged information from agency files. The district court ruled that once a government official seeks relief in a court of law, he "must be held to have waived any privilege, which he otherwise might have

---

119. Id. at 183, 184.
120. Id. at 184.
121. Id. at 185.
122. Id. at 197–98, 201, 209–11.
123. United States v. Nixon, 418 U.S. at 712 (Note 19).

had, to withhold testimony required by the rules of pleading or evidence as a basis for such relief."[124]

The court said it could not be disputed that if the lawsuit were between two private parties, "the plaintiff would be compelled to comply with the interrogatory. But, because the plaintiff here is a governmental agent, he considers himself exempt from the rule as to interrogatories."[125] The court rejected that analysis. The privilege claimed by the government conflicted with the rules of pleading and the rules of evidence. To gain the relief it sought, it was necessary for the government "to comply with the conditions precedent to the granting of such relief and, to that extent, surrender the right of secrecy." The Administrator of the Wage and Hour Division of the Labor Department had a choice: "He must either give up his privilege to withhold pertinent evidence or he must abandon his suit for relief."[126]

The same principle surfaced in a 1949 case after the United States sued the Cotton Valley Operators Committee and others for violating the Sherman Anti-Trust Act. In response to the government's failure to comply with a court order to produce documents requested by the defendants, the court dismissed the government's case.[127] Similarly, in 1958 the Eighth Circuit reviewed an action by the Secretary of Labor, who enjoined certain individuals from violating minimum wage, overtime, and record-keeping provisions of the Fair Labor Standards Act. A district court dismissed the lawsuit after the secretary refused to obey court orders directing him to produce for the individuals four statements taken by the Secretary's investigators. The secretary argued that the statements were privileged under the act. The Eighth Circuit, affirming the district court's decision, concluded that under the circumstances of the case, the question of privilege was left to the court.[128]

In a 1961 case, the National Labor Relations Board refused to permit testimony sought by a company charged with unfair labor practices. To the Fifth Circuit, "fundamental fairness" required that the company "be allowed to introduce testimony that may impeach the evidence offered against it. The N.L.R.B. cannot hide behind a self-erected wall evidence adverse to its interest as a litigant."[129] The case presented

124. Fleming v. Bernardi, 4 F.R.D. 270, 271 (D. Ohio 1941).
125. Id.
126. Id.
127. United States v. Cotton Valley Operators Committee, 9 F.R.D. 719 (D. La. 1949), judgment aff'd, 339 U.S. 940 (1950).
128. Mitchell v. Bass, 252 F.2d 513, 517 (8th Cir. 1958).
129. NLRB v. Capitol Fish Co., 294 F.2d 868, 875 (5th Cir. 1961).

an anomaly in our system of justice. The agency official charged with
responsibility for asserting the claim of privilege is also the prosecutor
whose successful prosecution of this case could depend on exclusion of
the evidence for which the privilege is claimed. And, he is one part, the
trial court (examiner) a second part, and the reviewing court (the Board)
a third part of one agency—the agency bringing the action. Impartiality is the life of justice. It is against all concepts of impartial justice for
the trial examiner to assume that the Board, through its regulations, or
the General Counsel, by virtue of his office, is the final arbiter to decide whether a Board attorney should testify. Responsibility for deciding the question of privilege properly lies in an impartial independent
judiciary—not in the party claiming the privilege and not in a party
litigant.[130]

A tax case in 1963 illustrates the right of a private party to agency documents. The government sued to recover over a million dollars in an allegedly
erroneous payment of a tax refund to a cement company, which then asked
to inspect intraoffice reports, memoranda, and other documents held by the
Internal Revenue Service. The government insisted that the documents occupied an executive or attorney-client privilege or were covered by the attorney
work-product doctrine. A district court held that the company was entitled to
see the documents, in part because "the Government itself is the moving party
and most certainly has an obligation to see that justice is done."[131] It would
be "unconscionable," said the court, for the government to be permitted to
prosecute the suit "challenging its own prior determination of defendant's tax
liability, and then invoke governmental or attorney-client privileges, or the
attorney's work-product doctrine, to deprive the defendant of matters which
might be material to its defense." In this type of case "the defendant should
not be kept in the dark, but . . . a full disclosure should be made."[132]
  The court explained that an in camera inspection showed that the documents requested by the company did not reveal any military or state secret or
"threaten the National Security in any way."[133] It is understandable that the
court would want to distinguish this case from *Reynolds* and other national
security decisions, but even the presence of military or state secrets would not
justify suing a private company on the basis of information that the govern-

130. Id.
131. United States v. San Antonio Portland Cement Co., 33 F.R.D. 513, 515 (D. Texas
1963).
132. Id.
133. Id.

ment keeps to itself. In such situations the government should be asked either to release the documents or drop the suit.

The next year, a district court held that when the government brings a civil suit, it waives any privilege, "including even the entirely legitimate privilege which the government might otherwise assert with respect to diplomatic and military service."[134] A year later, the Ninth Circuit reversed the decision of the National Labor Relations Board to block subpoenas issued by a company for agency documents and testimony. Initially, the NLRB argued that the agency general counsel had not consented to the subpoenas. It later claimed that some of the documents might be privileged. If the agency wanted to push in that direction, the court said it had a choice: "just as a plaintiff in a civil action could not obtain a judgment if it persisted in withholding evidence which the court determined should be produced, so the Board could not enter an enforceable order if it insists on withholding evidence which, under the rules of evidence in effect in federal district courts, is admissible."[135]

In 2005, the Supreme Court reviewed a disturbing case that had been bouncing around the Tax Court for a number of years. Secrecy was practiced not within an executive agency but inside the judiciary. Tax Court judges are appointed for 15-year terms, assisted by "special trial judges" who have no fixed term of office. Any case before the Tax Court may be assigned to a special trial judge for hearing. Special trial judges take testimony, conduct trials, rule on the admissibility of evidence, and render final decisions in small tax cases. The Supreme Court case involved taxpayers who had been charged by the government with failure to report certain payments on their individual tax returns and with tax fraud. They had reason to believe that a report submitted by a special trial judge—a document publicly available in earlier years—had been withheld from them. This report concluded that the taxpayers did not owe taxes and that the fraud penalty did not apply.[136]

The Tax Court ruled that the report (called a "preliminary draft") was not available to the taxpayers because it related to "the internal deliberative processes of the Court."[137] The Commissioner of Internal Revenue called the report an internal draft, "a mere 'step' in a 'confidential decisional process,' and therefore properly withheld from a reviewing court."[138] The Supreme Court rejected those arguments: "The Tax Court's practice of not disclosing the special trial judge's original report, and of obscuring the Tax Court judge's mode of reviewing that report, impedes fully informed appellate review of the

134. United States v. Gates, 35 F.R.D. 524, 529 (D. Colo. 1964).
135. General Engineering, Inc. v. NLRB, 341 F.2d 367, 376 (9th Cir. 1965).
136. Ballard v. C.I.R., 125 S.Ct. 1270, 1277–78 (2005).
137. Id. at 1278.
138. Id. at 1283.

Tax Court's decision."[139] Of course this practice of secret reports also denies private citizens the documents they need to prevail in court.

Civil Cases: Government as Defendant

When a private party brings a case against the government, as in a tort claims action, the government may be put in the position of either releasing requested documents or losing the case. In *Reynolds,* both the district court and the Third Circuit told the government that if it insisted on withholding the accident report and the survivor statements from the three widows, it would lose. Only at the level of the Supreme Court was the government allowed to both withhold documents and prevail on the merits. Cases since that time have not been as generous to the government. Whether the case is criminal or civil, plaintiffs have a right to obtain government documents needed to support their case. It does not matter whether the government brings the case or is the defendant. A trial court must at least conduct in camera review to independently assess the government's claim of privilege, including state secrets. "Any other rule would permit the Government to classify documents just to avoid their production even though there is need for their production and no true need for secrecy."[140]

In 1954, Weldon Bruce Dayton was offered a position as a research physicist at the Tata Institute of Fundamental Research, affiliated with the University of Bombay. The Director of the Passport Office advised him that his application for a passport had been denied because the Department of State "feels that it would be contrary to the best interest of the United States to provide you passport facilities at this time." He executed an affidavit stating that he was not, and never had been, a member of the Communist Party, and, with the possible exception of a brief association with the Joint Anti-Fascist Refugee Committee for a few months in 1941 and 1942, he had never been a member of any of the organizations designated on the Attorney General's list of subversive organizations. The director wrote to him that his affidavit had been given careful consideration, but in view of "certain factors" of his case "which I am not at liberty to discuss," the passport denial would stand. Later the director wrote to Dayton's lawyer:

> In arriving at its decision to refuse passport facilities to Mr. Dayton, the Department took into consideration his connection with the Science for Victory Committee and his association at that time with various com-

---

139. Id. at 1283.
140. American Civil Liberties Union v. Brown, 619 F.2d 1170, 1173 (7th Cir. 1980).

munists. However, the determining factor in the case was Mr. Dayton's association with persons suspected of being part of the Rosenberg espionage ring and his alleged presence at an apartment in New York which was allegedly used for microfilming material obtained for the use of a foreign government.[141]

Faced with what was "suspected" and "alleged," Dayton requested information from the Board of Passport Appeals concerning three items: his alleged association with various communists, his association with persons suspected of being part of the Rosenberg ring, and his alleged presence at the apartment in New York. The board provided the apartment address and some names, but it announced that it would prohibit him from examining "a confidential file composed of investigative reports from Government agencies."[142] Secretary of State John Foster Dulles issued a statement on October 4, 1956, providing additional details drawn from the open record and confidential information contained in departmental files. He warned that full disclosure of the confidential information "might prejudice the conduct of United States foreign relations."[143] The selective use of confidential information meant that the government could release what was necessary to damage an individual's reputation—to sustain the government's position in court—but not enough to allow the individual to analyze the source and mount an effective defense.

Dayton sued the government, arguing that he was entitled to a passport. The district court and the D.C. Circuit upheld the government.[144] The Supreme Court, divided 5 to 4, reversed, holding that Congress had not delegated to the Secretary of State the authority used to deny the passport.[145] In the companion case, spelling out in greater detail the delegation question, the Court pointed out that persons denied passports because of alleged contacts with communist organizations had "neither been accused of crimes nor found guilty."[146] Describing the right to travel abroad as constitutionally based, the Court said it would not "readily infer that Congress gave the Secretary of State unbridled discretion to grant or withhold it."[147]

A case somewhat less favorable to a private party was brought by Kaiser Aluminum against the government and decided by the U.S. Court of Claims

141. Dayton v. Dulles, 357 U.S. 144, 146 (1958).
142. Id. at 148.
143. Id. at 153.
144. Dayton v. Dulles, 146 F.Supp. 876 (D.D.C. 1956); Dayton v. Dulles, 254 F.2d 71 (D.C. Cir. 1957). See also Dayton v. Dulles, 237 F.2d 43 (D.C. Cir. 1956).
145. Dayton v. Dulles, 357 U.S. 144 (1958).
146. Kent v. Dulles, 357 U.S. 116, 130 (1958).
147. Id. at 129.

in 1958. Kaiser, thinking that its contract with the United States had been breached, sought and received from the General Services Administration a number of documents. Its request was fully complied with except for one document, which the government withheld because it was "contrary to the national interest." The court upheld the government's privilege in this particular instance, but it disagreed that the government had absolute authority to block access to such documents: "The power must lie in courts to determine executive privilege in litigation."[148]

In 1975, the U.S. Court of Claims weighed the competing arguments of the government and a private company on access to government documents in a civil case. Attorneys for former President Richard Nixon claimed that "there is a big difference between civil and criminal cases" as to executive privilege "because it can be invoked in the latter only at the price of letting defendant go free."[149] Still, Nixon's attorneys recognized that plaintiffs should be allowed to show that the documents (in this case not involving sensitive national security matters) are relevant to the litigation.[150] Comparing the dispute to *United States v. Nixon* (1974), involving a criminal case, the court concluded that "the same sort of balancing process would be applicable to an incumbent President's claim of privilege in a civil case, albeit the burden on the litigant seeking discovery might be heavier."[151] The court decided that the plaintiffs had shown the requisite need for the documents.[152]

A more sensitive case arose in 1977, when the government was sued after the arrest of approximately 1,200 persons demonstrating against the Vietnam War. The plaintiffs subpoenaed White House tapes in the possession of Nixon's attorney, who argued that the presidential privilege of confidentiality "was absolute in the context of civil litigation."[153] The D.C. Circuit rejected that position.[154] Even though this was not a criminal case, "there is also a strong constitutional value in the need for disclosure in order to provide the kind of enforcement of constitutional rights that is presented by a civil action for damages, at least where, as here, the action is tantamount to a charge of civil conspiracy among high officers of government to deny a class of citizens their constitutional rights and where there has been sufficient evidentiary

148. Kaiser Aluminum & Chemical Corp. v. United States, 157 F.Supp. 939, 947 (Ct. Cl. 1958).
149. Sun Oil Co. v. United States, 524 F.2d 1020, 1022 (Ct. Cl. 1975).
150. Id. at 1023.
151. Id. at 1024.
152. Id.
153. Dellums v. Powell, 561 F.2d 242, 244 (D.C. Cir. 1977).
154. Id. at 245–46.

substantiation to avoid the inference that the demand reflects mere harassment."[155]

Two cases before the U.S. Court of International Trade, in 1982 and 1983, illustrate how a court can independently examine a state secrets claim by the government and find it empty of privileged content. The first case involved a dispute over antidumping duties on steel exported from Romania. The Under Secretary of Commerce for International Trade insisted that two cables from the Commerce Department to the American Embassy in Bucharest remain confidential. After examining the documents in camera, the court said they "showed nothing in the nature of a state secret, nothing suggestive of delicate matters of foreign policy and nothing else of a dimension entitled to a privilege against disclosure under the existing case law."[156]

The next year, the court again rejected the government's contention that documents should be withheld because they contained state secrets. Dismissing the government's claim that the state secrets privilege is absolute, the court declared: "It is for this Court to determine whether the state secrets privilege applies."[157] In looking at the disputed material, the court found that it "does not consist of state secrets and does not achieve the status of a state secret by virtue of a request by a foreign government or international agency that it be kept confidential, or by this government's classification of it under Executive Order 12356, or by the opinion of the Secretary of Commerce that disclosure of the information to a party in this judicial review would damage international relations and reasonably be expected to damage national security."[158] There was "no need to transform confidential matters into state secrets in this area of litigation." To do so "would be a distortion of the state secrets privilege and an unjustified interference with the right of judicial review."[159]

When Government Is Not a Party

The issue of state secrets often arises in lawsuits where the United States is not a party, but it intervenes because a confidential government document might be made public. In a 1912 case between two steel companies, one firm had a contract with the United States to manufacture and deliver armor-piercing projectiles. Drawings of the projectiles, made by the Bureau of Ordnance for the Navy Department, were delivered to one of the companies on the

155. Id. at 247. For more on these arrests, see Apton v. Wilson, 506 F.2d 83 (D.C. Cir. 1974); and Sullivan v. Murphy, 478 F.2d 938 (D.C. Cir. 1973).
156. Republic Steel Corp. v. United States, 538 F.Supp. 422, 423 (1982).
157. United States Steel Corp. v. United States, 578 F.Supp. 409, 411 (1983).
158. Id. at 411–12.
159. Id. at 413.

condition that the drawings were confidential and could not be disclosed. A district court sustained a motion to strike the drawings from the record, on the ground of public policy and to prevent military secrets from being revealed. At the request of the Navy Department, a U.S. attorney appeared at the trial in support of the motion to prevent disclosure of the drawings.[160]

Similarly, in a 1939 dispute between two companies, one had entered into a contract with the federal government to construct sighting data for guns. At issue was the public disclosure of confidential drawings. The government, moving to intervene, filed a statement that the suit involved a military secret and that any disclosure would be detrimental to the national defense and the public interest. In a letter to the Attorney General, the Navy Department insisted that the company had contracted with the government after signing a pledge of secrecy not to disclose any information about the military devices. A district court ruled that the documents sought in court must be deemed privileged and were properly withheld from discovery.[161]

In a 1966 case, two companies contesting trademarks and trade names sought and it received some 4,500 documents from the federal government, including all government communications with outsiders as well as nearly all intragovernmental materials.[162] The government opposed a subpoena, requesting 49 documents from the U.S. Justice Department, on the ground that they consisted of memoranda that contained opinions, recommendations, and deliberations about departmental matters, including litigation strategy. A district court ruled that the documents were integral to the department's decisional and policy-making functions and were immune from disclosure. The court, treating this type of privilege as qualified and capable of being outweighed by a showing of need, supported the government's position. The court indicated that the result might have been different had there been charges of governmental misconduct or perversion of governmental power.[163]

These types of cases appear with some frequency. A 1985 case involved an individual who sued *Penthouse* magazine for publishing an article that charged him with espionage. The U.S. Navy intervened to advise the judiciary that the government had a national security interest that would not be protected by the two parties. After several rounds in the courts, the Fourth Circuit dismissed the case on the ground that continued litigation would result in disclosure of privileged state secrets. The court recognized that when the state secrets privilege is validly asserted, "the result is unfairness to individual

---

160. Firth Sterling Steel Co. v. Bethlehem Steel Co., 199 F. 353 (E.D. Pa. 1912).
161. Pollen v. Ford Instrument Co., 26 F.Supp. 583 (E.D. N.Y. 1939).
162. Carl Zeiss Stiftung v. V.E.B. Carl Zeiss, Jena, 40 F.R.D. 318, 327 (D.D.C. 1966).
163. Id. at 329.

litigants—through the loss of important evidence or dismissal of a case—in order to protect a greater public value."[164] The court did not take state secrets as an absolute privilege. The privilege comes into play only when the government "is able to convince the court that, due to the nature of proof to be presented in a case, the action presents a substantial threat that state secrets will be compromised."[165]

Other cases, where the government intervened to prevent state secrets from being made public, were decided in 1991 and 1993.[166] Depending on the case, a trial may proceed between two private parties after a court grants the government's motion to block access to secret documents. The case may not be one where the very subject matter of the litigation is itself a state secret, and the evidence protected from discovery may not be central to the question in court. In such cases, a fair trial can be had.[167]

State Secrets Flourish

In *Reynolds,* the Supreme Court cautioned the government that the state secrets privilege "is not to be lightly invoked."[168] That sense of self-restraint has long since disappeared. The federal government now invokes the privilege not merely for military and diplomatic secrets, or for national security in general, but for other categories that in the past would have been considered labored and far-fetched. For example, a Ninth Circuit decision in 1989 reviewed a lawsuit brought by a homosexual employee of a government contractor. He objected that the contractor's decision not to submit his application for security clearance deprived him of constitutional rights. The Secretary of Defense filed a motion to dismiss on the ground that the action could not be litigated without disclosing protected state and military secrets.[169] The political climate after 9/11 has emboldened the government to assert state secrets in an increasing number of cases.[170]

---

164. Fitzgerald v. Penthouse Intern., Ltd., 776 F.2d 1236, 1238 (Note 3) (4th Cir. 1985).
165. Id. at 1243.
166. Zuckerbraun v. General Dynamics Corp., 935 F.2d 544 (2d Cir. 1991); Bareford v. General Dynamics Corp., 973 F.2d 1138 (5th Cir. 1992), cert. denied, 507 U.S. 1029 (1993).
167. DTM Research, L.L.C. v. AT & T Corp., 245 F.3d 327 (4th Cir. 2001).
168. United States v. Reynolds, 345 U.S. at 7.
169. Weston v. Lockheed Missiles & Space Co., 881 F.2d 814, 815 (9th Cir. 1989).
170. OpenTheGovernment.org, "Secrecy Report Card 2005," at 7. These statistics are drawn from William G. Weaver and Robert M. Pallitto, "State Secrets and Executive Power," 120 Pol. Sci. Q. 1 (2005).

Richard Barlow

In 2002, the U.S. Court of Federal Claims decided the case of Richard Barlow, who in the late 1980s faced termination from the Defense Department and suspension of security clearances after disputes within the executive branch, and between the executive branch and Congress, over Pakistan's nuclear capabilities. Some central questions were whether executive officials had misled lawmakers, in secret briefings, regarding Pakistan's activities, and whether the Reagan administration had improperly certified to Congress that Pakistan did not have nuclear weapons.[171]

After a number of investigations by the Defense Department, several by agency inspectors general and another by the General Accounting Office regarding agency retaliations against Barlow's whistle-blower activities, a bill was introduced in the Senate to provide relief to Barlow.[172] The private bill included the sum of $1,100,000 to compensate him for losses due to the personnel actions taken against him and his separation from the Defense Department on February 27, 1992.[173] In 1998, the Senate referred the matter to the Court of Federal Claims requesting that it report back findings of fact and conclusions "that are sufficient to inform the Congress of the nature, extent, and character of the claim for compensation referred to in such bill as a legal or equitable claim against the United States or a gratuity."[174]

Barlow and his attorneys, through the discovery process, sought documents that they believed would show that Congress had been misled about Pakistan's capabilities. On February 10, 2000, CIA Director George Tenet signed a declaration and formal claim of state secrets privilege and statutory privilege. The declaration denied Barlow and his attorney access to any of the classified intelligence information under Tenet's control. Tenet said it would not be possible "to sanitize or redact in any meaningful way" the information that Barlow sought.[175] A separate declaration by Lieutenant General Michael V. Hayden, Director of the National Security Agency, also invoked the state secrets privilege to assert the agency's privilege over NSA intelligence reports

171. Seymour M. Hersh, "On the Nuclear Edge," New Yorker, March 29, 1993, at 56.

172. For a description of these investigations, see Barlow v. United States, 51 Fed.Cl. 380, 390–92 (2002).

173. S. 2274, 105th Cong., 2d Sess. (1998).

174. 144 Cong. Rec. 23357 (1998).

175. Declaration and Formal Claim of State Secrets Privilege and Statutory Privilege by George J. Tenet, Director of Central Intelligence, February 10, 2000, Barlow v. United States, Congressional Reference No. 98-887X, at 9 (hereafter "Tenet Declaration").

and information from intelligence reports contained in minutes of the Nuclear Export Violations Working Group meetings.[176]

These declarations did not automatically block Barlow's access to the documents. In fact, Tenet acknowledged that the branch that decides what evidence to admit in court is the judiciary, not the executive branch: "I recognize it is the Court's decision rather than mine to determine whether requested material is relevant to matters being addressed in litigation."[177] The Court of Federal Claims had several options. It could have ordered the government to provide a full public account of why disclosure of the information would harm national security.[178] It could have conducted "an *in camera* examination of the requested materials" and also asked that sensitive material be redacted to permit access by Barlow.[179]

In a decision filed July 18, 2000, and reissued August 3, 2000, the Court of Federal Claims initially treated the state secrets privilege as qualified, not absolute. Although it noted that some courts have held that state secrets are "absolutely privileged from disclosure in the courts,"[180] it stated correctly that "the mere formal declaration of the privilege does not end the court's inquiry."[181] Toward the end of this analysis, however, the court ruled that state secrets were absolute: "The privilege is absolute, the law having evolved to reflect a choice of secrecy over any balancing of risks and harms."[182] (There had been no evolution of total deference by the judiciary to executive branch claims.) The court concluded that the documents sought by Barlow, "to the extent not already produced or located, are privileged *in toto.*"[183] He was not denied some of the documents. He was denied all.

The court continued the trial and allowed the government to introduce the documents and testimony to support its case, while at the same time denying Barlow access to documents and testimony he requested to support his position. On May 4, 2000, Barlow's attorneys, Paul C. Warnke and Diane S. Pickersgill, objected that the state secrets privilege should not apply to congressional reference cases to prevent Barlow and the court access to "key

176. Declaration of Lieutenant General Michael V. Hayden, United States Air Force, Director of the National Security Agency, February 2000, Barlow v. United States, Congressional Reference No. 98-887X.

177. Tenet Declaration, at 7.

178. Ellsberg v. Mitchell, 709 F.2d 51, 60–64 (D.C. Cir. 1983).

179. Id. at 64.

180. Barlow v. United States, No. 98-887X, 2000 WL 1141087, at 4, citing Halkin v. Helms, 690 F.2d 977, 990 (D.C. Cir. 1982).

181. Barlow v. United States, 2000 WL 1141087, at 4.

182. Id. at 8–9.

183. Id. at 9.

evidence."[184] Warnke and Pickersgill asked the court to review the documents in camera.[185] In an opposition filed on May 9, 2002, Barlow's attorney, Joseph A. Ostoyich, pointed out that during the discovery phase the government "blocked Mr. Barlow's access to thousands of pages of documents containing the facts he alleges were concealed from Congress by invoking the state secrets privilege over every word in those documents."[186] On May 31, 2002, two days before the trial, Ostoyich objected that

> the Government seeks to prevent the Court carrying out its mission, to prevent the Congress from finding out whether it was misled, and to thwart Mr. Barlow's case by asserting the state secrets privilege over virtually all classified information relevant to the Pakistani nuclear program—even the most generalized conclusions about the facts known to the Executive Branch—regardless of the fact that much of it is already public and none of it threatens to jeopardize a source or method of U.S. intelligence gathering.[187]

No case, he said, "has ever granted the Executive Branch such a broad—and irrational—invocation of the state secrets privilege and this Court should decline to do so."[188]

The U.S. Court of Federal Claims noted that it had "previously ruled that the defendant successfully invoked the state secrets privilege."[189] Not only had the government prevailed on that question but the court had treated the privilege as absolute. To accept the privilege as absolute implies that the trial is being turned over to the executive branch and the plaintiff is no longer in a courtroom operated by an independent judge. By deferring absolutely to the privilege, the Court of Federal Claims acknowledged that a "limited amount of information and testimony was thus removed beyond even the court's access."[190] How much of that "limited amount" of information and testimony was crucial to Barlow's case cannot be known.

184. Plaintiff's Opposition to Defendant's Motion for a Protective Order, Barlow v. United States, Congressional Reference No. 98-887 X, at 1.

185. Id. at 9.

186. Plaintiff's Opposition to the Government's Motion *in Limine,* Barlow v. United States, Congressional Reference No. 98-887 X, at 1–2.

187. Plaintiff's Opposition to the Government's Motion for Clarification Regarding the State Secrets Protective Order, Barlow v. United States, Congressional Reference No. 98-997 X, at 1.

188. Id. at 2.

189. Barlow v. U.S., 51 Fed.Cl. 380, 384 (Note 6) (2002).

190. Barlow v. U.S., 53 Fed.Cl. 667, 669 (2002).

Sibel Edmonds

Sibel Edmonds, hired as a contract linguist by the FBI after 9/11, began listening to recorded wiretaps and making translations from Turkish, Farsi, and Azerbaijani. She told supervisors that she thought a colleague was covering up illegal activity involving Turkish nationals. Working through agency channels, she eventually reported her concerns to the FBI Office of Professional Responsibility and the Inspector General (IG) of the Justice Department.[191] Within weeks of making those reports, she was fired. At that point, she turned to the courts for relief, filing several lawsuits under the Privacy Act, the Freedom of Information Act, and the Federal Tort Claims Act. She sought damages for the wrongful and unauthorized disclosure of agency records to third persons.

When she pursued FBI documents concerning her whistle-blower activity, Attorney General John Ashcroft on October 18, 2002, relied on the state secrets privilege to prevent her from gaining access to agency records. His classified declarations in 2002 and again in 2004 argued that the privilege needed to be invoked to protect the foreign policy and national security interests of the United States. The second set of declarations was designed to block her from being deposed in a case brought by families of 9/11 victims. The declarations were submitted to district court for ex parte, in camera review. The district court decided against Edmonds and the D.C. Circuit affirmed without a separate written opinion.[192]

Senators Charles Grassley (R-Iowa) and Patrick Leahy (D-Vt.) wrote to the Inspector General of the Justice Department on June 19, 2002, inquiring about its investigation into the firing of Edmonds. They suggested a number of issues that could be pursued.[193] In a floor statement, Leahy underscored a paradox: "It is not a good management practice for the FBI to fire a person who reports a security breach while nothing happens to the person who allegedly committed the breach. That could mean if you commit a breach, you might get away with it, but if you report it, you are out of here."[194]

---

191. James V. Grimaldi, "2 FBI Whistle-Blowers Allege Lax Security, Possible Espionage," *Washington Post*, June 19, 2002, at A10.

192. Edmonds v. Department of Justice, No. 04-5286 (D.C. Cir. May 6, 2005); John Files, "Appeals Court Backs Dismissal of Suit on FBI," *New York Times*, May 7, 2005, at A12; Edmonds v. U.S. Dept. of Justice, 323 F.Supp.2d 65 (D.D.C. 2004); Burnett v. Al Baraka Inv. & Development Corp., 323 F.Supp.2d 82 (D.D.C. 2004); Edmonds v. F.B.I, 272 F.Supp.2d 35 (D.D.C. 2003); David Rose, "An Inconvenient Patriot," *Vanity Fair*, September 2005, at 264–82.

193. 148 Cong. Rec. S5843-44 (daily ed. June 20, 2002).

194. Id. at S5842.

On July 21, 2004, FBI Director Robert Mueller wrote to Senator Orrin Hatch, chairman of the Senate Judiciary Committee, to summarize a classified report prepared by the IG office on Edmonds's case. Mueller said he was concerned by the IG's conclusion that Edmonds's allegations "were at least a contributing factor in why the FBI terminated her services." Moreover, the IG criticized the FBI for failing to adequately pursue her allegations of espionage by one of her colleagues. Mueller explained that Edmonds, as a contract employee, did not qualify for whistle-blower protection. Nevertheless, he said he would encourage all FBI employees, including contractors and detailees, to report "good faith concerns about mismanagement or misconduct." One of Mueller's first official communications was to state that he would not tolerate reprisals or intimidation by any agency employee against those who make protected disclosures, and he now extended that protection and policy to contractors and detailees.[195]

The IG office released an unclassified summary of its Edmonds investigation in January 2005. It charged that the FBI conducted "a cursory investigation" of her allegations.[196] It found that many of her allegations charging her coworker with possible espionage "were supported by either documentary evidence or witnesses other than Edmonds." It further concluded that had the FBI "performed a more careful investigation of Edmonds' allegations, it would have discovered evidence of significant omissions and inaccuracies by the co-worker related to these allegations. These omissions and inaccuracies, in turn, should have led to further investigation by the FBI." Edmonds "was justified in raising a number of these concerns to her supervisors." With respect to an allegation "that focused on the co-worker's performance, which Edmonds believed to be an indication of a security problem, the evidence clearly corroborated Edmonds' allegations."[197]

Instead of investigating her allegations "vigorously and thoroughly," the FBI regarded Edmonds as a "disruption and terminated her contract."[198] The IG office concluded that the FBI, confronted with her allegations about

195. Letter from FBI Director Robert S. Mueller III to Senator Orrin G. Hatch, chairman of the Senate Committee on the Judiciary, July 21, 2004; http://www.pogo.org/m/hsp/hsp-040721-Mueller.pdf.

196. Office of the Inspector General, U.S. Department of Justice, "A Review of the FBI's Actions in Connection with Allegations Raised by Contract Linguist Sibel Edmonds," January 2005, at 1; http://www.fas.org/irp/agency/doj/oig/sedmonds.html. See also Eric Lichtblau, "Inspector General Rebukes F.B.I. over Espionage Case and Firing of Whistle-Blower," New York Times, January 15, 2005, at A8; and Dan Eggen, "Official Faults FBI Probe of Translator's Complaint," Washington Post, January 15, 2005, at A13.

197. IG report, at 9.

198. Id.

possible espionage by the coworker, pursued an inquiry that was "seriously deficient."[199] The Security Officer's investigation of her claims against the coworker was "significantly flawed," he conducted "a superficial investigation," and he seemed not to appreciate or investigate the allegation that the coworker "may have been committing espionage." The Security Officer did not refer the allegations of potential espionage elsewhere in the FBI, regarding a referral to be pointless. "Our review revealed that a thorough investigation by the Security Office would have shown otherwise."[200]

On her last day of work, Edmonds prepared a memo that documented additional performance problems with the coworker, which she believed bolstered her underlying security concerns. A supervisor requested verification of the facts in the memo. The "follow-up confirmed that Edmonds' description of the facts was accurate," but the supervisor took no further action.[201] Had Edmonds been an FBI employee instead of a contractor, her allegations "would clearly qualify as protected disclosures under the FBI Whistleblower regulations." The key issue would be whether her disclosures were a "contributing factor" in her being fired. Under agency regulations, the FBI would have to prove by "clear and convincing evidence that it would have taken the same action absent her disclosures." The IG report concluded from its investigation that the FBI "could not show, by clear and convincing evidence, that at the time the decision was made it would have terminated Edmonds' contract absent her disclosures."[202]

Although Edmonds was fired on March 22, 2002, the IG's unclassified report of January 2005 stated that the FBI did not, "and still has not, adequately investigated" her allegations of espionage by the coworker. After a lapse of almost three years, the FBI "has not carefully investigated the allegations about the co-worker to determine if the co-worker compromised any FBI information." The IG report noted: "we believe the FBI should not discourage employees or contractors from raising good-faith allegations of misconduct or mismanagement and the FBI's termination of Edmonds' services may discourage others from raising such concerns."[203]

In his letter to Senator Hatch, Director Mueller attempted to allay these fears. However, Mueller's general policy announcements and promises, by themselves, are of little value. Every agency of government tolerates mismanagement if the overriding goal is to close ranks and protect the agency, as it generally is. In response to charges of mismanagement and misconduct, an

199. Id. at 10.
200. Id. at 12–13.
201. Id. at 18.
202. Id. at 25.
203. Id. at 28.

agency will resist parting with documents that might put it in a bad light. At the same time, agencies will routinely declassify documents and leak sensitive information if they decide it is in their interest. Loyalty to the agency generally trumps loyalty to the country (and to the Constitution).

The same agency that jealously and fiercely blocks access to internal records will turn on a dime and release them to congressional committees and the public to advance agency interests. Employees (or contractors) within the agency who threaten to embarrass coworkers and supervisors can expect a range of sanctions: loss of security clearance, reassignment, agency leaks to discredit them, and dismissal. Retribution comes no matter how valid the employee's information, and regardless of its importance to national security. It is rare in such instances to find an abusive manager sanctioned.

CONCLUSIONS

In *United States v. Reynolds,* the Supreme Court had two valid avenues before it. It could have followed the path taken by the district court and the Third Circuit, deciding in favor of the three widows because the government declined to release the accident report and the statements of the surviving crew members. The financial cost to the government would have been minimal. End of story. No need to carve out a new constitutional doctrine without adequate facts. The second legitimate choice would have been to ask that the government submit the disputed document to the Court for in camera review. Only through that examination could the Court be satisfied that the statements signed by Finletter and Harmon were solidly based.

Instead, the Court unnecessarily selected a third option that was the least justified. It assumed, on the basis of two ambiguous statements, that the government's claim of privilege had merit. In so doing, it resorted to a jumbled reasoning process that greatly broadened executive power in the fields of foreign and military affairs. Chief Justice Vinson may have thought he was prudently finding a middle ground between the two parties, giving something to each side. He said that the Court was faced with two broad propositions. On the one hand, the government urged that department heads had the power to withhold any documents in their custody from judicial view if they deemed it to be in the public interest. Counsel for the three widows insisted that the executive's power to withhold documents had been waived by the Federal Tort Claims Act. Vinson wrote: "Both positions have constitutional overtones which we find it unnecessary to pass upon, there being a narrower ground for decision."[1]

What Vinson did was to produce an unnecessary new doctrine that is incoherent, contradictory, and tilted away from the rights of private citizens and fair procedures and supportive of arbitrary executive power. After a department head makes a formal claim of privilege, "after actual personal consideration," the court itself "must determine whether the circumstances are appropriate for the claim of privilege, and yet do so without forcing a disclosure of the very thing the privilege is designed to protect."[2] The logical answer

1. United States v. Reynolds, 345 U.S. 1, 6 (1953).
2. Id. at 8.

would be for a court to look at the documents in camera to assure that the department's judgment was on reasonable grounds. Judicial scrutiny of the documents might reveal that the official could not have personally considered the affidavit, because the documents had no remote relationship to national security or military secrets. In such a situation, a judge must be willing to challenge the determination of an executive official. If judges conclude that they lack the competence to carry out the review function, the choices are unacceptable—either to capitulate to the executive branch, and say so; or to decide for the opposing party whenever the government raises a claim of state secrets privilege.

That is the problem with Vinson's analysis. He never makes it clear how executive officials are to be held accountable for their decisions and how courts can protect the legitimate rights of private citizens to gain access to needed documents. The court, he says, "must be satisfied from all the evidence."[3] If the evidence is merely a self-serving affidavit prepared by someone in the executive branch for a department head to sign, and the affidavit is filled with the ambiguities that Finletter put his name to, the court has no evidence worth its name. The only evidence that could satisfy a court would be the documents that justified the affidavit, and in the *Reynolds* case it would be the accident report and the survivors' statements. The district court and the Third Circuit insisted on that procedure. Vinson did not. Yet he writes: "If the court is so satisfied, the claim of the privilege will be accepted without requiring further disclosure."[4] Satisfied with the affidavit? The Court remained at arm's length from the evidence, expressing satisfaction with a shadow rather than the substance. It is not even clear what Vinson meant by "without requiring further disclosure." Disclosure to the court, for in camera inspection? Disclosure to the opposing party? Disclosure to the public? It is anyone's guess.

Vinson presents what he calls a "formula of compromise." He warns that judicial control over the evidence in a case "cannot be abdicated to the caprice of executive officers."[5] There should be little doubt that the Court did precisely that. Here the reasoning gets more tortured. Vinson said he "will not go so far as to say that the court may automatically require a complete disclosure to the judge before the claim of privilege will be accepted in any case. It may be possible to satisfy the court, from all the circumstances of the case, that there is a reasonable danger that compulsion of the evidence will expose military matters which, in the interest of national security, should not be divulged."[6] Without access to the documents, to be read in camera, how would

3. Id. at 9.
4. Id.
5. Id. at 9–10.
6. Id. at 10.

it be possible to satisfy the court? By an affidavit? Why should compulsion of the evidence to a judge, in chambers, risk divulging military matters? Judges should be assumed to protect military secrets with the same care as executive officials, if not more so. Judges take the same oath to protect and defend the Constitution, and judges are not tempted, as executive officers are, to selectively leak classified and secret documents to the public when it is advantageous to the administration.

Yet Vinson envisions situations where the executive branch can bar judges from seeing evidence and documents regardless of what precautions are taken to prevent disclosure. When there is a danger of divulging military secrets, "the occasion for the privilege is appropriate, and the court should not jeopardize the security which the privilege is meant to protect by insisting upon an examination of the evidence, even by the judge alone, in chambers."[7] This shows both a remarkable lack of trust in the judiciary and an inordinate faith in executive officials.

At this point in his opinion, Chief Justice Vinson draws attention to the current Cold War with the Soviet Union: "In the instant case we cannot escape judicial notice that this is a time of vigorous preparation for national defense. Experience in the past war [World War II] has made it common knowledge that air power is one of the most potent weapons in our scheme of defense, and that newly developing electronic devices have greatly enhanced the effective use of air power." He continues:

> It is equally apparent that these electronic devices must be kept secret if their full military advantage is to be exploited in the national interests. On the record before the trial court it appeared that the accident occurred to a military plane which had gone aloft to test secret electronic equipment. Certainly there was a reasonable danger that the accident investigation report would contain references to the secret electronic equipment which was the primary concern of the mission.[8]

In fact, there was never a danger that the secrecy of the electronic devices would be endangered by the litigation. The government could either withhold the documents and lose the case, as it was willing to do in district court and in the Third Circuit, or hand the documents over to the Court for examination in chambers. There was no risk that any secret information about the electronic devices would be divulged and exploited by the enemy. As to the record of the trial court showing that the accident occurred to a military plane that had gone aloft to test secret electronic equipment, that was known

7. Id.
8. Id.

by newspaper readers. It is the last sentence that is particularly off base. There was no "reasonable danger" that the accident investigation report would contain references to the secret electronic equipment. That was an implied assertion by the government. The Court never bothered to check it. We know now that the accident report had no references to the secret electronic equipment. There was a "reasonable danger" only because the Court chose to accept at face value the ambiguous Finletter statement and therefore abdicate judicial control to the executive branch.

The next paragraph tilts again to executive power: "when the formal claim of privilege was filed by the Secretary of the Air Force, under circumstances indicating a reasonable possibility that military secrets were involved, there was certainly a sufficient showing of privilege to cut off further demand for the documents on the showing of necessity for its compulsion that had then been made."[9] There was a "reasonable possibility" that military secrets were involved because it was common knowledge throughout the country. No one doubted the nature of the mission and the confidential equipment it carried. However, there was *not* a reasonable possibility that the requested documents contained military secrets. The Court denied itself the facts and the evidence to make an informed judgment.

Vinson closed by insisting that even if private parties showed a need for documents to make their case, and even if a judge wanted to see the documents in chambers, an assertion by the government could block all access. Where private parties make a strong showing of necessity for documents, "the claim of privilege should not be lightly accepted, but even the most compelling necessity cannot overcome the claim of privilege if the court is ultimately satisfied that military secrets are at stake."[10] How is a court to be satisfied that military secrets are at stake unless it looks at documents? In recommending that the three widows return to district court and depose the surviving crew members, Vinson seemed to leave open the possibility that access to the accident report might be possible. It should be possible for the widows to determine "the essential facts" that caused the accident "without resort to materials touching upon military secrets."[11] Implicit in this process is the possibility that evidence obtained from the crew members might uncover some tangible leads that would justify access to further documentation, including the accident report. The record indicates that the depositions were taken by the attorneys representing the widows, but it was decided not to litigate again in district court to request the documents.

9. Id. at 10–11.
10. Id. at 11.
11. Id.

The result is an exceptionally poorly reasoned decision by the Court that helped to launch a state secrets privilege that had no boundaries at the time, and not much now. What *Reynolds* did was to send an ominous signal that in matters of national security, the judiciary is willing to fold its tent and join the executive branch. Litigants have little reason in such cases to expect judges to exercise the independence they claim to possess. In such cases, the courtroom is not a place where the private litigant has a fighting chance. The private party is pitted against two superior forces: the executive branch joined with the judiciary.

The presumption in Congress and the courts should not be deference to executive claims about national security secrets. The performance of executive officials in *Reynolds* and subsequent cases does not merit deference. It warrants skepticism and close scrutiny by lawmakers and judges. The government's position is that when there is a "reasonable danger" that disclosing information would expose state secrets that, in the interest of national security, should not be divulged, "the privilege applies and is absolute."[12] The state secrets privilege must be regarded as qualified, not absolute. Otherwise there is no adversary process in court, no exercise of judicial independence over what evidence is needed, and no fairness accorded to private litigants who challenge the government.

If the government believes that a plaintiff's access to agency documents would endanger national security, a fair resolution would be for the courts to decide in the plaintiff's favor, as the district court and the Third Circuit did in *Reynolds*. Disposing of a case in that manner may reward plaintiffs who have unproven cases, but it also puts the government on notice that asserting state secrets comes at a price. That principle is understood in criminal proceedings. If the government refuses to release documents needed by the defendant, it must agree to drop the case. The accused goes free. In *Reynolds,* the government lost a civil case in district court and in the Third Circuit because it refused to turn over the accident report. The government was free to assert a privilege if it was willing to lose the case.

In civil cases, the government is invoking the state secrets privilege at little cost to itself and at great disadvantage to private individuals who press their claims. The government should not be placed in such a favored position. In some of these cases, the government denies a plaintiff access to agency documents while at the same time it releases agency information to the public to discredit the plaintiff. Government should not have it both ways.

12. Brief for the Respondents in Opposition, Edmonds v. Department of Justice, No. 05-190, on petition for a writ of certiorari to the D.C. Circuit, October 2005, at 8.

Preserving Judicial Integrity

Broad deference by the courts to the executive branch, allowing an official to determine what documents are privileged, undermines the judiciary's duty to assure fairness in the courtroom and to decide what evidence may be introduced. The person running the trial is the judge, not the executive official. The general rule is clear: the privileges of government are "governed by the principles of the common law as they may be interpreted *by the courts* of the United States in the light of reason and experience."[13] Although the Supreme Court in *Reynolds* did not follow the general principle it announced, the principle remains sound: "Judicial control over the evidence in a case cannot be abdicated to the caprice of executive officers."[14] The problem in *Reynolds* was the caprice of the judiciary, willing to craft high principles and then abandon them.

Some lower courts since 1953 have more clearly established the duty of a judge to be the final arbiter of what evidence to allow at trial. In a 1963 case against the government, the Secretary of the Air Force claimed a privilege against producing reports concerning an aircraft accident in which a crew member was badly injured. Certain documents and photographs were given to the plaintiff, but not everything he requested. While agreeing with the government that disclosure of investigative reports can hamper the efficient operation of a government program and even impair national security, a district court also recognized that it had a duty to give plaintiffs access to needed documents. When the secretary persisted in making only limited disclosure of reports, the D.C. Circuit affirmed the lower court and determined that his "offer" constituted inadequate compliance with the court order. It could not accept "the notion that the Secretary should himself decide what portions of the reports are or are not privileged. This is ordinarily a task for the court."[15] It acknowledged that in *Reynolds* the Supreme Court did not require the government to submit the disputed accident report to the Justices for their independent evaluation, but whatever "military secrets" the Court might have sensed were present, the D.C. Circuit concluded that "no substantial harm could result from submission of the report to judicial scrutiny."[16]

The D.C. Circuit in 1971 went beyond the judiciary's obligation to decide questions of evidence to broader issues of whether an executive official is operating in accordance with constitutional and statutory authority. It said that an "essential ingredient of our rule of law is the authority of the courts

13. Rule 501, 28 U.S.C. App. (2000) (emphasis added); 88 Stat. 1933 (1975).
14. United States v. Reynolds, 345 U.S. at 9–10.
15. Machin v. Zuckert, 316 F.2d 336, 341 (D.C. Cir. 1963).
16. Id.

to determine whether an executive official or agency has complied with the Constitution and with the mandates of Congress which define and limit the authority of the executive. Any claim to executive absolutism cannot override the duty of the court to assure that an official has not exceeded his charter or flouted the legislative will."[17] To grant an executive official or agency absolute authority to determine what documents may be given to the courts would empower the head of an executive department "to cover up all evidence of fraud and corruption when a federal court or grand jury was investigating malfeasance in office, and this is not the law."[18]

In the Watergate cases, District Judge John Sirica in 1973 held that it was necessary for the administration to produce presidential tape recordings to the court to be inspected in camera. Given the criminal investigations at stake, he asked: "Would it not be a blot on the page which records the judicial proceedings of this country, if, in a case of such serious import as this, the Court did not at least call for an inspection of the evidence in chambers?"[19] Unlike the Supreme Court in *Reynolds*, Sirica insisted that the tapes be delivered to him in chambers, at which point he—not the White House—would decide whether to excise portions of material that he concluded were privileged.[20]

On that procedure he was upheld by the D.C. Circuit, which called for the disclosure "of all portions of the tapes relevant to matters within the proper scope of the grand jury's investigations, unless the Court" judges that the public interest served by nondisclosure of particular items would outweigh the grand jury's needs.[21] The Supreme Court, affirming, also recognized that questions of what material needed to be excised would be left in the hands of the trial judge.[22] The following year a district court underscored the point: "The Court, not the executive officer claiming privilege, makes the judgment whether to uphold or overrule the claim."[23]

In *Reynolds*, the Supreme Court established a number of requirements for the government when it invokes the state secrets privilege: "There must be a formal claim of privilege, lodged by the head of the department which has control over the matter, after actual personal consideration by that officer. The court itself must determine whether the circumstances are appropriate for the claim of privilege, and yet do so without forcing a disclosure of the very

17. Committee for Nuclear Responsibility, Inc. v. Seaborg, 463 F.2d 788, 793 (D.C. Cir. 1971).
18. Id. at 794.
19. In re Subpoena to Nixon, 360 F.Supp. 1, 14 (D.D.C. 1973).
20. Id.
21. Nixon v. Sirica, 487 F.2d 700, 718 (D.C. Cir. 1973). See also id. at 720, 721.
22. United States v. Nixon, 418 U.S. at 714–15. Also id. at 715 (Note 21).
23. Kinoy v. Mitchell, 67 F.R.D. 1, 7 (S.D.N.Y. 1975).

thing the privilege is designed to protect."[24] The Court might have satisfied the latter requirement had it actually looked at the accident report and the survivor statements, but it chose not to, preferring to accept the word of the administration and the ambiguous affidavits it submitted.

As for the first requirement, there is little reason to expect the head of an executive department to have the time or expertise to give "actual personal consideration" of the claim. Subordinates draft an affidavit or declaration and the agency head signs it. A district court in 1975 concluded that it did not appear that Attorney General Elliot Richardson "personally considered the material as to which he lodged this claim of privilege and decided that it was a military or state secret."[25] What triggered the court's skepticism is not explained, but certainly substantial doubt is justified. It is not enough for a court to accept an affidavit at face value. It must be willing to look at classified information, in camera, to see whether it supports the affidavit. In this case, Richardson in his affidavit said it would be "a practical impossibility" to submit to the court all of the facts, circumstances, and other considerations that he used to justify authorization of electronic surveillance, and further certified that it "would prejudice the national interest" to disclose the facts contained in a sealed exhibit. However, he agreed to give the sealed document to the court to be examined in camera.[26] If a judge finds an affidavit too general or abstract, it can require the head of a department to lodge a claim of privilege that is more specific and detailed.[27]

In a case where an individual is suing the government and encounters the state secrets privilege, if the documents are needed by the private party a court should be able to compel the government to submit the documents to the court for in camera review. That is the only way the court can determine that the government properly classified the documents as "secret." Any other procedure would permit the government "to classify documents just to avoid their production even though there is need for their production and no true need for secrecy."[28] Some courts still treat state secrets as "*absolutely privileged* from disclosure in the courts," even for in camera review.[29] Such decisions put the executive branch in charge of the courtroom.

To cope with thousands of pages of classified documents, district judges have appointed a special master to develop representative samples of documents, summarize each party's actual or potential arguments, and present

24. United States v. Reynolds, 345 U.S. at 7–8.
25. Kinoy v. Mitchell, 67 F.R.D. at 9.
26. Id. at 7 n.17, para. 4.
27. Id. at 14.
28. American Civil Liberties Union v. Brown, 619 F.2d 1170, 1173 (7th Cir. 1980).
29. Halkin v. Helms, 690 F.2d 977, 990 (D.C. Cir. 1982) (emphasis in original).

this organized material to the judge without making recommendations. The master, of course, would need sufficient security clearance to look at the documents. Appellate courts have held that this type of arrangement and procedure is not an abuse of discretion on the part of the trial judge.[30]

Coram nobis suits give the judiciary an opportunity to check and correct misleading statements in court. False and deceptive affidavits by the government lead to incorrect and unjust decisions. To allow or countenance fraud in the courtroom does damage to the independence and reputation of the judiciary. The danger is especially grave when the affidavits are prepared by the government, which is the principal litigant in court. *Coram nobis* is a judicial instrument for holding the executive branch accountable. In cases of national security and state secrets, the absence of accountability permits the executive branch to manipulate the courts at no cost to itself. The damage inflicted on the judiciary, litigants, and democratic government is deep and far-reaching.

When *Reynolds* was relitigated in 2003, the Third Circuit decided to take two competing constitutional principles and elevate one to first place. After announcing the basic facts, it opened with these two sentences: "Actions for fraud upon the court are so rare that this Court has not previously had the occasion to articulate a legal definition of the concept. The concept of fraud upon the court challenges the very principle upon which our judicial system is based: the finality of a judgment."[31] The judicial system is not based solely on judicial finality. It is based also on the belief that a litigant has the chance to find fairness and honesty in the courtroom, even when the opposing party is the government. To have that hope dashed in national security cases sends the message that the judiciary is not an independent branch but functions as an agency of the executive branch.

Placing the emphasis on judicial finality cheapens the courtroom, making it look like a factory busily grinding out decisions regardless of whether a court knew what it was doing or whether the facts, revealed later, justified the ruling. Judicial finality means don't look back at *Reynolds* to see where the government misled the courts, deliberately or not, and thus changed the outcome of a judicial ruling that produced a new constitutional doctrine based on wrong facts. Look ahead at the next batch of cases coming your way.

The cloudiness and ambiguity of the Finletter and Harmon statements were well known in lower court. True, it was the responsibility of the plaintiffs to confront that head-on and insist on a clear statement from the government. But how difficult was it for the Justices, once they decided to rely on the Finletter statement, to tell the government: "We're not sure what it means. The parts of the statement talking about the secret mission and the confidential equipment are of no value or interest. Everyone in the country who read newspaper stories about the crash were aware of the mission and the equipment. Tell us in plain terms: Are there state secrets in the accident report? Are there state secrets in the statements of survivors? If you can't speak clearly on those questions you lose the case."

The ambiguities were never resolved, leading to the Third Circuit's decision in 2005. It is pathetic to know that the key issue for the Third Circuit, when examining the Finletter statement, was the meaning of "its." Courts that reason in that manner are not entitled to respect. The impression is that they are either intimidated by state secret issues or are essentially in league with the executive branch. Litigants in such cases are entitled to regard the judiciary as a dependent, not independent, branch. The contest moves from an already difficult task of private litigants against an executive agency to the inherently unequal one of private litigants against both the judicial and executive branches.

There is no justification for a court to take at face value affidavits and declarations signed by agency heads, and no justification to allow agencies to excise materials from documents before they are submitted to courts for in camera review. The framers adopted separation of powers and checks and balances because they did not trust human nature and feared concentrated power. To defer to agency claims about privileged documents and state secrets is to abandon the independence that the Constitution vests in Congress and the courts, placing in jeopardy the individual liberties that depend on institutional checks.

CHRONOLOGY

October 6, 1948	Midair explosion of B-29 aircraft over Waycross, Ga.
June 21, 1949	Widows of three civilians killed in the crash file a lawsuit in district court in the Eastern District of Pennsylvania.
June 30, 1950	District Judge William H. Kirkpatrick decides that the widows have good cause to see the Air Force accident report and statements of three survivors, and rejects the government's reliance on the Housekeeping Statute to prevent plaintiffs from obtaining the documents.
August 7, 1950	Judge Kirkpatrick orders the government to release the documents to the plaintiffs.
September 21, 1950	Judge Kirkpatrick issues an amended order, directing the government to produce the documents for his examination, to be read in his chambers.
October 12, 1950	After the government's refusal to give him the documents, Judge Kirkpatrick issues an order that the facts be taken as established in favor of the plaintiffs.
November 27, 1950	Judge Kirkpatrick hears testimony on the compensation due the widows.
February 27, 1951	He awards $80,000 each to Phyllis Brauner and Elizabeth Palya and $65,000 to Patricia Reynolds.
December 11, 1951	The Third Circuit upholds Judge Kirkpatrick's decision.
March 1952	The government appeals.
April 7, 1952	The Supreme Court agrees to hear the case.
October 21, 1952	Oral argument.
October 25, 1952	Justices meet in conference to discuss the case.
March 9, 1953	Court decides that the Air Force had a valid claim of privilege to withhold the documents from the plaintiffs.
June 22, 1953	Widows settle their cases with the government, receiving a total of $170,000, or $55,000 less than the original judgment.
February 10, 2000	Judith Palya Loether discovers declassified accident report on the Internet and finds that it contains nothing that would have been detrimental to national security.

February 26, 2003   Family members of the three civilians killed in 1948 petition the Supreme Court to reinstate the original district court judgment, holding that the government had deceived the Court about the contents of the accident report and the statements of survivors.

June 23, 2004   Court refuses to take the case, forcing plaintiffs to return to district court.

September 10, 2004   District court decides against plaintiffs.

September 22, 2005   Third Circuit decides against plaintiffs.

December 21, 2005   Plaintiffs file cert petition with the Supreme Court.

May 1, 2006   Supreme Court denies cert.

ARCHIVAL SOURCES

For insights into how the Supreme Court decided the case, I reviewed the manuscripts of five Justices whose papers are kept in the Library of Congress: Hugo Black, Harold Burton, William O. Douglas, Felix Frankfurter, and Robert H. Jackson. For the papers of Justice Tom Clark, I turned for help to Michael Widener and Addy Sonder at the Tarlton Law Library of the University of Texas at Austin and received many valuable documents. Rebecca Cape of the Lilly Library of Indiana University advised me that the collection for Justice Sherman Minton contained nothing on *Reynolds*. It's important to know that nothing is there. For the two remaining members of the *Reynolds* Court, Chief Justice Fred M. Vinson and Justice Stanley Reed, Roger Hamperian of the Public Policy Archives of the University of Kentucky located a number of helpful documents that explain their participation and deliberation.

At the Library of Congress, I rely extensively on three wonderful divisions: the manuscript division, the newspaper reading room, and the Law Library. I made extensive use of those collections, all ably and professionally staffed. On a number of occasions I turned for help to the Supreme Court Library and received valuable information. To Brian Stiglmeier and other members of the Court's staff: My thanks. Gail Farr at National Archives in Philadelphia located several hundred pages of documents on the *Reynolds* litigation. Daniel Linke, archivist of the Mudd Library at Princeton University, sent me the link to the set of oral history interviews with Justice William O. Douglas. I mined those materials with much profit. Appreciation also to James Britton, reference librarian at the Okefenokee Regional Library, Waycross, Ga., and Linda Aaron of the University of Georgia, for locating documents and forwarding them to me.

From E. Glenn Parr, Air Force Legal Services Agency, I received a number of documents related to the B-29 crash. They were forwarded to him by James S. Howard, archivist for the Air Force Historical Research Agency, Maxwell Air Force Base, Ala. Also from the Air Force Historical Research Agency, I received extensive help from Lynn Gamma.

BIBLIOGRAPHY

Abel, Elie. Leaking: Who Does It? Who Benefits? At What Cost? (New York: Priority Press Publications, 1987).

Abshire, David M. Saving the Reagan Presidency: Trust is the Coin of the Realm (College Station: Texas A&M University Press, 2005).

Alterman, Eric. When Presidents Lie: A History of Official Deception and Its Consequences (New York: Viking, 2004).

Ambrose, Stephen E. Eisenhower: Soldier, General of the Army, President-Elect 1890–1952 (New York: Simon & Schuster, 1983).

Andrew, Christopher. For the President's Eyes Only: Secret Intelligence and the American Presidency from Washington to Bush (New York: HarperCollins, 1995).

Arendt, Hannah. "Lying in Politics: Reflections on the Pentagon Papers," in Hannah Arendt, Crises of the Republic (New York: Harcourt Brace Jovanovich, 1972).

Asbill, Mac and Willis B. Snell "Scope of Discovery Against the United States," 7 Vanderbilt Law Review 582 (1954).

Ball, Howard. Justice Downwind: America's Atomic Testing Program in the 1950s (New York: Oxford University Press, 1986).

Berger, Margaret A. "How the Privilege for Governmental Information Met Its Watergate," 25 Case Western Reserve Law Review 747 (1975).

Berger, Raoul, and Abe Krash. "Government Immunity from Discovery," 59 Yale Law Journal 1451 (1950).

Beveridge, Albert J. The Life of John Marshall (3 vols., Boston: Houghton Mifflin Co., 1919).

Biographical Directory of the Federal Judiciary, 1789–2000 (Lanham, Md.: Bernan, 2001).

Bissell, Richard M., Jr. Reflections of a Cold Warrior (New Haven, Conn.: Yale University Press, 1996).

Bok, Sissela. Lying: Moral Choice in Public and Private Life (New York: Pantheon Books, 1978).

———. Secrets: On the Ethics of Concealment and Revelation (New York: Pantheon Books, 1983).

Borchard, Edwin M. "Government Liability in Tort," 34 Yale Law Journal 1, 129, 229 (1924–25).

Brachtenbach, Robert F. "The Privilege Against Revealing Military Secrets," 29 Washington Law Review 59 (1954).

Carrow, Milton M. "Governmental Nondisclosure in Judicial Proceedings," 107 University of Pennsylvania Law Review 166 (1958).

Christoph, James B. "A Comparative View: Administrative Secrecy in Britain," 35 Public Administration Review 23 (1975).

Coleman, Gregory S. "*Touhy* and the Housekeeping Privilege: Dead But Not Buried?," 70 Texas Law Review 685 (1992).

Cross, Harold L. The People's Right to Know: Legal Access to Public Records and Proceedings (New York: Columbia University Press, 1953).

Davis, Kenneth Culp. "Tort Liability of Governmental Units," 40 Minnesota Law Review 751 (1956).

Devins, Neal, and Louis Fisher. "The Steel Seizure Case: One of a Kind?," 19 Constitutional Commentary 63 (2002).

DuVal, Benjamin S., Jr. "The Occasions of Secrecy," 47 University of Pittsburgh Law Review 579 (1986).

Ehlke, Richard C., and Harold C. Relyea. "The Reagan Administration Order on Security Classification: A Critical Assessment," 30 Federal Bar News & Journal 91 (1983).

Ellsberg, Daniel. Secrets: A Memoir of Vietnam and the Pentagon Papers. (New York: Viking, 2002).

Fein, Bruce E. "Access to Classified Information: Constitutional and Statutory Dimensions," 26 William and Mary Law Review 805 (1985).

Fisher, Louis. American Constitutional Law (6th ed., Durham, N.C.: Carolina Academic Press, 2005).

———. "Confidential Spending and Governmental Accountability," 47 George Washington Law Review 347 (1979).

———. "Congressional Access to Information: Using Legislative Will and Leverage," 52 Duke Law Journal 323 (2002).

———. "Congressional-Executive Struggles over Information Secrecy Pledges," 42 Administrative Law Review 89 (1990).

———. "Invoking Executive Privilege: Navigating Ticklish Political Waters," 8 William & Mary Bill of Rights Journal 583 (2000).

———. Nazi Saboteurs on Trial: A Military Tribunal and American Law (Lawrence: University Press of Kansas, 2003).

———. The Politics of Executive Privilege (Durham, N.C.: Carolina Academic Press, 2004).

———. Presidential Spending Power (Princeton, N.J.: Princeton University Press, 1975).

———. Presidential War Power (2d ed., Lawrence: University Press of Kansas, 2004).

Flynn, Sean C. "The *Totten* Doctrine and Its Poisoned Progeny," 25 Vermont Law Review 793 (2001).

Franck, Thomas M., and Edward Weisband, eds. Secrecy and Foreign Policy (New York: Columbia University Press, 1974).

Frankel, Max. "The 'State Secrets' Myth," Columbia Journalism Review, September/October 1971, at 22–26.

Freedman, Abraham L. "The Writ of Error Coram Nobis," 3 Temple Law Quarterly 35 (1929).

Gardner, J. Steven. "The State Secret Privilege Invoked in Civil Litigation: A Proposal for Statutory Relief," 29 Wake Forest Law Review 567 (1994).

Gellhorn, Walter, and Louis Lauer. "Federal Liability for Personal and Property Damage," 29 New York University Law Review 1325 (1954).

———. "Congressional Settlement of Tort Claims Against the United States," 55 Columbia Law Review 1 (1955).

Gellhorn, Walter, and C. Newton Schenck. "Tort Actions Against the Federal Government," 47 Columbia Law Review 722 (1947).

Griswold, Erwin N. "The Pentagon Papers Case: A Personal Footnote," Yearbook 1984, Supreme Court Historical Society, at 115.

———. "Secrets Not Worth Keeping," Washington Post, February 15, 1989, at A25.

Gromley, Charles R. "Discovery Against the Government of Military and Other Confidential Matters," 43 Kentucky Law Journal 343 (1955).

Hearon, Robert J., Jr. "Federal Courts—Discovery-Requiring Production of Documents by the Government," 30 Texas Law Review 889 (1952).

Hersh, Seymour M. "On the Nuclear Edge," New Yorker, March 29, 1993, at 56.

Hudson, F. G. "The Federal Tort Claims Act," 22 Tulane Law Review 299 (1947).

Ichter, Cary. "'Beyond Judicial Scrutiny': Military Compliance with NEPA," 18 Georgia Law Review 639 (1984).

Irons, Peter. The Courage of Their Convictions: Sixteen Americans Who Fought Their Way to the Supreme Court (New York: Free Press, 1988).

———. Justice at War (New York: Oxford University Press, 1983).

Jaffe, Louis L. "Suits Against Governments and Officers: Sovereign Immunity," 77 Harvard Law Review 1 (1963).

Jost, Kenneth. "Government Secrecy," CQ Researcher, vol. 15, no. 42, December 2, 2005, at 1005–28.

Kenny, Gerard J. "The 'National Security Wiretap': Presidential Prerogative or Judicial Responsibility," 45 Southern California Law Review 888 (1972).

Kincaid, John. "Secrecy and Democracy: The Unresolved Legacy of the Pentagon Papers," in Watergate and Afterward: The Legacy of Richard Nixon, edited by Leon Friedman and William F. Levantrosser (Westport, Conn.: Greenwood Press, 1992).

King, Wilbur Branch. "Military Secrets as an Evidentiary Problem in Civil Litigation," 4 Journal of Public Law 196 (1955).

Labovitz, John R. Presidential Impeachment (New Haven, Conn.: Yale University Press, 1978).

Ladd, Bruce. Crisis in Credibility (New York: New American Library, 1968).

Landmark Briefs and Arguments of the Supreme Court of the United States: Constitutional Law, edited by Philip B. Kurland and Gerhard Casper (Arlington, Va.: University Publications of America, 1978–).

Levin, Ronald M. "In Camera Inspections Under the Freedom of Information Act," 41 University of Chicago Law Review 557 (1974).

Liebman, Charles, ed. Directory of American Judges (Chicago: American Directories, 1955).

Lively, Don. "Government Housekeeping Authority: Bureaucratic Privileges Without a Bureaucratic Privilege," 16 Harvard Civil Rights–Civil Liberties Law Review 485 (1981).

Lundy, James P. "Executive Privilege and the Air Force," 1 JAG Bulletin 13 (1959).

Maher, Christopher M. "The Right to a Fair Trial in Criminal Cases Involving the Introduction of Classified Information," 120 Military Law Review 83 (1988).

Mann, Theodore R. "History and Interpretation of Federal Rule 60(b) of the Federal Rules of Civil Procedure," 25 Temple Law Quarterly 77 (1951).

McCartney, James. "What Should Be Secret?," Columbia Journalism Review, September/October 1971, at 40–44.

McCloskey, Paul N., Jr. Truth and Untruth: Political Deceit in America (New York: Simon & Schuster, 1975).

Melanson, Philip H. Secrecy Wars: National Security, Privacy, and the Public's Right to Know (Washington, D.C.: Brassey's, 2001).

Mink, Patsy T. "The Cannikin Papers: A Case Study in Freedom of Information," in Thomas M. Franck and Edward Weisband, eds., Secrecy and Foreign Policy (New York: Oxford University Press, 1974).

Mitchell, John J. "Government Secrecy in Theory and Practice: 'Rules and Regulations' as an Autonomous Screen," 58 Columbia Law Review 199 (1958).

Moore, James Wm., and Elizabeth B. A. Rogers. "Federal Relief from Civil Judgments," 55 Yale Law Journal 623 (1946).

Moorman, William A. "Executive Privilege and the Freedom of Information Act: Sufficient Protection for Aircraft Mishap Reports?," 21 Air Force Law Review 581 (1979).

Moynihan, Daniel Patrick. Secrecy: The American Experience (New Haven, Conn.: Yale University Press, 1998).

Nagle, James F. A History of Government Contracting (2d ed., Washington, D.C.: George Washington University Law School, 1999).

Nather, David. "A Rise in 'State Secrets,'" CQ Weekly Report, July 18, 2005, at 1958–66.

"National Security and the Public's Right to Know: A New Role for the Courts Under the Freedom of Information Act," 123 University of Pennsylvania Law Review 1438 (1975).

Note. "Access to Official Information: A Neglected Constitutional Right," 27 Indiana Law Journal 209 (1952).

Note. "Discovery Under Federal Tort Claims Act—Privilege for Defense Secrets Upheld Without Requiring Disclosure," 21 George Washington Law Review 792 (1953).

Note. "Evidence—Government Agencies—Right to Determine Privilege of Non-Disclosure of Records," 6 Miami Law Quarterly 509 (1952).

Note. "Evidence—State Secrets Privilege—Discovery Under Federal Tort Claims Act," 28 New York University Law Review 1188 (1953).

Note. "The Executive Evidential Privilege in Suits Against the Government," 47 Northwestern University Law Review 259 (1952).

Note. "Federal Courts—Rules of Civil Procedure—Secretary of Air Force Subject to Discovery in Suit Under Federal Tort Claims Act," 65 Harvard Law Review 1445 (1952).

Note. "Federal Tort Liability for Experimental Activity," 6 Stanford Law Review 734 (1954).

Note. "*In Camera* Inspection of National Security Files Under the Freedom of Information Act," 26 Kansas Law Review 617 (1978).

Note. "Judicial Control of Secret Agents," 76 Yale Law Journal 994 (1967).

Note. "Keeping Secrets: Congress, the Courts, and National Security Information," 103 Harvard Law Review 906 (1990).

Note. "The Military and State Secrets Privilege: Protection for the National Security or Immunity for the Executive?," 91 Yale Law Journal 570 (1982).

Note. "National Security and the Public's Right to Know: A New Role for the Courts Under the Freedom of Information Act," 123 University of Pennsylvania Law Review 1438 (1975).

Note. "Power of the President to Refuse Congressional Demands for Information," 1 Stanford Law Review 256 (1949).

Note. "Practice and Procedure—Discovery—Government Priviledge [*sic*] in Litigation Under the Federal Tort Claims Act," 36 Minnesota Law Review 546 (1952).

Note. "Procedure—Discovery Against the Government—Privilege for State Secrets," 100 University of Pennsylvania Law Review 917 (1952).

Note. "The Touhy Case: The Governmental Privilege to Withhold Documents in Private Litigation," 47 Northwestern University Law Review 519 (1952).

Olmsted, Kathryn. Challenging the Secret Government: The Post-Watergate Investigations of the CIA and FBI (Chapel Hill: University of North Carolina Press, 1996).

Olson, Keith W. Watergate: The Presidential Scandal that Shook America (Lawrence: University Press of Kansas, 2003).

O'Reilly, James T. Federal Information Disclosure (2 vols., 3d ed., Eagan, Minn.: West Group, December 2000).

O'Reilly, John D., Jr. "Discovery Against the United States: A New Aspect of Sovereign Immunity?," 21 North Carolina Law Review 1 (1942).

Orfield, Lester B. "Criminal Law—Procedure—Judgment—Applicability of Writ of Error Coram Nobis in Nebraska," 10 Nebraska Law Bulletin 314 (1932).

———. "Criminal Law—Procedure—Judgment—Writ of Error Coram Nobis in Nebraska—An Addendum," 11 Nebraska Law Bulletin 421 (1933).

———. "The Writ of Error Coram Nobis in Civil Practice," 20 Virginia Law Review 423 (1934).

Orman, John M. Presidential Secrecy and Deception (Westport, Conn.: Greenwood Press, 1980).

Parks, Wallace. "Secrecy and the Public Interest in Military Affairs," 26 George Washington Law Review 23 (1957).

Pfiffner, James P. The Character Factor: How We Judge America's Presidents (College Station: Texas A&M University Press, 2004).

Pike, James A., and Henry G. Fischer. "Discovery Against Federal Administrative Agencies," 56 Harvard Law Review 1125 (1943).

Pines, Daniel L. "The Continuing Viability of the 1875 Supreme Court Case of *Totten v. United States,*" 53 Administrative Law Review 1273 (2001).

Prados, John, and Margaret Pratt Porter, eds. Inside the Pentagon Papers (Lawrence: University Press of Kansas, 2004).

Rauh, Joseph L., Jr., and James C. Turner. "Anatomy of a Public Interest Case Against the CIA," 11 Hamline Journal of Public Law and Policy 307 (1990).

Relyea, Harold C. "The Coming of Secret Law," 5 Government Information Quarterly 97 (1988).

———. "Government Secrecy: Policy Depths and Dimensions," 20 Government Information Quarterly 395 (2003).

———. "Increased National Security Controls on Scientific Communication," 1 Government Information Quarterly 177 (1984).

Riordan, Theodore Francis. "Contract Law—*Totten* Doctrine—Judicial Sabotage of Government Contracts for Sabotage Services," 13 Suffolk Transnational Law Journal 807 (1990).

Rourke, Francis E. Secrecy and Publicity: Dilemmas of Democracy (Baltimore, Md.: Johns Hopkins Press, 1966).

———. "Secrecy in American Bureaucracy," 72 Political Science Quarterly 540 (1957).

———, ed. "A Symposium: Administrative Secrecy: A Comparative Perspective," 35 Public Administration Review 1 (1975).

Rudenstein, David. "The Book in Retrospect," 19 Cardoza Law Review 1283 (1998).

———. The Day the Presses Stopped: A History of the Pentagon Papers Case (Berkeley: University of California Press, 1996).

Sanford, William V. "Evidentiary Privilege Against the Production of Data Within the Control of Executive Departments," 3 Vanderbilt Law Review 73 (1949).

Schuck, Peter. Suing Government: Citizen Remedies for Official Wrongs (New Haven, Conn.: Yale University Press, 1983).

"Separation of Powers and Executive Privilege: The Watergate Briefs," 88 Political Science Quarterly 582 (1973).

Seymour, Whitney North, Jr. "At Last, the Truth Is Out," 19 Cardoza Law Review 1359 (1998).

Shils, Edward A. The Torment of Secrecy: The Background and Consequences of American Security Policies (Chicago: Elephant Paperbacks, 1996 ed.).

Sibley, Katharine A. S. Red Spies in America: Stolen Secrets and the Dawn of the Cold War (Lawrence: University Press of Kansas, 2004).

Simpson, John W. "Use of Aircraft Accident Investigation Information in Actions for Damages," 17 Journal of Air Law and Commerce 283 (1950).

Sirica, John J. To Set the Record Straight (New York: Norton, 1979).

Street, Harry. "State Secrets—A Comparative Study," 14 Modern Law Review 121 (1951).

Taubeneck, T. D., and John J. Sexton. "Executive Privilege and the Court's Right to Know—Discovery Against the United States in Civil Actions in Federal District Courts," 48 Georgetown Law Journal 486 (1960).

Tell, Larry. "The Cloak-and-Dagger Court," National Law Journal, August 10, 1981, at 1.

Temple, Hollee S. "Raining on the Litigation Parade: Is It Time to Stop Litigant Abuse of the Fraud on the Court Doctrine?," 39 University of San Francisco Law Review 967 (2005).

Theoharis, Athan G., ed. A Culture of Secrecy: The Government Versus the People's Right to Know (Lawrence: University Press of Kansas, 1998).

Thompson, Robert T. "Right of Discovery Against the United States Government," 1 Journal of Public Law 235 (1952).

The Tower Commission Report (New York: Random House, 1987).

Ungar, Sanford G. The Papers and the Papers: An Account of the Legal and Political Battle over the Pentagon Papers (New York: E. P. Dutton & Co., 1972).

U.S. Department of Justice. Freedom of Information Act Guide and Privacy Overview (Washington, D.C., May 2004).

Warren, John H., III. "Administrative Law—Judicial Review, State Secrets, and the Freedom of Information Act," 23 South Carolina Law Review 332 (1971).

Weaver, William G., and Thomas Longoria. "Bureaucracy that Kills: Federal Sovereign Immunity and the Discretionary Function Exception," 96 American Political Science Review 335 (2002).

Weaver, William G., and Robert M. Pallitto. "State Secrets and Executive Power," 120 Political Science Quarterly 85 (2005).

Weber, Max. Economy and Society: An Outline of Interpretive Sociology, edited by Guenther Roth and Claus Wittich (New York: Bedminster Press, 1968).

Welch, William J. "Evidence: Privilege Against Revealing State Secrets," 10 Oklahoma Law Review 336 (1957).

Wetlaufer, Gerald. "Justifying Secrecy: An Objection to the General Deliberative Privilege," 65 Indiana Law Journal 845 (1990).

Wigmore, John Henry. Evidence in Trials at Common Law (10 vols., Boston: Little, Brown, 1940).

Wise, David. The Politics of Lying: Government Deception, Secrecy and Power (New York: Random House, 1973).

Wittes, Benjamin. "Surveillance Court Gets New Powers," Legal Times, November 7, 1994, at 1.

Wolkinson, Herman. "Demands of Congressional Committees for Executive Papers," 10 Federal Bar Journal 103, 223, 319 (1949).

Wright, Benjamin Fletcher, ed. The Federalist (Cambridge, Mass.: Harvard University Press, 1961).

Wright, Charles Alan, and Kenneth W. Graham Jr. Federal Practice and Procedure, vols. 26 and 27 (St. Paul, Minn.: West Publishing Co., 1992).

Yoo, John C. "The First Claim: The Burr Trial, United States v. Nixon, and Presidential Power," 83 Minnesota Law Review 1435 (1999).

Zagel, James. "The State Secrets Privilege," 50 Minnesota Law Review 875 (1966).

Zedalis, Rex J. "Resurrection of Reynolds: 1974 Amendment to National Defense and Foreign Policy Exemption," 4 Pepperdine Law Review 81 (1976).

INDEX OF CASES

SUBJECT INDEX

Supreme Court, U.S. (*continued*)
  Reynolds plaintiff's brief in (1953), 99–104
  Tax Court case and, 239–40
  Totten case, 221–22, 223, 224–25, 226
  writ of error *coram nobis* by *Reynolds* plaintiffs
    and, 176–88, 211, 264

Taft, William Howard, 130
Taft-Hartley Act, 92
Taliban, 27
Tax Court, U.S., 239–40
Taylor, Stuart, 109
Tenet, George, 246–47
Tenth Circuit, 175
Texas Law Review, 88
Third Circuit, 40
  on accident report of B-29 crash, 184, 197
  judges in *Reynolds* case (1951), 59–60
  Reynolds decision (1951), 79–86, 87–91, 113,
    191, 240, 263
  Reynolds government's brief (1951), 60–73,
    184, 197
  Reynolds plaintiffs (2005) appeal to, 187, 200–
    211, 261, 262, 264
  Reynolds plaintiffs brief (1951) and, 73–79
  Supreme Court on 1951 *Reynolds* ruling by,
    105, 107, 109, 115, 185
Thys, Fred, 169
Tort claims, 11–12. *See also* Federal Tort Claims Act
Touhy, Roger, 65
Tower Commission Report, 26
Treasury, U.S. Department of, 46–47, 146, 231
Truman, Harry, 25, 92–95, 101, 154
Tucker, John, 11

U.S. Court of International Trade, 243
U.S. Information Agency, 131

Underhill, Charles Lee, 13
University of Pennsylvania Law Review, 88
USA Patriot Act, 150

Van Antwerpen, Franklin S., 206
Vanderbilt Law Review, 121
Vietnam War, 26
Vinson, Frederick, 94, 102, 105, 106–7, 110–14,
  119, 120, 121, 253–56

Walton, Reggie B., 213, 214, 220, 221
War Department, U.S., 172, 173
Warner Robins Air Force Base, 1
Warnke, Paul C., 247–48
Warren, Earl, 140
Washington, George, 54
Washington *Evening Star*, 131, 187
Washington Law Review, 122
Washington Post, 93, 120, 154
Watergate tapes case, 124, 158–60, 220–21, 259
Waycross, Ga., 1
Waycross Journal-Herald, 202
Weber, Max, 18
Whistle blowing cases, 246–48, 249–52
Wigmore, John Henry, 48, 49, 111
Wilkinson, General, 213–17, 219, 230
Wilmington, Del., 7
Wiretapping, 146, 147–48, 149, 150–51
Wise, David, 26
Wolkinson, Herman, 69–70, 90, 108, 213
Writ of error *coram nobis. See* Coram nobis,
  writ of

Yousef, Ramzi, 27

Zuckert, Eugene M., 51, 64